Corruption and Anti-Corruption

CORRUPTION AND ANTI-CORRUPTION

**Peter Larmour and Nick Wolanin
(editors)**

Australian
National
University

E PRESS

ANU
E PRESS

Published by ANU E Press
The Australian National University
Canberra ACT 0200, Australia
Email: anuepress@anu.edu.au
This title is also available online at http://epress.anu.edu.au

---

National Library of Australia Cataloguing-in-Publication entry

Title: Corruption and anti-corruption / Peter Larmour and Nick Wolanin (editors).
ISBN: 9781922144768 (pbk.) 9781922144775 (ebook)
Notes: Includes bibliographical references and index.
Subjects: Misconduct in office.
            Political corruption--Economic aspects.
            Political corruption--Prevention.
            Misconduct in office--Prevention.
Other Authors/Contributors:
            Larmour, Peter.
            Wolanin, Nick, 1962-
Dewey Number: 364.1

First published by Asia-Pacific Press 2001.

Contents

Tables

Figures

Box

Abbreviations

AFP	Australian Federal Police
ASEAN	Association of Southeast Asian Nations
ATM	automatic teller machine
AV	Annual Valuation
BPI	bribe payers index
CC	Constitutional Court
CCMC	Counter Corruption and Malfeasance Commission
CCN	corruption, crony capitalism and nepotism
CDA	Constitutional Drafting Assembly
CESCR	Committee on Economic, Social and Cultural Rights
CIA	Central Intelligence Agency
CJC	Criminal Justice Commission
CPI	corruption prevention index
DPRK	Democratic People's Republic of Korea
DTI	Direct Trader Input
EDI	Electronic Data Interchange
EFTPOS	electronic funds transfer at point of sale
EU	European Union
IBRD	International Bank for Reconstruction and Development
ICAC	Independent Commission Against Corruption
ICCPR	International Covenant on Civil and Political Rights
ICESCR	International Covenant on Economic, Social and Cultural Rights
IMAC	International Mutual Assistance in Criminal Matters
IMF	International Monetary Fund
INTERPOL	International Criminal Police Organisation
IOC	International Olympic Committee
IT	information technology
LAPD	Los Angeles Police Department
MP	Member of Parliament
MRP	Moral Recovery Program

NCCC	National Counter-Corruption Commission
NGO	non-governmental organisation
NHRC	National Human Rights Commission
NPKC	National Peacekeeping Council
NSW	New South Wales
OAS	Organisation of American States
OECD	Organisation for Economic Cooperation and Development
OLRS	Online Release System
PCGG	Presidential Commission for Good Government
PEAC	Public Ethics and Accountability Committee
PIN	personal identification number
RICO	Racketeering Influenced Corrupt Organization
SEZ	special economic zone
TI	Transparency International
UDHR	Universal Declaration of Human Rights
UN	United Nations
UNDP	United Nations Development Programme
UNDCP	United Nations Drug Control Programme
UNGA	United Nations General Assembly
VAT	value-added tax
WTO	World Trade Organization

Contributors

Borwornsak Uwanno is Secretary General of King Prajadhipok's Institute, Professor of Laws, Faculty of Law Chulalongkorn University, former secretary and rapporteur of the Drafting and Scrutiny Committee of the present Constitution, the Constitutional Drafting Assembly.

Zoe Pearson is a doctoral student at the Faculty of Law, The Australian National University.

Flavio M. Menezes is Senior Lecturer at the Department of Economics, Faculty of Economics and Commerce at The Australian National University.

John McFarlane is Special Adviser with the Office of the Deputy Commissioner, Australian Federal Police and AFP Visiting Fellow at the Australian Defence Studies Centre, Australian Defence Force Academy.

Peter Larmour is Director of Graduate Studies in Development Administration at the National Centre for Development Studies, The Australian National University.

Peter Grabosky is Director of Research at The Australian Institute of Criminology.

Angela Gorta is Research Manager at the NSW Independent Commission Against Corruption. Previously she was Chief Research Officer with the NSW Department of Corrective Services and lectured in psychology at Macquarie University.

David A. Chaikin is chairman of Cyberbrief Consultants. He is international adviser to a number of governments and financial institutions, and more recently has acted as a special legal adviser to the Anti-Graft League of the Philippines in relation to the recovery of the illicit assets of former Philippines President Ferdinand E Marcos. He is a former Senior Assistant Secretary in the Australian Federal Attorney-General's Department and former Senior Fraud Officer of the London-based diplomatic body, the Commonwealth Secretariat.

Andrew Brien is a Senior Research Officer in the Department of the House of Representatives, in the Parliament of the Commonwealth of Australia. He has held academic positions in New Zealand and Australia, where he lectured in social and political philosophy, ethical theory, as well as business, professional and applied ethics.

Barry Hindess is Professor in the Political Science Program, Research School of Social Sciences at The Australian National University.

Vicki Klum is a Senior Corruption Prevention Officer at the NSW Independent Commission Against Corruption. Previously she worked in a wide range of management, policy development, regulation and consumer protection roles within the NSW public sector.

Catherine Boardman is a Senior Corruption Prevention Officer at the NSW Independent Commission Against Corruption. Previously she worked in the Federal and NSW State public sectors in the fields of Territories Administration, regulatory law enforcement, management, consumer protection, public funding programs and policy development.

John Warburton is a Senior Investigator at the NSW Independent Commission Against Corruption. Previously he was a Detective with the Australian Federal Police working in the fields of fraud and organised crime. He is currently a part-time doctoral student at the Faculty of Economics, University of Sydney.

Nick Wolanin is Principal Corruption Prevention Officer at the NSW Independent Commission Against Corruption. Previously he was a research scientist at BHP Steel International before serving with the Australian Federal Police as a fraud and white collar crime detective.

Guillermo Parayno Jr is former Commissioner of the Philippines Customs Service.

Asim Barman is the Municipal Commissioner for Calcutta.

Introduction

Peter Larmour and Nick Wolanin

New attention to the old problem of corruption has several characteristics. First it is international. Previously corruption was mainly the concern of domestic agencies, like the police or auditors. Now it appears on the agenda of international organisations, like the World Bank or the OECD. The internationalisation of controlling corruption has been led by a non-government organisation, Transparency International (TI), which has campaigned to outlaw the bribery of foreign officials. Transparency International devised a controversial 'Corruption Perceptions Index', which ranked countries according to how corrupt they were perceived to be. It followed this up with a Bribe Payers Index, which ranked countries according to their propensity to offer bribes (Transparency International 2000:13–14).

Second, it is economic. Previously, corruption was largely the concern of lawyers and criminologists. Now the lead is being taken by economists. They look at the costs of corruption, and its effect on economic development (Rose-Ackerman 1999). They also apply the methods of economic analysis to the problem of corruption—the assumption that people are rational and calculating, and will respond to incentives and disincentives. This approach is well summarised in Robert Klitgaard's (1988) formula

Monopoly + Discretion − Accountability = Corruption

Third, the new interest in corruption is less patient with cultural explanations. Previously corruption in developing countries might be explained by traditions of gift giving, or the obligations of kinship. Now many people in these countries are less tolerant of such excuses. A draft bill to establish an anti-corruption commission in Papua New Guinea, for example prescribes bluntly 'custom [is] not to be a defence' (Papua New Guinea 1998, s.40). A brisk distinction between gifts and bribes has been given by the Nigerian President, Olusegun Obasanjo, who said that

> ...the gift is usually a token. It is not demanded. The value is usually in the spirit rather than the material worth. It is usually done in the open, and never in secret. Where it is excessive, it becomes an embarrassment and it is returned. If anything corruption has perverted and destroyed this aspect of our culture (quoted in Pope 1997:5)

Fourth, it is suspicious of state action. Previously, a corruption scandal might lead to a government sponsored crackdown or inquiry. An 'independent' commission might be established, but it would report directly to the Prime Minister or the President. Now there is more suspicion that those at the top may also be involved. The Independent Commission Against Corruption (ICAC) in New South Wales, for example, reports to a bipartisan committee of the legislature, rather than to the government which established it. It went on to investigate the State Premier, leading to his resignation (though the Supreme Court later found the ICAC Act did not apply to the Premier in the circumstances).

Suspicion of state action has led to greater emphasis on the role of civil society, and the private sector in preventing corruption. Transparency International has supplemented its international action against business corruption by franchising national chapters, constituted like other domestic non-government organisations, each campaigning in a different way—monitoring the privatisation program in Panama, for example, or establishing advice centres in Bangladesh. Transparency International has also attracted financial support from (among others) large international companies who are tired of paying bribes. Where the private sector used to be regarded as one of the causes of corruption, it now casts itself as a victim.

Fifth, it is as much concerned with education and prevention as with investigation and prosecution. Corruption is difficult to investigate. It typically takes place in secret, without witnesses, between willing partners. Prosecutions are hard to bring, and there is sometimes suspicion that governments are selectively targeting their political enemies. Like other crime, more corruption probably takes place than is ever investigated or prosecuted. Additional resources might therefore be better spent 'upstream', in reforming administrative systems to reduce opportunities for corruption, and in educating citizens against accepting it. Transparency International's mandate specifically precludes it from taking up individual cases.

These five characteristics of the new interest in corruption are linked to broader tendencies. The rapid rise of Transparency International is part of a process of globalisation. The involvement of non-governmental organisations (NGOs) and the private sector is characteristic of modern forms of governance, in which order is seen as the result of the interaction between hierarchies, markets and communities. The economic analysis of corruption is part of a wider intellectual movement to apply the assumptions of rational choice to social and political institutions. There are links between the characteristics, but also tensions between them. Neoliberal economists and NGO activists, for example, may share a suspicion of state action, but differ over the value of moralistic appeals. Disciplined secretive organisations like the police force may be uncomfortable with the new emphasis on management reform and civil society.

This book reflects these new approaches to corruption, but it is also critical of them. It deals with the international dimensions of corruption, as a human rights issue (Pearson), in the recovery of assets that corrupt leaders have hidden abroad (Chaikin), and in the links between corruption and transnational crime (McFarlane). It includes an original piece of economic analysis (Menezes). It is designed to be read by people without formal training in economics, and provides a guide to further reading. Other chapters draw on different intellectual and professional traditions, particularly criminology (Grabosky). Angela Gorta's research for the ICAC draws on broader social science methodology. Hindess' initial chapter is critical of the narrowness of current economic approaches to understanding corruption, while Warburton's final chapter on corrupt networks draws on politics, sociology and social psychology.

The title of the book comes from a four-week short course, designed and taught jointly by academics at the Australian National University and public servants at the New South Wales Independent Commission Against Corruption. Its creation was stimulated by Transparency International, on behalf of Indonesian NGOs looking for anti-corruption training before the fall of Soeharto. It has been taught annually since 1998 as part of a Masters in Development Administration degree, taken by students from audit offices, public service commissions, anti-corruption commissions and NGOs from a range of countries in East Asia, Africa and the South Pacific.[1] Versions have been taught in shorter training courses in Jakarta, Phnom Penh, and Manila. These workshops were sponsored by the Centre for Democratic Institutions at the Australian National University, which also commissioned Zoe Pearson's chapter on corruption and human rights.

Most of the authors have taught in the course, and the chapters are based on lectures and workshops they designed for it. Peter Grabosky's involvement led to the publication of this volume jointly with the Australian Institute of Criminology. The three case studies—of Calcutta, the Philippines and Thailand—were originally presented at a seminar organised by the Asian Development Bank (ADB), and moderated by one of the editors. We are grateful for the permission of the ADB and the authors for their inclusion.

............g about their chances of being caught.
- there are different types of crime. Remedies for one kind may have no impact on others.
- offenders try to justify, rationalise and neutralise what they do. People will say, for example, 'everybody does it' or 'I did it for my family'.
- organisational factors affect whether crime takes place. These include the informal culture of an organisation, as well as formal rules and regulations.

These theories of crime in turn suggest their own remedies for corruption, which are described in Gorta's chapter.

Corruption control in practice

Different schools of thought have been reflected in the development of thinking about corruption prevention, which is reflected in the curriculum of the ANU/ICAC course on Corruption and Anti-Corruption. We will call these 'interventionism', 'managerialism' and 'organisational integrity', the last of which is described in more detail in the chapter by Catherine Boardman and Vicki Klum.

Interventionism

Most western methods of policing wait for a crime to be committed and then intervene in the conduct of the offender. 'Catching crooks' is how most law enforcement agencies still see themselves. This approach prevails in the so-called law and order auctions when political parties compete to show they are 'tough on crime' at election times. It is easy to measure in the statistics of conviction and crime clear-up rates.

It is assumed that society is protected by preventing the offender from continuing or repeating the offence. Intervention kicks off processes such as compensation, retribution, rehabilitation or quarantine. There is an assumed measure of deterrence for the offender as recidivist, and also for others contemplating similar conduct.

There are, however, many weaknesses in this approach, particularly when applied in isolation. First, harm done cannot be undone. Second, most crime

Corruption and Anti-corruption

Definitions, explanations and remedies

There are several kinds of definitions of corruption. Some turn on the idea of the 'public interest', and deviations from it. Others turn on popular understandings, noticing cultural and other differences in what people regard as corrupt. Corruption is often, but not always, against the law in many countries, even if the law is hard to enforce. Different explanations for corruption suggest different remedies, just as different diagnoses of a disease suggest different cures. Klitgaard's formula, quoted above, for example, suggests the break up of government monopolies, reduced official discretion, and more accountability.

Some of these explanations are quite traditional, but the cures they suggest remain plausible. Barry Hindess' chapter goes back to the classical foundations of Western political theory. Corruption has also been a concern of non-Western theory. Syed Alatas' pioneering sociology of corruption described the philosophy of Wang An Shih (AD 1021–1086) who argued that corruption was caused by a combination of bad systems and bad men. Ibn Khaldun (AD 1332–1406) argued that it was caused by luxurious living within the élite (Alatas 1990). The recent scandals surrounding the Olympic games show how reliance on the virtue of 'good people', such as former athletes, is insufficient unless good systems are also in place. 'Luxurious living' suggests close attention to the office car park, bank accounts, and the lifestyles of leaders and their families.

Transparency International influentially defines corruption in terms of the use of public office for private gain (Pope 1997:1). The distinction between 'public' and 'private' matters is often associated with the rise of the modern bureaucratic state. Corruption is seen as the result of the failure to distinguish private matters from public ones—appointing relatives, rather than on merit; or diverting public money to private purposes. Municipal reformers in the United States also saw corruption arising from politicisation of properly bureaucratic activities. The remedy was professional administration, at arms length from politicians, even-handedly applying legislation. Typical public administration remedies include independent commissions.

As Hindess' chapter

Corruption and Anti-corruption

goes unreported. Its particular conspiratorial characteristics mean an even smaller percentage of crimes of corruption are likely to come to notice. The 'happy giver–happy receiver' situation and the absence of a victim at the scene of the crime mean most corruption is invisible. Effective intervention is therefore the exception rather than the rule.

Third, its demands on resources are unlimited. As with taxation, full compliance might only be possible if every person is engaged in the supervision of everyone else. The abject failure of interventionism to deal with the trafficking of narcotics is a widely recognised example of the limits of resources. If the resources will never be available to match the scale of the problem, there must be selectivity in applying what resources are to hand. Thus we confront the issues of biased target selection, and uncertainty of detection.

Fourth, the interventionist may not notice the offence, or not treat it seriously. If attending to street violence is an electoral priority, then white-collar, environmental or industrial crimes may go unchallenged, despite their potential for causing a greater harm to society. For example, the law enforcement sector has been slow to realise the damage done by e-crime. Selective enforcement may also apply along socioeconomic, racial, ethnic, gender, age or political lines, sometimes unwittingly but also deliberately and corruptly. Individuals affected can include a government's political opponents.

Fifth, if most crime and even more corruption goes undetected, unreported and hence unrestored, what measure of deterrence can exist? Interventionism assumes that a potential offender exercises rational judgment about behaviour and consequences. She supposedly compares the gain to be had from an illegal or corrupt act with the probability of detection and the severity of punishment, if detected, and then acts on the result of that notional equation. The slim possibility of detection means that corruption is almost risk free. Hence confidence in the deterrent effect of intervention might be misplaced.

Rational choice is often assumed as an explanation. However, many crimes, like murder, are not well understood as rational choices. Similarly, the association between corruption and gambling has led to a contrary view about rationality. The conventional construction is that a gambler might turn to corruption in order to service debts. However, it may be that the propensity to engage in risk-taking behaviour is what attracts certain types of people to gambling. It may also attract them to corruption. If engaging in corruption is merely another form of risk-taking, or a gamble on the consequences versus the rewards, then it is likely that gambling and corruption are behavioural neighbours rather than a causal couple.

Deterrence has an intuitive appeal to those who are close to the processes of law enforcement. They see the unhappy results of detection, prosecution and imprisonment. They would not want themselves to be caught up in the harshness of the system. However, experience and criminological research suggests deterrence is a more elusive phenomenon in the minds of offenders. To rely on this as a sole means of controlling crime or corruption is problematic.

Managerialism

The managerialist model of corruption control assumes that those who seek to misbehave can be discouraged or prevented from doing so by the erection of appropriate systems, procedures and protocols. It also assumes that preventing the harm from occurring in the first place is more desirable than chasing the consequences of the harm after the fact. Prevention is often said to be better than cure.

Managerialism sees the world as made up of opportunities and exploiters of opportunity. Reduce or eliminate opportunity and misconduct will be reduced or disappear. For example, cash boxes are locked away, every purchase order is double-checked, audit trails are kept and reviewed, and so on. A key advantage of the approach over interventionism is that it can realistically hope to capture a larger proportion of misconduct. It can defeat outright some attempted abuses. It may enhance deterrence by presenting a greater chance of detection.

The limitation of this approach is its failure to recognise and deal with the interactivity of systems and human nature. It sees humans operating a machine which will only permit correct operation but not permit incorrect operation, rather like an electrical socket which can only work one way. However, people are an integral part of any system and organisations are much more complex than electrical sockets.

For example, requiring all cars to be fitted with seat belts is a typical 'managerialist' solution to the problem of road accidents. A reckless driver wearing a seatbelt should be prevented by the system from being injured in the inevitable accident. Ensuring that people use seat belts is another story. Managerialist solutions also tend to deal with idealised or standardised workplace situations. To call again on the car safety analogy, the seat belt solution is inappropriate for a heavily pregnant woman or for an infant but the system, because it is designed for the widest possible application, fails to be effective when it most needs to be—for those users who are most vulnerable. Similarly, a crime or corruption control system needs to be most effective in opposing the most serious instances of abuse. A system which only catches the insignificant abuse but which fails to deal with infrequent but critically damaging incidents is not serving the organisation.

The failings of managerial approaches turn our attention to the character of the people operating the systems. Most people who work in organisations can be seen to fit into three broad categories. In Category 1 there are those who want to do the right thing and need varying degrees of guidance about what the right thing is to do. Category 2 people are those who are too timid to take the risk of operating outside the rules. Paradoxically, they limit any deviance to technical, sometimes clever compliance with rules. Finally, in Category 3, there are those who simply are crooks and will operate outside the rules entirely.

Let us look at a commonly used system which is assumed (often incorrectly) to prevent bribery by limiting the amount of money an official can receive in the form of a gift. People in Category 1 already know not to accept gifts, and a corrupt official in Category 3 is not going to declare the receipt of a 'gift' whatever its value. So having a system of controlling gifts merely creates a means by which Category 2 officials can legitimise corrupt rewards. How? If the rule says one can accept a gift up to $50, in order to receive a $100 bribe, you just register them as two separate gifts of $50. If the rule is consequently amended to stipulate that only up to $50 can be accepted on the same day from the one person, the corrupt official merely has to wait two days or take the bribe in two lots from two different people acting in concert. Or over three days from three people, and so on.

If the prohibition is then applied to cash gifts in any amount, the giver simply spends the cash on a good or service before delivering it to the official. And so on. The point is that whatever regime of rules is established, it can be subverted. By engaging in a futile battle of rule-setting, response and then rule-hardening, the runaway growth in the number and complexity of rules can eventually lead to the stifling of all legitimate business activity.

A burgeoning base of rules, characteristic of excessively managerialist systems, seems to lead to several effects. The first is to breed a culture of 'approval through omission'. Where impermissible conduct is carefully and comprehensively described, people tend to adopt a 'what's not proscribed is permissible' attitude.

The second effect is that where clearly impermissible conduct can be made to fit the rules, it can 'launder' the misconduct. For example, if a travelling allowance rule requires a journey of no less than 50kms to trigger entitlement, the system merely encourages people to work harder for their misconduct, if they are so minded, perhaps by driving 50kms around in circles.

Managerialist corruption control approaches also tend to ignore market forces. Say for argument's sake a group of public officials is corruptly selling confidential information. Each piece of information leaked earns the corrupt official 100 illicit dollars. If managerialist corruption prevention controls are applied with alacrity, the leaking of such information becomes more difficult and more risky. Some of the corrupt officials, unwilling to take the risk, drop out of the market. However, basic economic theory contends that if the supply of a commodity falls but demand remains unchanged, the price per item goes up. The control measure has not dampened the corruption but merely created a more vigorous market because the remaining suppliers who are willing to take the risk can now command a higher price.

Other similar effects can be seen in wider crime prevention practice. Banks which 'target harden' against armed robbery by the use of bullet proof screens, armed guards, dye bombs, etc do not reduce crime, but merely displace it into other areas. Petrol stations, post offices and convenience stores have become the new targets of armed robberies until target hardening in those locations acts again to shift the crime elsewhere. Similarly, sophisticated anti-theft measures in motor cars create sophisticated car thieves. It enables them to steal a commodity for which there is high demand but limited supply because of effective anti-theft measures. They can command an even higher price for their crime because they no longer have to compete with the unsophisticated thieves.

The same economic theory also contends that an increase in price will cause more suppliers to enter a market which will again achieve an equilibrium, but at higher price levels and with fewer suppliers. So, at best, the managerialist prevention measure distorts a market which simply responds in a recognisable way. At worst, the risk takers become more sophisticated in their methodology to avoid detection and the consequences. Paradoxically, the prevention measure can have the effect of professionalising or increasing the sophistication of the corruption hence making it more difficult to detect and control. By ignoring the interactivity of systems, the managerialist approach tends to change the nature and location of corruption rather than prevent it.

Excessive reliance on systems can also engender complacency. Those who are convinced that a system is foolproof tend to look away, falsely believing they have successfully prevented corruption. A rule based, managerialist approach to controlling corruption may also generate responses in which strict compliance becomes an end in itself, displacing the outcome intended by the rules. A good example can be found in the way most conflicts of interest are handled. Many organisations require the disclosure of actual or potential conflicts of interest as a rule. The outcome intended is that officials sense the organisation's interests, not their own personal interests. Because many conflict of interest rules focus on declaration, there is a common attitude that the declaration itself purges the conflict. Having declared the conflict, the official then goes on to serve their private interest and defends any subsequent accusations of corruption by pointing to the declaration. Even worse, is that many people accept the defence because there was compliance with the rules.

Another example is in procurement. Procurement rules often require the seeking of multiple quotations directly or by public tender in order to ensure best value for money is obtained and to lessen the chance of a corrupt arrangement emerging between an official and a particular provider of goods or services. When auditing records against procurement rules, often a check is made to see if, say, three quotes have been obtained where it is necessary to do so. There are many cases where such audits have missed corruption because the three quotes have been present on the files but, unknown to the auditor, two of them were forged. Here the rules and their application, extending even into the audit methodology, have helped to hide corruption. How? The three quote rule when abused through prima facie compliance means that a corruptly favoured contractor enjoys the cover of having been the 'best' bidder each time bids were called. Cosy relationships, without the obfuscating documentation required by managerialist methods, might be questioned sooner.

Many organisations deal with corruption risks by relying on some interventionist activities coupled with some measure of managerialist controls. Responsibility for implementation tends to lie with a specialised subsection of the corporate affairs portfolio, or be an additional responsibility of the internal audit function. Thus corruption control is marginalised. That is not to say that interventionist and managerialist measures have no place. The choice of measures and their strategic applications, however, form part of the organisational integrity approach outlined briefly below, and explained in greater detail in the chapter by Catherine Boardman and Vicki Klum.

Beyond managerialism—organisational integrity

Organisational integrity is a term used to label an approach to minimising corruption. It refers to the integration of an organisation's operational systems, corruption control strategies and ethical standards. In other words, it is about establishing a social norm in an organisation which accurately defines and resists corruption. That norm, in the case of a public agency, must be one which serves the public interest. The use of the word 'integrity' is similar to its use when describing a building or a bridge as having structural integrity, which is to say a robust stability founded in an informed use of physical laws.

One of the conceptual underpinnings for the approach can be found in John Braithwaite's theory of reintegrative shaming (1989). Braithwaite contends that the incidence of deviance is largely governed by the dynamics of shame in the community. Hence, if criminal behaviour is nourished by not subjecting it to shame, it tends to be encouraged as a group norm. A similar relationship is thought to exist between crime in the community and corruption in an organisation.

A key assumption in the organisational integrity approach is that deviance stems largely from the nature of the organisation rather than the nature of the individual.

[T]he ability to behave ethically in the workplace may be related more to aspects of the organisation than to attributes of the individual (Zipparo 1998:10).

It is the inverse of the 'rotten apple theory', which blames corruption on the attributes of individuals. If Zipparo is correct, then measures which target the individual are less likely to be effective than those which address the organisational context in which individuals operate. Corruption must be seen in the context of a social organism. The organisational integrity approach seeks to achieve high corruption resistance in the way an organisation functions according to a clearly defined schema of ethical values.

Business and government have been learning that failure to manage an organisation along ethical lines can have a negative impact on the organisation's objectives. For example, if treating employees with care and dignity leads to greater levels of customer service, this in turn can lead to a more profitable business that enhances shareholder value. For a public company, the root ethic might be one of service to shareholders. For a public sector organisation, the root ethic must be one of serving the public interest. A group of second order ethical values can then be identified such as customer service, sustainable development, workplace safety and so on, but they must permeate universally the organisation's practices before an observable culture of ethical management, based on that particular ethical schema, can emerge. For an organisation to operate without corruption, careful selection and promotion of appropriate ethical values must be made.

In the public sector, serving the public interest should be the defining ethic, which can be expressed in terms of public duty values. A government agency which operates on the Organisational Integrity model will have public duty values built in at every level, no matter where and how deeply one drills down. For example, for procurement to serve the public interest it must be conducted free of the personal interest of those administering the process. Procurement policies and procedures must, among other things provide the framework and guidance for officials to do their work in such a way that they cannot exploit the process for personal gain. The key is to deal with the corruption risks integrally with the procurement process.

In contrast, the interventionist and managerialist approaches see the corruption problem as somehow separate and to be dealt with outside the procurement process. The difference is between having a fraud control policy and ensuring fraud control measures are built in to all policies, procedures and plans. Fraud and corruption control is not something to bolt on to a procurement system, it needs to be part of the procurement system. Organisations which make that leap in thinking across all areas of business appear to have the best chance of minimising corruption.

The choice of anti-corruption approaches seems to depend partly on the size of an organisation, and can be thought of (following Klitgaard 1988) in principal–agent terms. In a very small organisation, say a sole proprietor with one or two employees all located together, it is possible and cost effective for the owner to ensure her interests are being served by adopting an interventionist approach. She can conceivably monitor most or all of her employees' behaviour and when an instance of wrongdoing occurs, she can take any necessary action to minimise loss.

Where the organisation is larger and perhaps distributed over more than one location, it is not possible for the owner or owners to maintain total surveillance and control over all employees' behaviour. However, a managerialist approach can be adopted to minimise the range of behaviour which requires surveillance and possible intervention.

A cost–benefit analysis must be applied in the sense that much in the way of resources could be spent dealing with threats which in a medium-sized organisation might never occur. Falling back on interventionist methods in the event of a threat becoming a reality is probably a better use of resources. Hence, a suitable combination of these two anti-corruption methods is likely to serve best an organisation of medium size and complexity.

For example, the organisation may be small enough to reserve all purchasing decisions for the owners rather than vesting them with employees. This managerialist control might prevent gross oversupply frauds, but is less likely to be able to stop an employee corruptly leaking valuable information to a tenderer. An interventionist approach is the only practical and cost effective alternative.

In a very large and highly distributed organisation a managerialist solution will not be able to deal with all situations requiring control. A key advantage in the organisational integrity approach is that without a clear procedure for completing a task correctly, the right decision can be made by the application of a previously established global ethical framework. The interventionist model caters only for what has happened. The managerialist model caters for what might happen but is limited by the imagination and prescience of the system's designers. The inherently heuristic nature of organisational integrity, however, means the right decision can be inferred even if the problem was never anticipated or previously encountered.

The serving of ethical values needs to merge invisibly into every business system from Human Resources to waste management. Organisations which exhibit high levels of corruption resistance tend not to be obsessed with the rhetoric of fraud and controlling corruption and tend not to approach the problem by establishing discrete functional work groups (like anti-fraud sections). Instead, the corruption resistance emerges from the fact that dealing with corruption problems is a seamless part of the core business of the organisation. It is but one component, along with others like strong customer service values which in turn underpin higher order outcomes and, ultimately, stakeholder interests, public or private. Whichever business process one examines, at any level of complexity, public duty values must be factored in, both explicitly and implicitly, to ensure high corruption resistance in the public sector. Organisational integrity means being able to drill down into any part of an organisation, to any depth, and see evidence of the guiding ethics, whatever they might be.

A useful comparison is with fractal objects, which have an inherent property of self-similarity. Computer generated fractal art became popular in the 1990s because, no matter how closely one zooms in on a fractal image, the shape of the overall object is reflected in any component part. In a public sector agency, when the guiding ethical values of public duty can be observed to be operating at any level of inspection, the term organisational integrity can be applied. That it can better resist corruption is almost axiomatic. Of course, public sector organisations are invariably very complex social organisms. Unpacking and describing the precise factors which contribute to high corruption resistance is a difficult task and one which varies from organisation to organisation. The strength of a building can be described by reference to engineering principles based on the laws of physics. In the world of organisational strengthening, cause and effect are harder to define.

Note

[1] The authors wish to gratefully acknowledge the support for the course given by Irene Moss AO and The Honourable Mr Justice Barry O'Keefe AM, respectively the current and previous ICAC commissioners, as well as Grant Poulton and Peter Gifford, respectively the current and previous ICAC directors of Corruption Prevention, Education and Research. Acknowledgement is also due to ANU Visiting Fellow Grant McKay. Formerly of the ICAC, Mr McKay was a foundation member of the group teaching the course and was instrumental in establishing its content and direction.

1

Good government and corruption

Barry Hindess

Corruption today is commonly understood in economic terms, in relation both to its content (money in exchange for favours) and to its effects (on economic growth, development, and so forth). In other historical contexts, corruption has been understood more generally and I will raise the question of why this narrowly economic perspective has come to be so influential. Other chapters in this collection address the issues of how to identify corruption and how to deal with it when you find it. The aim of this chapter, in contrast, is to stand back from such concerns and to focus instead on how we think about corruption, especially in relation to other aspects of public life. Along the way I will raise some questions about the links between democracy and corruption and suggest ways in which what counts as corruption can be seen as a political issue.

Corruption as an economic issue

Susan Rose-Ackerman's *Corruption and Government* (1999) is a useful place to start since it presents a particularly clear example of the modern understanding of corruption as a predominantly economic issue. With only minor variations, her account is one that would be accepted not only by the World Bank and other international financial institutions but also by many aid agencies. Rose-Ackerman begins by asking why it is that so many countries have low or negative rates of economic growth, often in spite of the fact that they are well endowed with natural resources or with a highly educated labour force. She offers two different but complementary answers. One is that such countries have weak and poorly functioning public and private institutions.

They need institutional reform, but such reform is difficult. Constructing dams, highways, and port facilities is technically straightforward. Reforming government and nurturing a strong private sector are more subtle and difficult tasks that cannot be reduced to an engineering blueprint (Rose-Ackerman 1999:1).

Not so long ago, the assumption that economic growth requires a strong private sector would have been widely disputed, but it is now common currency amongst professional economists, and therefore also amongst the governments and other agencies that they advise. So too, unfortunately, is the economists' disdain for all too many technical skills—such as those involved in managing large-scale construction projects—other than those of their own profession.

Her second answer, of course, is corruption, which she understands as a condition in which people (politicians, public servants, businesses) use their privileged positions in order to pursue economic gain. The problem she identifies here is not the pursuit of self-interest as such but rather the manner in which it is pursued in such cases—that is, through the use of a privileged position. Thus she contrasts the pursuit of self-interest through competitive markets—where, she claims, it 'is transmuted into productive activities that lead to efficient resource use'—with 'situations where people use resources both for productive purposes and to gain an advantage in dividing up the benefits of economic activity—called 'rent-seeking' by economists' (Rose–Ackerman 1999:2). The problem in this latter case is that rent-seeking introduces costs and distortions with the result that a country will be 'poorer overall if corruption levels are high' (1999:3).

Rose–Ackerman also acknowledges, of course, that what counts as corruption often depends on the context: 'one person's bribe is another person's gift' (1999:5). Her aim is not to deny the reality of such cultural differences but rather to point out 'as an economist...when the legacy of the past no longer fits modern conditions' (1999:5). Here, the economist presumes to pass judgment over contemporary cultures and practices, dividing them up into elements that belong in the 'modern' world and those that should be discarded as really belonging in the past. While the latter may not always be seen as forms of corruption, the economist's perspective tells us that they have much the same effect.

Why do I think that this view of corruption is far too narrow? I can answer by way of a few examples, starting with two taken from recent issues of *The Washington Post*—excerpted in *The Guardian Weekly* of 9 March 2000. The first is an article on Brazil's civil and military police which claims that 'thousands of brutal slayings around the country are being blamed on corrupt civil and military officers'. The second, rather closer to home, refers to 'the worst corruption scandal' in the history of the Los Angeles Police Department. The *Washington Post* reports the LAPD's own internal inquiry as showing that the problem was caused, in large part, 'by its own poor management and a culture of mediocrity—creating the very conditions necessary for dirty cops to run wild'. Not surprisingly, the LAPD also insists, on the basis of the same inquiry, that 'only a small number of officers were directly involved in corrupt and criminal activities'. It is interesting to speculate about how much comfort the citizens of the United States could be expected to draw from the careful use of the word 'directly' in this last extract (how many employees in a large business organisation deal directly with its customers?).

For my purposes, however, what is most striking about these cases is that the word 'corruption' is used to describe the police activities in question, in spite of the fact that economic gain is obviously not the central issue. Even in Washington, home of the World Bank, there are times when it is clearly recognised that there is more to corruption than the pursuit of financial reward. Rose-Ackerman's treatment of corruption as if it were first and foremost an issue of financial gain and economic effect may not deny the existence of these other forms of corruption but it does suggest that they should be seen as something of a sideline. Thus, one problem with the narrowly economistic understanding of corruption concerns the value judgments—for example, that a few thousand brutal slayings may be ultimately less important than economic growth—which its technical language tends to disguise.

In fact, of course, the value judgments involved here are rather more complex than I have just suggested. On the one hand, it is often assumed that economic growth itself will reduce the incidence of violence in a society, and indeed of corruption more generally. The level of police brutality directed against members of the black community in the United States and the systematic corruption of the political systems in the most developed contemporary societies—Japan and the United States—suggest that this assumption may not be well founded. On the other hand, the contrast between economic and other forms of corruption—which the economistic definition tends to promote—should not be overdrawn. Police brutality is commonly directed against union organisers and other leftists, and against the poor more generally, and in that respect it has an obvious economic significance—although its effects in this regard will often be difficult to quantify. This point brings out another facet of the value judgments disguised in the economistic understanding of corruption—the issues highlighted by Rose-Ackerman's discussion are significant, not so much because their economic effects are more substantial than those of other forms of corruption, but rather because they can readily be analysed using the tools of contemporary economic theory. (An unkind critic might go further to suggest that, like the police themselves, economic theory often shows a marked social bias in its effects).

Now consider a few other cases of what some might regard as corruption.

- A government puts pressure on police and judiciary to protect its friends and to penalise its opponents.
- A ruling party appoints judges (at very high salaries) and uses the courts to destroy the political opposition. The practice is not uncommon, but Singapore is perhaps the best known example.
- A government acts illegally—that is, against its own laws—in order to influence the policies of other governments, to destabilise governments that it does not like or to prevent unfriendly governments coming to power. All powerful states do this—the United States is the best known example simply because it is by far the most powerful of all contemporary states and, unlike most other states, it has interests in all parts of the world.
- A government uses its powers to discriminate systematically in favour of some sections of the population and against others. Fiji, Northern Ireland and Quebec are well known contemporary examples, but all governments do this to some degree.
- Politicians and public servants are given high salaries relative to most of the population in order to make them less susceptible to bribes. This is one of the solutions to the problem of corruption canvassed by Rose-Ackerman. Why should one suppose that the political and economic effects of having the ruling stratum cut off from the majority in this way will be less damaging than the effects of bribery? Here, too, it is tempting to think that value judgments, rather than evidence and argument, may be at work.

I'll stop here, but it would not be difficult to extend the list of dubious political practices. What is significant about these examples is that they show how political, how contentious, the idea of corruption can be. Whether the practices I've listed are good or bad for the society in question is a matter of political dispute, and those who favour the latter view might be tempted to describe them as corrupt. But they would not be corrupt in Rose-Ackerman's terms. This point brings out yet another facet of the narrowly economistic understanding of corruption, namely, that it focuses on issues that are uncontentious. (Here again, as with the police and economic theory, an unkind critic might be tempted to suggest that this choice too disguises a certain political bias.)

A broader perspective

One way of taking a broader perspective on these issues is to go back into the history of the idea of corruption. The original, and still the most general use of the idea was to identify damaging impurity, some kind of intrusion or distortion which prevented something from being as it should—a foreign element in a chemical compound or a batch of seeds, stones in a packet of rice, talcum powder in cocaine, decay in meat or vegetables. In the case of government, then, corruption in its most general sense refers to anything that prevents government from being what it should (Euben 1989).

Thus, Aristotle, one of the earliest and most influential of Western political thinkers, distinguishes various forms of government—of oneself, of a household, of a slave or of a state—each of which has its own proper purpose and its own forms of corruption (1988). In his view, then, the government of oneself is corrupted if one gives in to unworthy desires or becomes a slave to one's passions. Again, the government of a household is corrupt if, instead of pursuing the interests of its members, the head of the household—assumed to be a male in Aristotle's discussion—uses his position simply for his own satisfaction. Similarly, if the government of a state pursues factional interests rather than the common interests of the community then it too should be seen as corrupt.

Of course, Aristotle's days are long past but this broad understanding of corruption continued to be influential in the West well into the modern period. Thus, when modern forms of representative government began to emerge towards the end of the eighteenth century many people were concerned that parties would be divisive and lead to the pursuit of merely partisan interests. David Hume, for example, notes that parties are

> plants which grow most plentifully in the richest soil; and though absolute governments be not wholly free from them, it must be confessed, that they rise more easily, and propagate themselves faster in free governments, where they always infect the legislature itself, which alone could be able, by the steady application of rewards and punishments, to eradicate them (Hume 1987:55–6).

The most notable feature of this passage is its view of partisan politics as a damaging infection. This fear of what partisanship might do to government is a continuing feature of liberal political thought but, by the end of the twentieth century, the term 'corruption' was no longer used to describe it. Another example appears in James Madison's comments on the danger of faction, which date from the early debates around the framing of the American Constitution. Faction, he tells us, is

> a number of citizens, whether amounting to a majority or minority of the whole, who are united and actuated by some common impulse...adverse to the rights of other citizens, or to the permanent and aggregate interests of the community (Madison 1857:43).

Notice that, in Madison's view, a faction might well consist of a majority of the population. This raises an obvious issue in the relationship between corruption and democracy since it suggests that the people themselves can be seen as a major source of governmental corruption. In fact, this view of the people has influenced the development of representative government in the West (Hindess 2000), where it is designed to limit the influence of the people themselves on the work of government, and it has been used by states, leaders of coups and the military in many parts of the world.

But, for the moment, the main points to notice are

1. that partisanship in government was once seen as a major source of corruption and even now, in the West, where political partisanship is commonplace, there is still a concern that the ruling party or coalition might go too far;

2. that while 'the common interest' or some such notion may be widely invoked, its substantive content is often a matter of political dispute, and that partisan groups commonly identify themselves as pursuing the common interest while describing their political opponents as representing merely factional interests.

Finally, before moving on to the next section, it is worth noting two further uses of the idea of political impurity. One concerns the identification of alien groups within the community—Albanians in Serbia, Indians in Fiji, Christians in India, etc. The sense of impurity invoked here suggests an obvious political solution, namely, 'ethnic cleansing'. This term may be a recent invention but the practices it refers to have played a major part in the history of the West, as indeed they have in other parts of the world. All contemporary Western states, with the partial exception of Britain—which engaged in extensive ethnic cleansing in other parts of the world—are the products of widespread population clearances (Mann 1999).

The other usage appears in the anti-élitism of populist politics. The underlying message here is that political and other élites pretend to speak for the people while actually representing only themselves—they offer a distorted representation of the common interest. Populism is often regarded as a kind of extremism but it is actually an endemic feature of modern politics—in which the rulers of all states claim to act in the interests of the people (Schedler 1997). Most successful political leaders resort to such populist appeals, suggesting that it is their political opponents who are out of touch with the people.

While the word 'corruption' is not often used in these cases, they appeal to the same underlying idea of impurity or distortion. I suggested earlier that the economistic understanding of corruption may be too narrow, that there are important issues which it fails to address. These last two cases suggest that there may be dangers in a broader understanding, that the invocation of impurity or distortion as something which ought to be corrected can sometimes have remarkably destructive effects. It is not obvious that 'corruption', in its most general sense, is necessarily a bad thing.

Why does it matter?

I have said enough to indicate why the economistic view of corruption may be too limited. I have also suggested, in passing, that going in the other direction may not be without dangers. But I have said very little about how or why this particular understanding of corruption has become so influential. Unfortunately, this question raises the more general issue of the role of economics in contemporary politics—and that is clearly too large an issue to address in a few paragraphs. For the moment, then, let me offer just a couple of observations. One, as in fact I have just suggested, is that the focus on economic corruption is part of a more general shift in governmental thinking over the last 50 years or so—a shift in which economic issues have become increasingly important to governments, so much so, in fact, that they are now widely seen as the central area of government policy.

The other observation is that development agencies were once content to live with a certain amount of corruption—as, indeed, were colonial governments before them—but that they have turned strongly against it over the last 30 years or so. And they have turned against it, not only in the narrow economic sense that I've been disputing, but also more generally. Thus, while not describing such issues in terms of corruption, these agencies now tend to favour human rights, free and fair elections, and so on.

This last development might seem to suggest that my critique has been misdirected, that the economistic understanding which I have disputed has developed alongside a concern for at least some of the issues that I would want to include within a broader understanding of corruption. This, in fact, returns us to the question of the relations between corruption and democracy which I mentioned earlier, and we should give some attention to the links that have recently been drawn between them.

Democracy was initially understood as one of only three basic forms of government. Aristotle, for example, defines a state as 'a body of citizens sufficing for the purposes of life' (1988:1275b, 21–2) and he goes on to say that the state may be ruled by the one, the few or the many. The last of these cases, rule by the many, is democracy. The modern idea of government by the people carries a similar sense—it is not a matter of government by a King, dictator or military junta. This idea, that the people are the ultimate source of political legitimacy for governments, raises one of the broader senses of corruption noted earlier: who belongs to the people and who does not—and it is partly for this reason that population cleansing has played such a prominent part in modern history.

But Aristotle was far from being an unequivocal supporter of democracy. On the contrary, all of the Greek philosophers who have anything to say about democracy regarded it as a potential source of a particular kind of political corruption—the corruption of government by the people themselves (Farrar 1988). The idea here is that government by the people is in danger of being dominated by the poor and poorly educated majority, in which case it could be expected to reflect their ignorance and their prejudices and the ambitions of unscrupulous demagogues.

In fact, this negative perception dominated Western discussion of democracy until well into the nineteenth century (Roberts 1994). When modern forms of representative government began to develop around the end of the eighteenth century it was not initially seen as a kind of democracy at all. It did give the people as a whole a limited role in government, and it was seen for that reason as a way of avoiding the kinds of corruption associated with rule by a King or aristocracy (government by the one or the few). But, because it gave the people a very limited role and left the work of government in the hands of a small minority of elected politicians and public servants, it was also seen as a way of avoiding the dangers which had traditionally been associated with democracy. The identification of representative government with democracy was a nineteenth century development, one that involved a radical transformation of the earlier meaning of democracy.

Unfortunately, it soon became clear that, in avoiding one form of political corruption, by the people in general, representative government opened the way for corruption of others kinds, that is, for the corruption of government by professional politicians and public servants—a form of corruption which has been the concern of populist politics on the one side and of public choice theory and contemporary neoliberalism on the other.

In fact, the history of representative government could be written as the history of attempts to minimise the effects of the new sources of corruption which it creates (Hindess 2000). Populism addresses the issue by attempting to replace professional politicians by politicians of a different kind—that is, by politicians who profess not to be professionals. Liberalism, inheriting the older tradition of distrusting the people, addresses the issue rather differently

1. by instituting a system of checks and balances, rational bureaucratic administration, codes of conduct for politicians and public servants, independent audits, among other things.
2. by reducing the temptations in various ways—for example, by offering relatively high salaries to elected politicians and public servants.
3. by reducing the opportunities for corrupt practice by taking government out of certain areas and reducing the scope for administrative discretion.

The last two categories are the prime targets of the economistic understanding of corruption, and I'll come back to them in a moment. But first, we should notice that when the World Bank and other agencies favour democracy, what they have in mind is a form of representative government that avoids the forms of corruption associated with dictatorship and military rule while giving a strictly limited role to the people themselves.

Let me conclude by observing that, in addition to the issues noted earlier, there are grounds for thinking that minimising economic corruption may not be the most important issue for government. Consider two possible remedies for economic corruption canvassed by Rose–Ackerman. She suggests that one way of reducing corruption is to reduce the amount of government itself, for example, by privatising government utilities and public services or by limiting the extent to which economic activity is regulated. Rose–Ackerman focuses on the advantages of such developments but they also have disadvantages, and it is far from clear that the former will outweigh the latter. There are, for example, well known problems associated with the process of privatisation itself—developments in Russia since the end of communist rule provide Western media with the most flagrant examples. There are equally well known problems of a decline in certain kinds of standards as a result of privatisation or a reduction of administrative regulation—safety, security of employment, service to less wealthy customers and so forth. My point here is not that privatisation is necessarily bad or that state provision and state regulation are always good. It is simply that minimising certain kinds of corruption should not be the only concern, and it is not obvious that it will always be the most important.

Another suggested remedy is to ensure that professional politicians and those working at higher levels of the public service receive salaries that are competitive with those in private business. The assumption here, which seems to me *prima facie* implausible, is that the better off will be less susceptible to bribery. But, even if it does have the desired effect, this remedy has the consequence noted earlier of creating a significant income gap between a cadre of professional politicians and senior public servants on the one hand and the majority of the population on the other. It leads, in other words, to another version of the problem of faction.

This last point brings us back to the older, more general view of corruption noted earlier. In contrast to this view, the economistic understanding of corruption seems both too narrow and too narrowly technical. It is too narrow because a focus on minimising the extent of economic corruption can obscure—and may sometimes exacerbate —more general problems in the workings of government. It is too narrowly technical because the identification of these more general problems depends on how we identify the common interest—and that, as we have seen, is commonly open to dispute. Thus, to treat the problem of corruption as if it were really amenable to technical solution is also to ignore the fundamentally contentious character of political life.

2

Research

A tool for building corruption resistance

Angela Gorta

With the increasing attention that is being given to corruption internationally, calls to 'combat the cancer of corruption' or to 'stop the scourge of corruption' have become more frequent. In order to begin to control corruption two basic questions need to be addressed

- where does one start in order to attack corruption?
- how does one start to attack corruption?

There are many possible answers to these questions, depending on one's understanding of the causes and manifestations of corruption, resources available and the legislative framework within which one is operating.

The 'hidden' nature of corruption means that much corruption remains undetected. This, in turn, highlights the importance of seeking to intervene before the corrupt conduct has been reported. More proactive methods of preventing future corruption (that is, how to increase corruption resistance) are required to supplement the investigation of reports of corruption once they are received.

This chapter illustrates how the NSW Independent Commission Against Corruption (ICAC) has used empirical research methods to improve efforts to build a more corruption-resistant public sector by identifying *where* and *how* to intervene. The basic theme of this chapter is that the more information one has about corruption the better equipped one is to prevent it.

The NSW Independent Commission Against Corruption

The New South Wales (NSW) Independent Commission Against Corruption (ICAC)[1] was established in March 1989 to expose and minimise corruption in the NSW public sector. It seeks to promote high standards of integrity in public administration. All public officials[2] in NSW government departments, statutory bodies and local councils, as well as judges, magistrates and elected officials fall within the ICAC's charter. Its jurisdiction also extends to those in the private sector and the general community when they deal with the public sector.

The ICAC has three main statutory functions,

- **to investigate allegations of corruption**—investigating and reporting on matters in order to expose and deter corrupt conduct and discover the deficiencies in systems and procedures which allowed the conduct to occur
- **corruption prevention**—reducing opportunities for corruption by advising and working with public sector agencies on improvements to procedures, policies, work systems and ethical culture
- **education**—educating the community and the public sector about the proper conduct of those in public office, the detrimental effects of corruption and the benefits which flow from action to reduce corruption.

In addition to these statutory functions, the ICAC uses empirical research as a tool to help it better understand corruption in the NSW public sector. ICAC research extends the information base on which the three statutory functions are carried out by conducting original empirical research on corruption and related issues, providing research support for major investigations, monitoring and/or evaluating anti-corruption initiatives, and providing the link to researchers working in related areas.

Such research might take the form of surveys or focus groups to discover public sector or community views. It might also involve an analysis of the existing academic literature. The research methodology is critical to its effectiveness. For example, survey samples are selected in such a way that results (from a relatively small portion of the public sector) can be generalised to the entire public sector. Care is taken in the design and administration of any surveys to minimise the possible impact on the results of the study being conducted by the ICAC. For example,

- some ICAC surveys have stressed their focus on exploring the range of *personal* views held about corruption (thus, there are no right or wrong answers)
- responses are returned directly to the researchers rather than through senior officers where respondents work
- respondents are assured that neither they nor their employers could be identified at any stage.

ICAC researchers are able to access operational information that would not be available to other corruption researchers such as those working in a university. ICAC research enables decisions about corruption-resistance strategies to be based on tested propositions rather than anecdotal evidence or untested assumptions about public sector behaviour.

Through this multi-strategy approach (of investigation, corruption prevention, education and research), the ICAC seeks to make the NSW public sector more resistant to corruption.

What is corruption?

While people agree that 'corruption' is bad and most can nominate examples of corruption, there is no one agreed definition of what constitutes corruption. There is a very large literature about different definitions of corruption (for a summary of this literature see, for example, Gorta and Forell 1994:4–24; Independent Commission Against Corruption 1997a:22–32).

The literature distinguishes different types of definitions of corruption. 'Formal definitions' (such as those provided in legislation, government guidelines and codes of conduct) frequently do not correspond to 'social definitions' (such as community and workplace views about what is corrupt). Even at the formal level, no one definition of corruption is universally accepted.

It has been argued that public opinion or social definitions are more salient in governing behaviour than are formal definitions. As has been repeatedly observed (Hollinger and Clark 1983; Werner 1983; Johnston 1986; Greenberger, Miceli and Cohen 1987), the influence of co-workers' attitudes on the behaviour of employees is significant. Hollinger and Clark, for example, have stated

> …these empirical results confirm…that employee deviance is more constrained by informal social controls present in primary work-group relationships than by the more-formal reactions to deviance by those in positions of authority within the formal organisation (1983:126).

The definition of corruption used by the NSW ICAC is provided in sections 7–9 of the ICAC Act (1988). It should be noted that the main role of these sections is to define the ICAC's jurisdiction—the range of conduct on which the ICAC can focus—rather than to clarify for the broader community what is meant by the term 'corruption'.

Broadly speaking, 'corruption', as specified within the ICAC Act, is the conduct of any person that adversely affects the honest and impartial exercise of the functions of NSW public officials. Corruption involves the misuse of public office. It also involves the misuse of information gained while performing public office. Commonly it involves the dishonest or biased use of power or position resulting in one person being advantaged over another. The ICAC definition of corruption takes into consideration the seriousness of the conduct. Only matters that amount to a criminal offence, a disciplinary offence, or conduct which would warrant a dismissal would be considered to be corrupt conduct by the ICAC. The ICAC definition includes the behaviour of private sector employees or community members if that behaviour is aimed at subverting a public official's performance of his/her public duty.

The Importance of dividing 'corruption' into its specific forms

It is common for commentators writing about the problem of corruption and causes of corruption to discuss it as if it were a single phenomenon. 'Corruption', however, is a term which encompasses many different forms of misuse of power or misuse of office. It is not a single issue, nor a single problem. For example, the term corruption can be used to describe behaviours as varied as bribing an inspector to license an unqualified person to operate machinery that might put lives in danger, theft of office resources for use at home, and police assisting criminals to commit crimes. In order to be able to begin to reduce corruption, it is important to have a clearer target (or targets) than the broad, nebulous concept of 'corruption'. If 'corruption' is viewed as a single problem it seems too large and amorphous to tackle effectively.

In their attempts to minimise crime, criminologists advocate taking a crime-specific approach in order to tailor prevention strategies (Gorta 1998a). For example, one would not use the same strategies to minimise shoplifting as one would to reduce physical assaults. The same is the case for minimising corruption. If corruption is viewed as a single problem it obscures the fact that specific strategies are best employed to deal with different forms of corruption. In order to combat corruption it is important that specific forms of corrupt conduct which pose the most serious risks (to the area of interest—or example, state/organisation/process/country) are identified. Until one has some understanding of what forms corruption takes and how it comes about, one can do little to control it.

Since there is no well-defined or universally-accepted taxonomy of different types of corrupt conduct, the first step is to identify a useful classification system for different types of corrupt conduct. The ICAC has used research techniques to establish a categorisation system for coding allegations of corrupt conduct to enable it to analyse patterns in the information it receives. This classification system involves summarising each allegation by pairing an area of workplace activity (for example, 'tendering', 'development applications', 'licensing', 'use of government information') with a type of corrupt conduct (for example, 'bribery', 'misuse or theft of public resources', 'favouritism'). Hence allegations are summarised in pairs such as 'favouritism in tendering', or 'bribery in licensing'. This is one method that the ICAC uses to clarify the specific forms of corruption that occur in the NSW public sector.

Finding out about corruption

In order to decide where best to intervene one needs to understand the nature of the corruption which is or may be occurring.

This is made difficult by the hidden nature of corruption. Corrupt activities tend to be carried out in secret with few witnesses. Unlike the victim in many forms of criminal conduct (for example, robbery or assault), the potential victim of corruption is unlikely to know that it has occurred.

Figure 2.1 provides an outline of how one might obtain information about potential corruption. This figure also illustrates how the corruption which does occur is filtered, with only some being reported. As is evident from this diagram, opportunities and motivation must exist for corruption to occur. Once corruption does occur it will only be reported if all of the following occur

- the corrupt conduct is witnessed or detected in some other way
- the conduct is labelled as 'corrupt'
- the witness decides that it is worth taking action about the conduct
- that action includes reporting the conduct.

One possible strategy to improve our understanding of the nature of corruption is to analyse the allegations received about corrupt conduct (see item 9 on the flowchart). Reports of corruption that are received by anti-corruption bodies such as the ICAC are, however, only a subset of all of the corruption which occurs. The reported allegations of corrupt conduct are those that are more easily detected and labelled as corrupt. Hence that which is reported is not representative of all the corrupt conduct which occurs.

The 'hidden' nature of corruption means that the examination and investigation of individual allegations of corruption, while important, is not sufficient to prevent future corruption. Any strategy that relies solely on investigating and prosecuting individuals who have been reported as engaging in corrupt conduct is disadvantaged by the necessity for corruption first to have occurred, be detected, and then identified as 'corrupt' before it can be tackled. Such a strategy is also limited because it can never detect all those who are acting corruptly.

Figure 2.1 Finding out about corrupt conduct

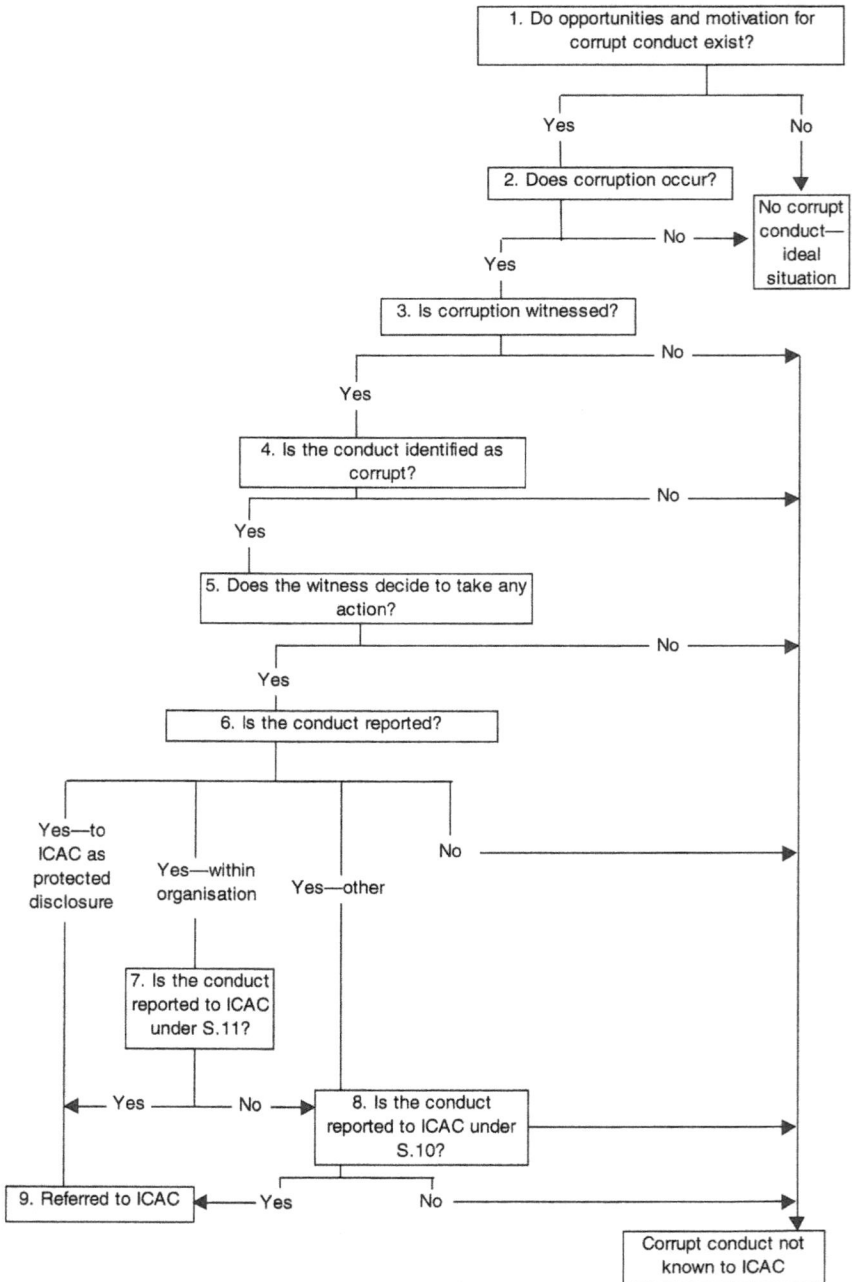

One consequence of the hidden nature of corruption is the importance of intervening before the corrupt conduct has been reported. Other more proactive methods of determining strategies to prevent corrupt conduct, such as undertaking empirical research, are required to supplement the investigation of reports of corruption once they are received.

The outline depicted in Figure 2.1 provides suggestions for identifying where to intervene before the corruption occurs to make the public sector more resistant to corruption and for making more visible the corrupt conduct which does occur. The process depicted in Figure 1 suggests that areas to explore in order to improve our understanding of corruption and to promote corruption resistance in the NSW public sector include

- opportunities and motivations for corrupt conduct to occur (see item 1 in the flowchart in Figure 2.1)
- making corruption more observable (item 3)
- making it easier to identify corrupt conduct (item 4)
- promoting action against corrupt conduct (item 5).

The sources of information used by ICAC research to explore these areas are described in the following section.

Types of research conducted by the ICAC

ICAC research uses a variety of approaches to aid efforts at building corruption resistance.

Considering the employees' perspective. The ICAC has found that surveys of employees' views can contribute to the formulation of strategies which assist in minimising corruption.

Employees' views are important for several reasons. Personal beliefs about corruption (social definition) have been found to have a greater impact than legislation or organisational policy documents in determining which types of conduct people identify (item 4 in Figure 2.1) and respond to as corrupt (item 5 in Figure 2.1). If people do not recognise an activity that they witness, or participate in, as 'corrupt', or at least as 'undesirable', then they are unlikely to take action against it. If they do recognise the behaviour as 'corrupt', but believe that, for example, such behaviour is appropriate given the circumstances, they are also unlikely to attempt to change their behaviour.

Since employees are in the best position both to engage in corrupt conduct and to witness any corruption that takes place at work and take action about it, it is important to consider their attitudes and beliefs. Examples of the use of this approach can be found in Coulter (1999), Gorta and Forell (1994, 1995), Independent Commission Against Corruption (2000a), Zipparo (1997a, 1997b), and Zipparo and Cooke (1999).

Identifying and disseminating strategies that some managers have found useful. Another strategy is to learn from those who have experience in attempting to minimise corruption. Drawing on the experience of those who have successfully fought corruption within their agencies (items 3 to 6 in Figure 2.1), advice can be disseminated to others in the public sector. This can **propagate** useful new strategies for reducing corruption and promote discussion of how best to minimise corruption. An example of the use of this approach can be found in Zipparo, Cooke and Bolton (1999).

Learning from others by reviewing the literature. Although corruption research is still in its infancy, there is already extensive material on factors contributing to corruption. Along with related areas of literature, such as those pertaining to ethical behaviour, crime prevention and organisational change, this material can provide a basis for identifying corruption risk factors (item 1 in Figure 2.1), and shaping corruption-resistance strategies (Gorta 1998a, 1998b; Zipparo 1998).

Analysing the types of allegations of corruption made to the ICAC. Soon after an allegation is received, the ICAC assesses the merits of investigating each matter individually. Analysis of aggregated allegations (item 9 in Figure 2.1) can usefully supplement the assessment of individual matters. The analysis of aggregated allegations to determine patterns and trends is important because it provides a mechanism for identifying public sector corruption risk areas and corruption-related issues that are relevant to a range of different agencies. It also enables the identification of agencies for whom the issues examined in specific investigations will be relevant. Examples of such analysis can be found recent ICAC annual reports (Independent Commission Against Corruption 1999b, 2000b).

Fostering community awareness and support for the minimisation of corruption. Based on the belief that a community which refuses to accept corruption is an important element in the fight against public sector corruption, community attitudes surveys can provide an informed basis for attempts to enhance public sector corruption resistance.

The ICAC collects information for these surveys through telephone interviews with a random sample of approximately 500 NSW adults. Each of the ICAC community attitude surveys conducted to date has contained two sets of questions—the first exploring general attitudes and perceptions about corruption, and the second seeking information about awareness of, and support for, the existence of the ICAC (Independent Commission Against Corruption 1994, 1995, 1996b, 1997b and 1999a).

Over the years these surveys have explored a range of issues, including
- perceptions of the effects of public sector corruption
- opinions of what is considered acceptable in the public sector compared with what is considered acceptable in the private sector

- attitudes to corruption
- awareness of possible responses to corruption
- attitudes to reporting corruption, and
- factors which would affect people actually taking action against corruption.

Examples of findings from such surveys include the finding that the majority of community members believe that they, as ordinary members of the public, are able do something about corruption in the NSW public sector and that they were most likely to make the effort to take action about corruption when they perceive the corruption affects them or their family (Independent Commission Against Corruption 1996b).

For any individual project, the type of research conducted by the ICAC depends upon the nature of the questions to be answered. It may include quantitative or qualitative empirical research and/or research using information from primary or secondary sources. As noted earlier, the research methodology is crucial to its effectiveness. ICAC research might take the form of

- surveys or focus groups with public sector employees or members of the community
- literature reviews to determine what can be learnt from the work of others
- analysis of the types of allegations of corruption made to the ICAC.

Some lessons from the research about how and where to intervene

ICAC research assists in building a more corruption-resistant public sector by identifying strengths to build upon and areas where further attention is required. Examples of identified strengths and areas for intervention are discussed below in terms of the following questions.

- What assists in the conduct being identified as 'corrupt'?
- How can taking action against corrupt conduct be promoted?
- What promotes an ethical culture?
- How does one to start to build corruption resistance more generally?

What assists in the conduct being identified as 'corrupt'?

As stated earlier, individual public sector employees' perceptions of what is considered to be corrupt impact upon the perpetuation of corrupt practices. If people do not recognise an activity as 'corrupt', or at least as 'undesirable' or 'harmful', then they are not likely to attempt to change the behaviour.

Examples of some of the identified strengths available for the NSW public sector to build upon when communicating about corruption include the fact that the majority of public sector employees

- do not restrict their definition of what may be corrupt to that which is prohibited by law (73 per cent in 1999) (Gorta and Forell 1994; Independent Commission Against Corruption (forthcoming))
- do not accept rationalisations that something cannot be called corrupt if everyone does it (94 per cent in 1999) or that the ends justify the means (79 per cent in 1999) (Gorta and Forell 1994; Independent Commission Against Corruption (forthcoming))
- do not condone petty theft from the government (92 per cent in 1999) (Gorta and Forell 1994; Independent Commission Against Corruption (forthcoming)).

Some examples of the areas identified through the research as possible places for intervention, together with the specific research findings follow.

Lessons from ICAC research

ICAC research has found that it is important to foster a common definition of what is corrupt in order to address the current lack of shared understanding by

- identifying and addressing 'grey' areas where employees are unsure of the appropriate behaviour
- focusing on the consequences or harmfulness of the behaviour as a useful educational strategy for communicating messages about corruption
- identifying, then challenging, explanations used to excuse or ignore corrupt behaviour
- providing specific training to address the needs of those participating in selection panels
- addressing educational messages across all subgroups of public sector employees.

Furthermore, public sector agencies should raise the awareness among contractors of the public sector's ethical expectations when these contractors are engaged to undertake public sector work.

Research findings on which lesson is based

ICAC surveys have

- found that NSW public sector employees differ in the types of behaviours that they consider to be corrupt. Thus, what any one public sector employee understands as 'corrupt' may not be shared by his or her colleagues. This research finding suggests that, when communicating to employees, it is not enough to have messages such as 'this organisation does not tolerate corruption' or 'report corruption'. Such messages leave open the response 'Yes, I know corruption should not be tolerated—but what I am doing isn't corrupt, it is just...'. A prior step to using these messages is to foster a common understanding throughout the organisation of what 'corruption' is.

- identified some behaviours where respondents were not clear whether or not the behaviour should be labelled as 'corrupt' (for example, in the case of theft with mitigating circumstances and for scenarios where rules were not followed yet a 'reasonable' outcome was reached).

- found that the perceived harmfulness of the behaviour was the variable which most frequently and best distinguished between those who consider a behaviour to be corrupt and those who do not. These results suggest that corruption, as an abstract term, is understood when translated into the more tangible context of the consequences of the behaviour

- provided insight into the criteria and justifications some public sector employees use when considering which behaviours are corrupt. For example, some respondents equate corruption with breaking the rules—as long as procedures are followed the behaviour cannot be corrupt; some suggest that if there is no personal gain the behaviour cannot be corrupt. ICAC surveys have also found a clear link between considering the behaviour as justified and the choice to do nothing about that behaviour (Gorta and Forell 1994, 1995; Independent Commission Against Corruption (forthcoming)). The literature on corruption and workplace crime indicates that, where an organisation does not clearly specify what is acceptable, there is more scope for employee deviance, including corruption (Horning 1970; Cressey 1986; Mirrlees-Black and Ross 1995; Hollinger and Clark 1983).

From the scenarios used in one survey, recruitment stood out as an area of decisionmaking in need of further attention in order to minimise corruption risks. Approximately one-third of the respondents considered that it was not corrupt to use one's public sector position to get a friend a job, irrespective of the respondent's experience in recruitment. This perception is inconsistent with the NSW public sector recruitment system which seeks to go fairly to the market, get the best person available, and leave no room for corruption or unfair advantage. Hence this perception needs to be addressed in both agency policy and training for those who participate in recruitment panels (Independent Commission Against Corruption (forthcoming)).

The relative unimportance of background characteristics of respondents in influencing perceptions of the scenarios and attitudes to what is corrupt suggests that educational messages and corruption resistance strategies should be directed across all subgroups of public sector employees (Gorta and Forell 1994, 1995; Independent Commission Against Corruption (forthcoming)).

Public sector rules are more likely to be perceived as negative or pointless by contractors engaged to undertake public sector work when there is a lack of understanding about the relationship of those rules to public duty and ethical work practices (Zipparo and Cooke 1999).

How can taking action against corrupt conduct be promoted?

In order to build a corruption-resistant public sector, public sector employees must be aware of the options for taking action and be prepared to take such action if they witness workplace misconduct.

Among the strengths available for the public sector to build upon when responding to potential workplace misconduct are that

- the majority of NSW public sector employees (86 per cent) indicated that they considered it their responsibility to report corruption (Zipparo 1997a)
- ICAC survey results strongly refute the notion that any reluctance to report corruption is due to peer pressure or that the Australian culture is opposed to reporting corruption (Gorta and Forell 1994; Zipparo 1997a, 1997b; Independent Commission Against Corruption (forthcoming))
- the majority of public sector employees believe that it is worth reporting corruption both because something *can* and something *will* be done about it (Gorta and Forell 1994; Zipparo 1997a, 1997b; Independent Commission Against Corruption (forthcoming))
- those in a position to take action (that is, supervisors, those in the higher salary categories, those who participate in recruitment and tender selection) are the ones who are most likely to believe that something *can* and *will* be done about corruption (Independent Commission Against Corruption (forthcoming))

- those with some experience in particular areas of work (such as recruitment and tendering), and therefore more likely to be in a position to observe corruption in such work, are more likely to say that they would report the behaviour within their organisation than those without such experience (Independent Commission Against Corruption (forthcoming))
- public sector employees are less likely to believe that people who report corruption are likely to suffer for it than they were in the past (Independent Commission Against Corruption (forthcoming)).

Lesson from ICAC research

The basic steps to equipping employees with a capacity to act if they witness workplace misconduct is for individual agencies to ensure that

- they have reporting mechanisms in place
- these reporting mechanisms include protection for those who use them
- they inform all employees of the existence of these internal reporting mechanisms and how they work, about external reporting channels available to the employees, and about the *Protected Disclosures Act 1994*, paying particular attention to induction training.

Management needs to take, and be seen taking, effective action against corrupt behaviour (including systemic change) in order to convince employees of the value of reporting corruption.

An organisational culture must be created in which employees feel safe to report corruption.

Research findings on which lesson is based

Each of the following was seen as a definite or likely deterrent from reporting corruption.

- Absence of formal reporting channels (by 55 per cent of the public sector employees surveyed).
- Not knowing anyone they could trust to whom to make a report of corruption (71 per cent).
- Lack of legal protection from negative consequences (76 per cent).
- Not being sure if their identity would be kept confidential (65 per cent)
- Not having enough proof (82 per cent) (see Zipparo 1997a).

A lack of knowledge of how to report corruption was found to be related to negative attitudes toward reporting corruption (see Zipparo 1997a, 1997b).

Recent survey results identified that it is those who are not supervisors, on lower salaries, and who have been employed for shorter periods, who consider that they are most in need of information about how and where to report corruption (Independent Commission Against Corruption (forthcoming)).

The belief that there is no point in reporting corruption as nothing useful will be done about it is a major deterrent to reporting corruption. Thus, if people are to be encouraged to take action about corruption, they must feel that their contribution will make a difference to the situation. While safe reporting channels are necessary, they are not sufficient (Gorta and Forell 1994, 1995; Independent Commission Against Corruption (forthcoming)).

Not being sure if their report of corruption would be taken seriously was seen as a definite or likely deterrent from reporting corruption by most of the public sector employees surveyed(61 per cent) (Zipparo 1997a).

Not being convinced that making a report will help to stop corruption was cited by 53 per cent of the public sector employees surveyed as a major deterrent to reporting (see Zipparo 1997a).

Managers acknowledged that being seen to punish perpetrators is extremely important for setting the tone of what is acceptable behaviour in organisations. On the other hand, those who perceive that their organisation does nothing about corruption say this sends a clear message to staff that corruption is acceptable to the organisation (Zipparo, Cooke and Bolton 1999).

Behaviours associated with the workplace being perceived as being honest include appropriate action being seen to be taken when wrongdoing is reported and appropriate action being taken against those who act dishonestly (Independent Commission Against Corruption 2000a).

One-third of public sector employees did not believe that their organisation would respond appropriately to a report of corruption and 54 per cent did not know whether their organisation was serious about protecting them from negative consequences if they were to make a disclosure (Zipparo 1997a).

Significantly fewer employees in 1999 than in 1993 agreed that people who report corruption are likely to suffer for it. The substantial number still agreeing with this statement suggests, however, that significant work remains for public sector managers to create organisational cultures in which employees feel and are safe to report corruption (Gorta and Forell 1994, 1995; Independent Commission Against Corruption (forthcoming)).

Lack of faith in how their organisation might handle reports was associated with employee perceptions that dishonest behaviour occurred in their organisation and that it was likely to go unpunished (Independent Commission Against Corruption 2000a).

What promotes an ethical culture?

Corruption occurs within a context. Some aspects of organisational culture facilitate corruption, others impede it. The lessons summarised above outline some of the steps to promote an organisational culture which impedes rather than facilitates corruption. The material which follows describes some more general lessons about promoting an ethical culture.

A literature review was undertaken to examine empirical evidence (as opposed to merely stated opinion) of how ethical culture impacts on the efficient functioning of an organisation as well as to identify which organisational factors impact upon ethical culture (Zipparo 1998). This analysis revealed that emphasising ethical work practices has a positive impact on the efficient functioning of an organisation. For example, it was found that the ethical tone of an organisation impacts upon efficiency and effectiveness, decisionmaking processes, employee commitment and job satisfaction, employee stress, and employee turnover. From this analysis of the literature, it was also apparent that, when it comes to making workplace decisions, aspects of the organisation appear to have more influence on the individual's ethical behaviour than do the individual's personal values. This provides a very positive message in terms of the capacity of organisations to influence the behaviour that occurs within them.

Lesson from ICAC research

A number of strategies for promoting ethical culture wthin an organisation can be derived from ICAC research. These include
- examining the organisational culture since the ethical culture of an organisation is critical to its performance.
- focusing on the example set by management.
- identifing corruption risk factors within the organisation, educating people within the organisation about these factors, and taking actions to minimise the risk.
- using tools such as codes of conduct and clearly stated values to communicate the organisation's ethical stance

Research findings on which lesson is based

Organisational culture and ethics research has shown that the ethical tone of an organisation impacts upon efficiency and effectiveness, decisionmaking processes, staff commitment and job satisfaction, and reduces staff stress and staff turnover (Zipparo 1998). The organisation has the potential to make an ethical person act unethically or an unethical person behave ethically (Zipparo 1998).

ICAC survey results confirm the importance of creating a workplace which emphasises and demonstrates ethical behaviour. Perceptions of an ethical workplace were found to be related to positive outcomes, such as staff saying they had better work relationships, greater job satisfaction, were less fearful to speak out, and were less likely to leave the organisation (Independent Commission Against Corruption 2000a).

In building an ethical culture, public sector managers advocate that 'tone at the top' is important. Appropriate behaviour must start at the top of the organisation and be transmitted down the hierarchy. The consistent and overwhelming message from public sector managers was that corruption prevention strategies require thought, effort and commitment from the top of the organisation (Zipparo, Cooke and Bolton 1999).

In this respect, public sector managers considered targeting education strategies towards CEOs and General Managers to be important, in addition to having education strategies for all other levels in the organisation (Zipparo, Cooke and Bolton 1999).

Behaviours associated with the workplace being perceived as being honest include supervisors and senior executives being seen to act honestly and practise what they preach, encouraging and emphasising honest behaviour in the workplace, treating all staff fairly and equally, and supervisors allowing staff to make decisions about how to conduct their own work and encouraging new ideas from staff (Independent Commission Against Corruption 2000a).

The most critical aspect of creating an ethical workplace is the behaviour of leaders (both senior executives and managers). The perception that leaders were honest was associated with staff having positive perceptions about colleagues, their job, and the workplace as a whole (Independent Commission Against Corruption 2000a).

Corruption risk factors are of interest because they present possible points of focus for corruption-resistance strategies. A review of the literature revealed the following corruption risk factors.

- The nature of the work performed, such as discretion exercised by position, position in the organisation and whether the work or service performed is associated with delays.
- Working conditions, such as the disputed role of salary and its relationship to need, lack of benefits for remaining with the employer, employee dissatisfaction, work pressures.
- Individual histories and dependencies, such as ethical decisionmaking history, dependence on employer, dependence on alcohol, drugs and gambling.
- Organisational culture, such as unclear messages about what is acceptable, attitudes of colleagues, example set by management, lack of reinforcement of ethical behaviour, other work practices.

- Other organisational factors, such as failure to identify the behaviour as wrong; existence, knowledge and perceptions of organisational reporting mechanisms; employee responsibility; organisational history in dealing with reports of corruption.

Other factors which affect whether action is taken against corruption, include individual beliefs about responsibility for taking action, beliefs about reporting being the appropriate thing to do, beliefs about whether benefits outweigh any costs, whether the employee has direct and convincing evidence of the wrongdoing, whether the wrongdoing is considered to be serious, whether the wrongdoing directly affects the employee (Gorta 1998b).

Survey results revealed that knowledge about codes of conduct, values, rules and procedures was related to employee perceptions that their organisation placed a strong emphasis on the importance of working honestly, had high levels of honesty among the executive, supervisors and staff, handled reports of wrongdoing appropriately, treated staff in a fair manner, and had values that matched their own (Independent Commission Against Corruption 2000a).

Public sector managers considered that it was important to have a written set of expectations (such as codes of conduct) that all staff are aware of in order to communicate the policies and standards set in the organisation (Zipparo, Cooke and Bolton 1999).

More general lessons on building corruption resistance

By exploring the crime prevention literature (Gorta 1998a), both general and specific lessons for minimising corruption were identified. In general terms, the crime prevention literature advocates taking an informed approach to corruption minimisation by understanding the process of engaging in corrupt conduct. Understanding the offender's perspective and considering different types of corruption separately are two strategies suggested to facilitate understanding the factors which underlie corrupt conduct. By examining individual types of corrupt conduct separately, those seeking to minimise corruption are better placed to tailor prevention techniques to match the various types of corruption.

Examples of some of the specific lessons for building corruption resistance which can be learnt from the crime prevention literature include

- not making assumptions that just because someone holds a particular position or has a particular background that they will be corruption-free
- asking offenders why they undertook the corrupt activity in order to identify circumstances which encourage corrupt conduct

- asking offenders about how they undertook the corrupt activity in order to understand in detail the process leading to the corrupt conduct and the necessary and sufficient conditions, in order to identify how and where to intervene in order to optimise the likelihood of prevention
- asking offenders whether they considered what they did acceptable and, if they did, why they did, in order that justifications can be identified and subsequently challenged
- after obtaining a better understanding of the dynamics and mechanics of corrupt conduct, consideration should be given to what recognised crime prevention technique, or set of techniques, might be most applicable to preventing a given type of corruption.

Conclusions

The basic theme of this chapter is that the more information and the better understanding one has about corruption, the better-equipped one is to prevent its occurrence. In order to combat corruption one needs to try to understand what forms it takes and how it comes about. Empirical research techniques provide methodologies for informing corruption-resistance strategies.

This chapter has illustrated the types of research the ICAC undertakes to inform efforts to minimise corruption in the NSW public sector and the reasons for such research. In particular, the following approaches are suggested as ways of informing corruption minimisation strategies

- consider the employees' perspective
- identify and disseminate strategies which other managers have found useful
- learn from others by consulting the literature
- analyse trends and patterns in allegations of corruption
- determine community awareness and support for the minimisation of corruption.

There are common themes which arise from the different ICAC research studies, undertaken using different methodologies. These common themes include the need

- to foster a common understanding of what behaviour is corrupt
- to identify and then challenge the rationalisations used to excuse or ignore corrupt behaviour

- for management to take, and be seen to take, effective action against corrupt behaviour
- for management to be committed and set an example
- to put effective and safe reporting mechanisms in place within organisations and inform employees about these reporting channels
- to examine organisational cultures and promote ethical culture.

When considering these research results in a broader context, it is important to recognise that the survey findings are based on samples (of public sector employees, private contractors or members of the community) from one Australian state. The public sector employees' views, no doubt, reflect their experiences in working in the NSW public sector and their knowledge of how allegations of corruption have been dealt with, within that arena, in the past. Despite this quite specific focus, many of the lessons from the ICAC's research work have broader implications. Over and above the specific research findings, you might also find helpful the broader concept of using research techniques to better understand different forms of corruption and how they come about in order to assist you build corruption resistance.

Notes

[1] The ICAC is based in Sydney, New South Wales (NSW). NSW has a population of approximately six million people, and an area of 801,428 square kilometres, and is the most populous state in Australia.
[2] Excluding police officers, whose conduct falls within the jurisdiction of the Police Integrity Commission.

3

An international human rights approach to corruption

Zoe Pearson

Corruption is a phenomenon that appears to be increasing throughout the world. It is a problem that affects both developed and developing countries to varying degrees, depending on the extent and type of corruption. There is a vast literature on the subject of corruption. Much of it approaches the problem from an economic or a political viewpoint, and the resulting analyses of the causes, effects and solutions to corruption reflect this approach. Corruption is viewed as having a deleterious effect on the economic growth and development of a country. This conclusion is generally accepted despite the limited empirical data. Corruption is also seen as a contributing factor to ongoing inequalities, whether in developed or developing countries.

It is important to extend the way in which corruption is analysed. It is argued here that current approaches that view corruption as exclusively an economic and political issue are inadequate and fail to give significance to the effect of corruption on people's lives and their rights. This chapter examines the effect of corruption on fundamental human rights. It argues that tolerance of corruption by states results in breaches of human rights and that existing international human rights mechanisms may therefore be useful in the fight against corruption. It does not propose the establishment of new human rights. Essentially, the fight against corruption and the fight for protection of human rights both rest on the need for accountable, representative government committed to equality and transparency.

The current approach

General Issues and approaches to corruption

Corruption is a phenomenon that human societies have experienced and attempted to overcome for thousands of years (Alatas 1990; Morgan 1998).

Alatas notes that the problem of corruption can be traced to the beginnings of humankind's social interaction and the development of social organisations. It is a problem that appears to be widespread. Despite the limited empirical evidence, most of the literature refers to corruption as being 'both pervasive and significant' throughout the world (Shleifer and Vishny 1993:599). It is important to emphasise that corruption is a worldwide phenomenon, experienced in both developed and developing countries. However, both the United Nations Development Programme (UNDP) and the World Bank note that the causes and effects of corruption vary from country to country, depending on the prevailing social, economic and political conditions (World Bank 1997b; UNDP 1999). Nye (1967:418) comments that while corruption is certainly not limited to developing countries, 'the conditions of [developing] countries are such that corruption is likely to have different effects than in more developed countries'.

While corruption and the campaigns against it are not new, the problem of corruption is emerging as an important global issue requiring global action. Glynn et al. comment that 'this decade is the first to witness the emergence of corruption as a truly political issue eliciting a global political response' (1997:7). Elliott, too, notes an increase in international action concerned with corruption this decade, with policies emerging to combat corruption from bodies such as the Organisation of American States (OAS), the International Chamber of Commerce, the World Bank (IBRD), the United Nations (UN), the International Monetary Fund (IMF), the World Trade Organization (WTO), and the Organisation for Economic Cooperation and Development (OECD) (Elliott 1997b:2–3). In addition, the growth of the non-governmental organisation Transparency International (TI) since its establishment in 1993 has been an important force in increasing the awareness of corruption as an international problem. Despite the limited empirical evidence on levels of corruption, the success and growth of international action against corruption indicates that there is real concern about corruption as an international issue.

The reasons for this increase in international awareness and action on corruption are varied. Commentators point to the increase in globalising tendencies as an important influence in the growth of awareness of corruption, with the increased interrelatedness of countries making corruption harder to hide (George et al. 1999). The end of the Cold War is also thought to have contributed to the emergence of corruption as an international issue (Glynn et al. 1997). Much of the literature discusses the increasing international integration in economic and trade arenas as important influences (Elliott 1997b; Joongi and Jong 1997). Other commentators point to the spread of values of democracy, and the increase in expectations of the accountability and transparency of states as influential (World Bank 1997a; Elliott 1997b). The increase in awareness of the importance of protection for human rights may also be a significant influence. The changing nature of the media in response to increased demands for transparency in the public arena, and the increased opportunities for communication due to advances in technology are also regarded as being important (Glynn et al. 1997; George et al. 1999). Glynn et al. believe that 'a new global standard appears to be taking shape in human consciousness, with potentially major ramifications for our institutions as well as our political and business lives' (1997:8).

Definitions

Definitions abound for corruption and nearly all mention the difficulties involved in formulating a definition. Gould (1991:467) notes that 'corruption has no single definition. It varies from region to region and remains largely contextual'. The World Bank (1997b) suggests that part of the reason for the difficulty in defining corruption lies in the complexity of the concept. Corruption is a phenomenon that may refer to many different human activities and behaviour in differing circumstances. As the causes and effects of corruption are different depending on the context of the country, it is perhaps not surprising that a single comprehensive definition that covers all the manifestations of corruption is difficult to formulate. As the Council of Europe notes, the result is that 'no precise definition can be found which applies to all forms, types and degrees of corruption, or which would be acceptable universally as covering all acts which are considered in every jurisdiction as contributing to corruption' (World Bank 1997b:20). The fact that corruption is studied from several different disciplines, including economics, law, sociology, political science and anthropology also contributes to the variety of definitions (Morgan 1998).

As a result of the difficulties of arriving at a universal definition, Morgan (1998) notes that much of the literature adopts a minimalist definition, concise and broad enough to be of use in most instances of corruption. The definition provided by the World Bank and also by Transparency International is an example of this, where corruption is defined as 'the abuse of public office for private gain' (World Bank 1997b:13; Transparency International website). Other institutions and authors have adopted similarly broad definitions (Morgan 1998:11–12). For the purposes of this chapter, such a broad definition of corruption will be adopted. It is worth noting that in most of these broad definitions, the focus is on corruption in the public sector, although there is recognition that corruption may also be present in the private sector. This may occur as a result of individuals engaging in corrupt behaviour within private companies for their own interest, and also as a result of individuals engaging in corrupt behaviour with public entities for their own private benefit. As the World Bank comments,

> the problem of corruption lies at the intersection of the public and private sectors. It is a two-way street. Private interests, domestic and external, wield their influence through illegal means to take advantage of opportunities for corruption and rent seeking, and public institutions succumb to these and other sources of corruption in the absence of credible restraints (1997a:102).

A distinction is often drawn between grand corruption and petty corruption. While grand corruption involves high public officials making corrupt decisions on large public contracts, petty corruption is generally said to involve public servants obtaining small extra payments—sometimes known as 'speed money'—from the public in return for the performance of their official duties (UNDP 1999). This chapter examines corruption as a systemic issue, and will thus consider the broader effects of corruption as a prevalent phenomenon, rather than concentrating on the differences between grand and petty corruption, both of which form a part of the larger picture of corruption within a society.

The broad definition can then be broken down further, distinguishing types of corruption by where it occurs (private or public sector), how it occurs (by extortion or consent), its intensity (high or low levels, depending on institutional mechanisms, governmental constraints and public tolerance of it), its prevalence (isolated or systemic occurrences), and what it involves (bribery, theft of assets, distortion of government expenditure, patronage, cronyism) (Morgan 1998:27–38; UNDP 1999:7–9; World Bank 1997b:13–15). Other distinctions are made depending on whether the corruption is local or national, personal or institutional, traditional or modern (Morgan 1998). In addition, distinctions are often also made in the literature between economic corruption and political corruption, though the two are necessarily often interlinked. Morgan comments that 'all of these various ways of dividing the concept of corruption into categories offer varying degrees of utility in identifying causes, consequences, and solutions. They suggest that the type of corruption determines the prognosis for solving the problem' (1998:12–13).

An examination of definitions of corruption often leads to discussion as to whether the definitions are universal across all cultural contexts. Morgan asks whether anti-corruption efforts represent a uniform standard of good governance or a misguided effort to impose subjective standards and values on countries and cultures where they are inappropriate (Morgan 1998:13). There is much discussion in the literature about the effects of cultural values and differing legal traditions and customs on whether certain practices are regarded as corruption. Due to these cultural differences, it is often argued that what constitutes corruption may differ between countries. For example, the literature notes that in some countries it may be customary to give a gift as part of a transaction, a practice which may often be regarded as bribery in other countries (Larmour 1997; Phongpaichit and Piriyarangsan 1994; Joongi and Jong 1997; UNDP 1999). However, some authors set out a clear distinction between gift-giving and bribery, noting that gifts are ceremonial, of a nominal value and presented in the open, compared to bribes which are secretive and often substantial (Alatas 1990). Larmour notes comments by a Nigerian Head of State, that 'the gift is usually a token. It is not demanded. The value is usually in the spirit rather than the material worth. It is usually done in the open, and never in secret. Where it is excessive, it becomes an embarrassment and it is returned' (Obasanjo quoted in Larmour 1997:3; UNDP 1999:8). Rose-Ackerman notes that often the critique of imposition of values is a mischaracterisation of local practices. She comments that many scholars of developing countries 'make it clear that traditions of gift giving do not translate into widespread acceptance of corrupt practices' and that widespread acceptance of corruption is not common (Rose-Ackerman 1999:177). However, issues of cultural relativity remain. Joongi and Jong comment, in the context of bribery as a form of corruption, that 'to create an international consensus to end the practice of bribery, these cultural differences cannot be disregarded and must be considered. Any efforts against international bribery will remain a contentious issue unless the fears that these cultural differences might be ignored in the process are allayed' (Joongi and Jong 1997:557).

Causes, effects and solutions

Due to the complexity of the phenomenon of corruption it is hardly surprising that the literature identifies many varied causes of corruption. The World Bank notes that the causes of corruption 'are always contextual, rooted in a country's policies, bureaucratic traditions, political development, and social history' (World Bank 1997b:14). Morgan summarises several widely accepted causes, noting that different methodological approaches identify different causes for corruption (Morgan 1998:13–15). At least three general classes of causes are identified: ethical or cultural causes (such as the changes to religious beliefs and public morality, the conflicts between traditional practices and colonial institutions), economic causes (examining the economic incentives for officials to act corruptly, and economic reasons for the private sector to tolerate, and engage in, corruption), and political causes (examining political systems and institutions, where weaknesses can lead to breakdown of formal rules and systems and lead to greater opportunities for corruption). There is also a growing approach in the literature that recognises that the causes of corruption are complex and interrelated, consisting of factors to do with institutional structures, civil liberties, governance, economic policies, country characteristics—including size—and existing inequalities between citizens (Morgan 1998).

Just as the causes of corruption are complex and varied, so too are the effects. Much of the literature approaches this issue from a political or economic viewpoint, looking at the consequences of corruption on a country's political or economic wellbeing. One of the primary foci in the literature is on the effect of corruption on the economic development of a country. In the past there has been limited empirical data, which has resulted in much theorising about whether corruption was in some circumstances good for the economic development of a country (Morgan 1998; Mauro 1997). However, more recently, emerging empirical studies have begun to show a negative correlation between corruption and long-term sustainable development. In particular, the work of Mauro indicates that corruption can slow development rather than be beneficial (Mauro 1997:83–107; Morgan 1998). Thus, there is increasing consensus on the negative effects of corruption on economic development (Shleifer and Vishny 1993; Morgan 1998).

Commentators point to the similarly negative effect on the strength and legitimacy of political institutions, and the consequences associated with this (Johnston 1997:61–82). For example, some authors note the effects of corruption on electoral processes and outcomes, and the subsequent political practices resulting from this (Etzioni-Halevy 1989:287–304). Nye notes that possible negative effects of corruption on governments include instability, reduction of administrative capacity, loss of legitimacy, waste of government resources and investment distortions (Nye 1989:967–73). The World Bank is also studying the links between good governance and development, especially with regard to anti-corruption (Kaufmann et al. 1997, 1999). One of the most widely discussed consequences of corruption on political and economic wellbeing is the distortion of government expenditure caused by corruption. This often results in public money being spent on large-scale projects—typically military or infrastructure projects—rather than on necessary public services such as health and education. The rationale behind this is that with large-scale expensive projects, more opportunities are presented for corrupt use of the funds (Mauro 1997, 1998; Morgan 1998). Related to this, the literature also notes that corruption exacerbates inequalities and poverty within societies. However, due to limited empirical data, these effects are not explored much beyond general statements (Elliott 1997b; Morgan 1998; UNDP 1999). As Morgan (1998:20) comments, 'additional empirical work to further develop our understanding of this complex issue is imperative. Understanding the full consequences of corruption is an important step in its eradication'.

The solutions to combat corruption suggested in the literature are similarly varied. The strategies used will necessarily be different depending on the type and cause of the corruption. Morgan (1998:20) notes that 'once the types of corruption and its determinants have been identified for a specific situation, anti-corruption reform is a two-step process. Policies must be developed that address the fundamental causes of corruption, not just symptoms. Then the political will must be created to implement reforms'. In deciding on ways to combat corruption, there is therefore a recognition that at the heart of the problem of corruption is the issue of good governance (UNDP 1999). Rose-Ackerman comments that

> combating corruption is not an end in itself. The struggle against malfeasance is part of the broader goal or creating a more effective government. Reformers are not just concerned with corruption per se but with its distortionary effect on development and society. Widespread corruption is a sign that something has gone wrong in the relationship between the State and society (1997b:34).

As a result of the focus on the economic and political consequences of corruption, the strategies that are commonly developed to combat corruption also adopt this approach. Morgan (1998:21) sets out the key strategies: 'serious and sincere commitments to counter corruption involve comprehensive institutional or administrative reform, reform of economic policy, legal or judicial reform, and in extreme cases of patronage and cronyism, reform of the political system'. Much of the literature discusses how to prevent officials from engaging in corrupt practices, through methods such as increasing the risks of getting caught, increasing the punishments involved for corruption, and limiting discretion of officials (Rose-Ackerman 1997b:46–55). This is also addressed at the international level with the development of new international agreements containing mechanisms to monitor and combat corruption of foreign public officials in the fields of international commerce and trade (Pieth 1997:119–31).

Corruption as an issue in the international arena

International action to combat corruption is very recent. Pieth notes that while some unsuccessful efforts began to develop international action on the subject in the 1970s, the topic of corruption has long been regarded as taboo due to its sensitivity (Pieth 1997; Klitgaard 1988). However, there have been several developments among international organisations this decade that have brought the issue of corruption onto the international agenda. One of the first initiatives to combat corruption on an international scale was the OAS Inter-American Convention Against Corruption, which was adopted in Venezuela in 1996. This Convention recognised the negative effects of corruption and the importance of coordinated efforts to combat it, and it has been widely adopted by the members of the OAS.[1] In addition, in 1997, the OAS adopted the Inter-American Program for Cooperation in the Fight Against Corruption, which sets out guidelines to implement the Convention and to combat corruption, working in four areas: legal, institutional, international, and civil society (OAS website).

Another important development in the international arena has been the development of the OECD Convention on Combating Bribery of Foreign Public Officials in International Business Transactions. This Convention was signed and adopted by the OECD in December 1997, after several years of negotiation and discussions, and came into force on the 15 February 1999. The Convention has now been signed by all 29 OECD countries as well as five non-OECD countries. Currently, 18 of these have ratified the Convention and the rest are in the process of ratification and implementation of new domestic legislation.[2] Australia has recently enacted legislation to incorporate the Convention. The Criminal Code Amendment (Bribery of Foreign Public Officials) Act No. 43 of 1999 came into force on 17 December 1999. The Convention represents an important part of the international effort to criminalise bribery in international business deals.

The United Nations has not played a major role in development of international instruments to combat corruption. Early attempts by the UN to address corruption as an international effort were stifled due to the lack of agreement and the atmosphere of distrust that prevailed at the time (Pieth 1997). However, the UN has remained part of the debate and has made efforts in its various forums and bodies to investigate and take steps to combat corruption. In 1996, the UN General Assembly (UNGA) adopted a Declaration Against Corruption and Bribery in International Commercial Transactions (Res.51/191, 16 December 1996). In addition, UNGA also adopted an International Code of Conduct for Public Officials in 1996, which recognised the seriousness of the problems posed by corruption and the importance of international cooperation in action against corruption (Res.51/59, 12 December 1996). Such resolutions are important in signifying broad political agreement in the international community. In 1997, UNGA adopted another resolution, on International Cooperation Against Corruption and Bribery in International Commercial Transactions (Res.52/87, 12 December 1997). George et al. (1999:39) note that it 'is by far the most extensive and significant declaration in support of the criminalization of bribery in international commercial transactions'. The most recent UNGA resolution concerning corruption— Action Against Corruption and Bribery in International Commercial Transactions—reaffirms the previous resolutions on corruption in international commercial transactions, and calls for national and international action against corruption by states (Res.53/176, 15 December 1998). All of these UNGA resolutions were adopted without vote. In addition, several UN programs and projects recognise the importance of addressing corruption as part of their programs. In particular, the UNDP takes an integrated and holistic approach to addressing corruption in its programs (UNDP 1999).

To date, the World Bank and other international financial institutions have been reluctant to address corruption as an issue. This reluctance is due largely to these institutions' perception of themselves as politically neutral, the limitations of their charters, and because of the sensitivities of many of their member states (UNDP 1999; Pieth 1997). Recently, however, this reluctance has changed, and both the IMF and the World Bank have increased their efforts to develop policies to combat corruption. This is welcome, as these institutions have long been linked with corrupt behaviour associated with their schemes and projects (Pieth 1997; UNDP 1999). The World Bank's approach to corruption is concerned only with the economic causes and effects of corruption. Due to the limits of its legal mandate, the Bank cannot concern itself with 'the exercise of State powers in the broad sense but specifically with the appropriate management of the public sector and the creation of an enabling environment for the private sector' (World Bank 1997b:24). The Bank sees itself as therefore limited to helping to design and implement government programs, by advising on economic policy reform and strengthening institutions, and also providing support in international efforts against corruption (World Bank 1997b). The IMF is also developing policies to combat corruption, one of which denies financial assistance to countries where corruption is likely to undermine economic recovery programs. The IMF has also recently adopted guidelines concerning its role in governance and promoting transparency and accountability in the public sector. The WTO has similarly begun to address corruption, with the establishment of a working group in 1996 focusing on transparency in government procurement (UNDP 1999; George et al. 1999).

Transparency International has had a major influence on increased action in the international arena in the fight against corruption. Transparency International's approach is to build national, regional and global 'coalitions', consisting of involvement of the state, international institutions, civil society and the private sector, to fight national and international corruption. It is founded on the principles of participation, decentralisation, diversity, accountability and transparency. Importantly, Transparency International does not seek to target individual cases of corruption, but rather to focus on building and supporting systems to combat corruption. The influence of Transparency International through its national chapters and its international conferences has been significant, both through increasing public awareness of corruption and through working with other international organisations to develop policies to combat it. Another important contribution of Transparency International has been the development of the Corruption Perceptions Index (CPI) which provides an indication of the levels of corruption believed to exist within countries. More recently, an important development by Transparency

International is the Bribe Payers Index (BPI) which provides an indication of levels of corrupt practices engaged in by transnational companies abroad.

Empirical data

As previously noted, one of the principal difficulties in discussing corruption is limited empirical data showing the prevalence and levels of corruption, and the effects that corruption has on countries. While this makes exact 'proof' of the levels and effects of corruption difficult, corruption is nevertheless widely accepted as a common phenomenon. It is recognised that measuring corruption is notoriously difficult owing to the nature of the phenomenon—corrupt behaviour is inherently secretive, which makes gathering empirical evidence difficult, if not impossible. Despite these difficulties, however, increasing numbers of empirical studies are emerging that attempt to measure levels and effects of corruption (Elliott 1997b:241–44).

Perhaps the most widely referred to is the Transparency International CPI, an annual report of Transparency International, which, in 1999, ranked 99 countries according to the perceived levels of corruption in the country (www.transparency.org). The CPI has been described as a 'poll of polls' and draws upon a large number of independent organisations' surveys of expert and general public views of the extent of corruption in many countries around the world. A number of countries are not included, however, due to insufficient availability of reliable data, and Transparency International stresses that it is an index of perceptions of corruption rather than a direct measurement of precise data. Importantly, Transparency International notes that the CPI shows that 'corruption is by no means perceived to be a plague confined to the developing countries. Numerous countries in transition in Central and Eastern Europe have very low rankings, while a number of leading industrial countries have scores that highlight the serious corruption problems that they must address' (www.transparency.org). The CPI is useful because it broadens the awareness of corruption, stimulates anti-corruption reform and influences the policies of international organisations, aid agencies and multinational corporations.

In addition to the CPI, Transparency International recently released a new index, the BPI. This index provides a ranking of 19 leading exporting countries in terms of the degree to which their corporations are perceived to be paying bribes abroad in order to win business opportunities. The BPI involved a survey in 14 leading emerging market economies.[3] The survey involved questioning senior executives at major companies, chartered accountancies, chambers of commerce, major commercial banks and law firms in each of the 14 emerging market economies about their perceptions of the levels of bribes being offered to their countries by corporations from abroad (www.transparency.org). The BPI is significant in that it attempts to show the responsibility and the role that industrial countries play in international anti-corruption efforts. Transparency International comments that 'the CPI only points the finger at the recipients of bribery. TI has always felt that this was inadequate, particularly since it does not reflect the responsibility of exporting countries for international corruption. The 1999 BPI is the first attempt to address this' (www.transparency.org). The BPI highlights the responsibility of industrial countries to take action to stop transnational corporations in their countries from engaging in corrupt behaviour abroad. The BPI is therefore a monitor of the effectiveness of the implementation of the OECD Anti-Bribery Convention.

Why combat corruption?

There has been some disagreement about the importance of combating corruption. Some authors have claimed that corruption may in some cases be desirable, facilitating and benefiting the development of a country (Morgan 1998). This view considers that corruption improves the efficiency of the country by providing a way around unnecessary, cumbersome regulations and bureaucratic delays. It is also seen as beneficial as it supplements the incomes of officials who may otherwise be poorly paid. This sort of view, however, is becoming less prevalent, as emerging empirical studies suggest that there is a negative correlation between corruption and the development of a country (Morgan 1998). The World Bank comments that such arguments are focused on the short term and therefore fail to take into account any objective other than enhanced efficiency in the short term. There are not only direct costs of corruption—diversion of money—but also indirect negative consequences, costly in the long term (Morgan 1998). The World Bank notes that in the long run, 'the results are likely to be costly in terms of economic efficiency, political legitimacy, and basic fairness' (World Bank 1997b:15). Such arguments also fail to address the underlying issue of what causes corrupt practices in the first place—the essential underlying structural inequalities and distortions within society that lead to corruption (Ward 1989).

Hence, there appears to be more of a consensus on the need to develop policies and measures to combat corruption, both in the literature, and also increasingly in practice at the national and international levels. While debates continue at the academic level about the definitions of corruption and on aspects of cultural relativity, it seems clear that corruption is a hindrance to the development and prosperity of a country. 'Governments can no longer deny its pernicious effects. Debunking this myth has been a crucial first step for building political will for any anti-corruption policy' (Morgan 1998:25; Shleifer and Vishny 1993:600). There is much discussion in the literature as to the possible benefits of eliminating corruption in countries, and these differ in emphasis depending on the discipline from which they come. On a general level, much of the literature focuses on the possibilities for increased development of countries. There is also focus on the opportunities for countries—and for the poor especially—arising from escaping the distortions of government expenditure on public services and infrastructure that are created by corruption. Those involved in business and trade anticipate benefits from the efficiencies of a corruption-free system, such as increased certainty in business transactions and increased opportunities for investment (Joongi and Jong 1997).

Possibly one of the most important reasons for combating corruption is the fundamental change in government that is required in some cases. Corruption is often associated with a lack of good governance: unrepresentative, autocratic, unstable and illegitimate regimes (Gould 1991; UNDP 1999). Corruption is often seen as essentially resulting from a bad system, rather than solely due to the influence of corrupt people in the system (Klitgaard 1988; Gould 1991). As Euben notes '... corruption is a disease of the body politic. It has less to do with individual malfeasance than with systematic and systemic degeneration of those practices and commitments that provide the terms of collective self-understanding and shared purpose' (1989:222–3). Much of the focus of the literature is on fighting corruption to improve good governance. Raising the standards of governance is thought to lead to many benefits for countries, especially in terms of economic, political and social development (UNDP 1999). It is seen as necessary for recognition of fundamental human rights, the rule of law, strengthening of institutions, political participation and strengthening of civil society and democracy (Ruzindana 1997; UNDP 1999). Much emphasis is also placed on the importance of strong leadership in efforts to combat corruption and promote good governance (Ruzindana 1997). Fighting corruption and promoting good governance is therefore crucial to developing an environment that facilitates the social, political and economic development of people within a country.

The inadequacies of current approaches

As previously noted, while corruption has been present in various forms in societies worldwide for thousands of years, it is only recently that coordinated efforts have begun at the international level to address the issue, and to discuss causes, effects and possible international solutions to the problem. Previously, the discussion of corruption as an international issue, both in the literature and in the international political arena, was negligible. It seems to have been regarded as a taboo matter (Pieth 1997). Until the mid 1970s, any analysis of corruption had a national focus (LeVine 1989). This appears to have been largely due to corruption being viewed as a domestic political issue which was the responsibility of individual states to address (LeVine 1989:686; Perry,

1997:36). Linked with the approach of regarding corruption as a national issue, there continue to be arguments that regard such international action as an unacceptable imposition of 'Western' values and customs on countries (Rose-Ackerman 1999; Pieth 1997). This continues to create tensions between developed and developing countries. As a result, Myrdal (1989:406) notes that the result is a certain 'general bias that we have characterized as diplomacy in research. Embarrassing questions are avoided by ignoring the problems of attitudes and institutions...The taboo on research on corruption is, indeed, one of the most flagrant examples of this general bias'.

This 'diplomacy in research', in addition to the general diplomatic approach on the international political level of non-interference with other state's domestic policies on corruption, has meant that the issue of corruption as an international problem was slow to be addressed. However, the enactment in 1977 of the US Foreign Corrupt Practices Act, and the subsequent attempts by the United States to get corruption on the international agenda marked the beginnings of an international movement to combat corruption. This 'opened a Pandora's box which much of the world—particularly those countries most affected by the revelations—would have preferred to have remained closed. On the other hand, the new transnational corruption, once revealed, had to be recognized for what it was—a new and dangerous challenge to the stability and predicability of the international market' (LeVine 1989:687). Increasingly, the focus turns to the responsibility and role of states in combating corruption, both internally and externally, for it is the efforts of states on the national and international level that are crucial in the elimination of corruption.

However, the examination of anti-corruption efforts by states remains limited, and to some extent a 'diplomacy in research' still exists. The current literature and action in the international domain approaches the causes, effects and solutions to corruption from largely an economic or political viewpoint. To some extent this reflects international practice in general, where consensus and action is more common and more readily arrived at in economic areas. In addition, much of the corruption literature and international action focuses on the actions of government officials only, and how to make these actors more accountable. For example, the OECD Convention focuses on combating bribery of foreign public officials in international business conventions; the four UNGA instruments concern adoption of an international code of conduct for public officials, and resolutions and a declaration concerning action and cooperation against corruption and bribery in international commercial transactions; and the World Bank's mandate is restricted to the economic causes and effects of corruption. Focusing solely on the actions of public officials often obscures the underlying wider responsibility of states to provide an environment in which corruption is not tolerated or condoned. The role of the state therefore seems marginalised, and the analysis restricted to economic concerns.

These approaches and strategies towards combating corruption are entirely valid and certainly necessary. The above comments are not intended to imply criticism of the usefulness of this approach *per se*. However, it is proposed here that this approach alone is inadequate. There is insufficient examination in the literature of the responsibility and role of the state to prevent corruption, both directly—by not engaging in corrupt behaviour through its officials— and indirectly—by not condoning an environment that tolerates or encourages corrupt behaviour by others. While current approaches address corrupt behaviour of officials and how to prevent and punish this sort of corruption, it is also important to address the corruption of the system as a whole that tolerates or condones corrupt behaviour, and to analyse the role and responsibilities of the dominant actor in this system, the state.

While general statements are often made about the effect of corruption on poverty and development, there is no explicit recognition that corruption is more than just wealth misappropriation or abuse of power. The effect of corruption on people's rights and needs has largely been left out of the corruption debate. There is little direct reference to human rights in the Preamble to the OECD Bribery Convention ('Considering that bribery…raises serious moral and political concerns, undermines good governance and economic development, and distorts international competitive conditions'); little in the Preamble to UNGA Resolution 51/59 of 1996 adopting a code of conduct for public officials ('Concerned at the seriousness of problems posed by corruption, which may endanger the stability and security of societies, undermine the values of democracy and morality and jeopardize social, economic, and political development'); and no mention in the Preamble to UNGA Declaration against Corruption and Bribery in International Commercial Transactions 51/191 of 1996. There is little reference to human rights concerns in the Preamble to the UNGA Resolution on International Cooperation Against Corruption and Bribery in International Commercial Transactions 52/87 of 1997 ('Convinced that such practices undermine the integrity of State bureaucracies and weaken social and economic policies by promoting corruption in the public sector, thus diminishing its credibility'); and only some mention in the UNGA Resolution on Action Against Corruption and Bribery in International Commercial Transactions 53/176 of 1998 ('Concerned at the seriousness of problems posed by corruption, which may endanger the stability and security of societies, undermine the values of democracy and morality and jeopardize social, economic, and political development').

The preamble to the OAS Inter-American Convention Against Corruption does make reference to the conviction that 'corruption undermines the legitimacy of public institutions and strikes at society, moral order and justice, as well as at the comprehensive development of peoples', and of 'the need to strengthen participation by civil society in preventing and fighting corruption'. The UNDP has also recently begun to consider the effect of corruption on governance. Overall, however, there is little reference to human rights in the corruption literature and in international action and instruments against corruption. Given the importance of human rights discourse in international law, an examination of corruption from a human rights perspective may shed some new light on the corruption debate, and provide some impetus for the way forward in anti-corruption efforts.

An alternative approach

A human rights approach

The growth of human rights discourse in international relations over the last 50 years has been impressive and is now universally recognised as a prominent aspect of international law. While there remain disagreements on aspects of the human rights jurisprudence, there is no longer debate on whether it is a legitimate subject for discussion between states (DFAT 1998). The basis of international human rights law rests upon the International Bill of Rights as the cornerstone of the human rights system, comprising the Universal Declaration of Human Rights (UDHR), the International Covenant on Civil and Political Rights (ICCPR) and the International Covenant on Economic, Social and Cultural Rights (ICESCR). These three instruments contain the fundamental rights and freedoms that are recognised as being universal in nature and essential to the enjoyment of life by all people. The two Covenants, which are binding on states that ratify them, have been widely accepted by the international community. One of the most important results of the development of the notion of universally applicable international human rights standards has been the recognition that human rights are a legitimate international concern.

Since the development of the UDHR, human rights have been regarded as inherent (that is, applying as a result of a person's humanity, rather than bestowed), inalienable (that is, cannot be taken or given away), and universal (that is, applying equally to all persons, regardless of race, nationality, status, sex, religious beliefs, and so on) (UDHR; DFAT 1998). There has been much discussion in the literature as to the relationship between the rights contained in the ICCPR and the ICESCR. Much has been made of the categorisation of the rights contained in the Covenants, and whether there is a hierarchy of rights. However, there is an increasing body of jurisprudence that takes a broad approach to human rights and argues against the categorisation of rights. This approach argues that the rights contained in the two Covenants are indivisible, interrelated and interdependent. The Vienna Declaration and Program of Action that were adopted at the Vienna World Conference of Human Rights in 1993 supports this approach and it is the approach endorsed by many countries, including Australia (DFAT 1998). This approach recognises that the values contained in the Covenants cannot be protected in isolation from each other, but that a more holistic approach should be taken in recognition of the interdependent nature of these rights and in the pursuance of the goal of human rights discourse—that of the pursuit of human dignity. Scott comments that

> [a] general conceptual analysis of human rights…should be approached with sustained attention to the underlying humanity of human rights and to the reality that human experience rarely confines itself to neat categories, much less highly abstract ones…By breaking out of overly rigid categories, human rights analysis can better focus on the underlying interests that rights should serve to protect…and the kinds of harm, practices, and systems that have historically generated the need for a discourse on human rights (1999:636–7).

The approach that is taken in this chapter is to transcend the categorisation of rights under the two Covenants, and to group the rights contained in those Covenants into categories that concentrate on people's inherent needs. There is no intention of suggesting that these groupings are in any way rigid, as the rights contained in the Covenants may be categorised in any number of ways. It simply represents an attempt to break from the rigid dichotomy drawn between the ICCPR and the ICESCR. This is useful for the purposes of this chapter, which explores human rights aspects of the complex phenomenon of corruption. The groupings serve as a productive way to examine how the fundamental needs of people are affected by corruption, and therefore how their rights are affected also. The groupings of rights used in this chapter are as follows

1. Rights to affiliation
   - right to self-determination
   - right to freedom of association
   - right to freedom of cultural belief and practice
   - right to freedom of religion
2. Rights to life, bodily health and integrity
   - right to freedom from torture
   - right to life, liberty, security of person
   - right to an adequate standard of living
   - right to health and wellbeing
3. Rights to political participation
   - right to freedom of expression
   - right to vote

4. Rights to non-discrimination and the rule of law
   - right to a fair trial and recognition as an equal person before the law
5. Rights to social and economic development
   - right to just and favourable conditions of work
   - right to education.

Examining a topic through a human rights lens involves focusing on the effects that a policy or practice has on the fundamental rights of people. It involves recognition that people have inherent rights, the protection of which must have consideration in states' policies and practices. It also involves examination of these policies and practices to determine their effectiveness or otherwise in protecting human rights. Therefore, this involves attention to the role and responsibilities of states in the creation of an environment that is conducive to the protection of human rights. Ultimately, for the successful prevention and elimination of corruption, it is necessary for the system as a whole to be involved. Transparency International notes that this must mean 'the involvement of all the stakeholders which include the State, civil society and the private sector' (Transparency International website). Moving from an economic and political perspective on corruption to a human rights approach involves shifting from viewing corruption as being a misappropriation of wealth and distortion of expenditure (that is bad for the economic and political stability of a country), to viewing corruption and the tolerance of corruption by states as also being a breach of fundamental human rights (due to the deleterious effects corruption has on people and on the state's ability to enforce these rights). Using the discourse of human rights enables the effects that corruption has on the ordinary person—especially in his/her contact with the state—to be recognised. Too often, the sufferings of people as a result of corrupt practices are hidden behind vague euphemistic statements of development and poverty levels that fail to draw national or international attention and stimulate the necessary action. It is proposed here that, by examining the human rights cost of corruption, added weight is given to anti-corruption efforts, as well as to human rights protection. A human rights approach to corruption provides an existing international procedural framework on which to base action against corruption to achieve minimum standards of protection of rights (HRCA 1995).

This chapter examines whether the generally recognised causes of corruption and the effects on people can be regarded as breaches of fundamental human rights, as grouped loosely into the categories broadly representative of necessary human needs. The issues that arise from recognising the role of states in tolerating corruption, both on the national and international levels, and the responsibility of states towards developing effective national and international mechanisms to combat corrupt behaviour are also important. Despite the limitations of the empirical data, there is an understanding that the phenomenon of corruption is widely recognised as prevalent, as is the usefulness of anecdotal evidence in this regard.

The Human Rights Covenants

While the rights noted above are grouped into categories in an attempt to use broad groupings based on the needs of people, it is recognised that the rights are drawn from two distinct Covenants. These Covenants place different obligations on states as to the realisation of the rights contained in the Covenants. The ICCPR provides that the state must respect and ensure the rights of individuals immediately; the ICESCR, by contrast, provides that the state must 'take steps…to the maximum of its available resources, with a view to achieving progressively the full realization of the rights' (Article 2 of both Covenants). However, there is increasing consensus in the literature and in the international arena—including the Committee on Economic, Social and Cultural Rights (CESCR)—that this difference in obligations does not indicate that states are free to delay the implementation of respect for the rights contained in the ICESCR. Rather, states must work towards the implementation of the rights, beginning with satisfying minimum standards (Yamin and Maine 1999:586–91). In addition, both the 1986 Limburg Principles on the Implementation of the International Covenant on Economic, Social and Cultural Rights (Limburg Principles) and the 1997 Maastricht Guidelines for Violations of Economic, Social and Cultural Rights (Maastricht Guidelines) indicate that states are required to move towards the full implementation of economic, social and cultural rights as soon as possible, and that the differing obligations contained in the ICESCR do not imply that states can defer efforts towards realisation of these rights.

What constitutes violation of the Covenants? Both the Limburg Principles and the Maastricht Guidelines provide guidance as to the nature and scope of the obligations contained within the ICESCR and also provide examples of what constitutes a violation of the Covenant. Both sets of guidelines were developed by a group of distinguished experts in international law, at meetings convened by the International Commission of Jurists (Geneva), the Urban Morgan Institute for Human Rights (Ohio, USA), and the Centre for Human Rights, Faculty of Law at Maastricht University (the Netherlands). Participants were a diverse range of experts from many countries, including academics, representatives of centres for human rights, non-governmental organisations, the International Commission of Jurists, staff members of the UN, and its Specialised Agencies and Committees.[4] The Limburg Principles have subsequently been adopted as an official UN document.[5] Both the Limburg Principles and the Maastricht Guidelines have been adopted widely as interpretive of the obligations in the ICESCR, and are useful for determining 'the general contours of possible violations of these rights' (Leckie 1998:89).

While both the Limburg Principles and the Maastricht Guidelines refer to rights in the ICESCR, they also accept the indivisibility and interdependence of the rights contained in both the ICESCR and the ICCPR. They also note that consideration must be given to the implementation and protection of all the rights contained in these Covenants, that a failure by a state to comply with an obligation in either Covenant is a violation under international law of that treaty, and that states are as responsible for violations of economic, social and cultural rights as they are for violations of civil and political rights. Therefore the guidelines provided in these documents are useful indicators of the kinds of behaviour by states regarded as a violation of either Covenant, and serve as guidelines for interpretation in addition to the relative clarity of provisions in the ICCPR as to violations of these rights. The Maastricht Guidelines are developed from the Limburg Principles and build on them, specifically providing guidelines as to the nature and scope of violations of economic, social and cultural rights. They are therefore a useful place to start when considering what amounts to a violation of a provision of the Covenants (Box 3.1).

The principles set up by the Maastricht Guidelines provide useful indicators as to what constitutes violations of rights in the ICESCR. Previously, there was some difficulty in determining what amounted to a violation as few standards of appropriate conditions were clearly set out, and this was compounded by the discussion as to what 'progressive realisation' meant. This was in contrast to the relative clarity of the rights and standards in the ICCPR, which was often backed up by indicators, bodies of national jurisprudence and precedent to draw upon as to what constituted appropriate conditions (Yamin and Maine 1999). As a result, these Guidelines may make things a little clearer concerning the responsibilities of states to protect rights, and states' culpability in certain circumstances of rights violations. Sometimes, due to the limited empirical evidence, it is difficult to establish a direct causal relationship between a state's actions or omissions and breaches of human rights. An example of this is in the case of corruption, where there is often a lack of evidence to establish a direct causal relationship with human rights breaches due to the secretive nature of corruption. These guidelines, however, indicate that states have responsibility both through action, and through countering inaction on the part of themselves and their agents, to provide an environment where human rights are respected, protected and fulfilled, and achieve a certain internationally-agreed standard.

Box 3.1   Maastricht Guidelines on violations of economic, social and cultural rights

---

II. The meaning of violations of economic, social and cultural rights...

14. Violations can occur through the direct action of States or other entities insufficiently regulated by states. Examples of such violations include
(a) The formal removal or suspension of legislation necessary for the continued enjoyment of an economic, social and cultural right that is currently enjoyed
(b) The active denial of such rights to particular individuals or groups, whether through legislated or enforced discrimination
(c) The active support for measures adopted by third parties which are inconsistent with economic, social and cultural rights
(d) The adoption of legislation or policies which are manifestly incompatible with pre-existing legal obligations relating to these rights, unless it is done with the purpose and effect of increasing equality and improving the realisation of economic, social and cultural rights for the most vulnerable groups
(e) The adoption of any deliberately retrogressive measure that reduces the extent to which any such right is guaranteed
(f) The calculated obstruction of, or halt to, the progressive realization of a right protected by the Covenant, unless the State is acting within a limitation permitted by the Covenant or it does so due to a lack of available resources or *force majeure*
(g) The reduction or diversion of specific public expenditure, when such reduction or diversion results in the non-enjoyment of such rights and is not accompanied by adequate measures to ensure minimum subsistence rights for everyone.

15. Violations can also occur through the omission or failure of States to take necessary measures stemming from legal obligations. Examples of such violations include
(a) The failure to take appropriate steps as required under the Covenant
(b) The failure to reform or repeal legislation which is manifestly inconsistent with an obligation of the Covenant
(c) The failure to enforce legislation or put into effect policies designed to implement provisions of the Covenant
(d) The failure to regulate activities of individuals or groups so as to prevent them from violating economic, social and cultural rights
(e) The failure to utilise the maximum of available resources towards the full realisation of the Covenant
(f) The failure to monitor the realization of economic, social and cultural rights, including the development and application of criteria and indicators for assessing compliance
(g) The failure to remove promptly obstacles which it is under a duty to remove to permit the immediate fulfilment of a right guaranteed by the Covenant
(h) The failure to implement without delay a right which it is required by the Covenant to provide immediately
(i) The failure to meet a generally accepted international minimum standard of achievement, which is within its powers to meet
(j) The failure of a State to take into account its international legal obligations in the field of economic, social and cultural rights when entering into bilateral or multilateral agreements with other States, international organisations or multinational corporations.

Note: The Limburg Principles and the Maastricht Guidelines set out examples of what amounts to violations. The failure of a state to comply with an obligation under either Covenant is a violation of the international obligations under that Covenant. Essentially, states have obligations to respect, protect and fulfil the rights contained in the Covenants. The Maastricht Guidelines provide some guidance as to what these obligations mean: the obligation to respect requires states to refrain from interfering with the enjoyment of the rights; the obligation to protect requires states to prevent violations of rights by third parties; the obligation to fulfil requires that states take appropriate legislative, administrative, budgetary, judicial and other measures necessary towards the full realisation of rights. The Maastricht Guidelines also note that there are then obligations on the state of conduct and result; the obligation of conduct meaning that the state must engage in conduct designed to realise the enjoyment of rights; and the obligation of result meaning that there is a requirement on the state to achieve a certain minimum standard of respect for rights as agreed in the international arena.
Source: International Commission of Jurists, 1998. 'Maastricht Guidelines on Violations of Economic, Social and Cultural Rights', *Human Rights Quarterly*, 20(3):695–97.

Classical notions of corruption and a human rights approach

An examination of corruption in terms of the effects that it has on human rights involves highlighting specific rights and how they may be violated. Sometimes there may be difficulties in this, as specific human rights are often bound up in broad concepts. For example, there is some discussion in the literature linking corruption and ideas of development, including aid, and also corruption and ideas of democracy. Currently, however, these analyses tend to focus on the economic and political costs to development and political stability, rather than examining to any great extent the human costs (Morgan 1998:15–20). As Alston points out, it is necessary to break down these broad terms such as 'development' and 'democracy' and to identify the values and rights contained within them in order to promote recognition of these rights. Alston goes on to note: '[w]e should affirm not that there should be 'democracy' and 'development', but that a range of quite specific values must be promoted and that those values, taken as a whole, will enable the realization of meta-norms of democracy and development' (HRCA 1995).

However, a human rights approach to corruption should also involve consideration of the broader, more systemic effects that corruption has on society as a whole. Examining corruption in terms of human rights highlights the obligations and accountability of states to facilitate the creation and the maintenance of a society in which human rights are respected and human dignity is promoted. To some extent this involves an analysis of existing discourses of the elements that are thought to be important for the idea of a good society, and the effect of corruption on these elements. It involves examination of ideas of democracy, development, the rule of law, accountability of power, and so on. While this involves looking at specific values, such as that proposed by Alston, it is also important to consider broad values that may be seen to be inherent in ideas of what a good society consists of, such as expectations of fairness, transparency, honesty and trustworthiness from those in a position of power within states. A corrupt state may be highlighted by discrepancies between what the state claims to do, and what actually happens, which in turn leads to distrust and cynicism by the people. Corruption may also lead to these legitimate expectations of society being violated as a result of lower standards that the state is prepared to enforce, including human rights standards. The lowering of standards in addition to general disillusion with corrupt practices in government may result in changes to society's attitudes and expectations, as reluctant acceptance of lower standards develops at a societal level. Therefore, an examination of the role of the state and society in considering the causes, consequences and methods of combating corruption is important. This recognition that corruption may be part of a broader societal problem rather than an individual economic one may be important for the success of anti-corruption efforts, and in particular for efforts to ensure protection for human rights against corruption.

The view that corruption is not simply an economic issue, but one that has broader societal origins and implications is an historical one. Heidenheimer et al. (1989:5) note that in ancient times, political theorists such as Aristotle regarded corruption as being primarily a moral issue, where corruption was used in an analysis of the structures and functions of society to characterise situations which were perceived to be 'marked by the decay of the moral and political order'. Aristotle's view of corruption involved looking at the ideals of a particular regime or political system; where the system fell short of these ideals, it was regarded as corrupt (Euben 1989). Euben notes that Aristotle's ideas of a healthy political system involved ideals of administration of justice, non-materialism in economic matters, diversity and unity, equality, higher guiding values of public interest over private values, and notions of citizenship (Euben 1989:227–30). Where these values were compromised, the system was viewed as corrupt. Corruption was viewed as 'a disease of the body politic', a degeneration and disintegration of the political system (Euben 1989:222; Friedrich 1989:18). Friedrich comments that corruption was therefore regarded as being 'a disintegration of the belief system upon which a particular political system rests' (1989:17). This view of corruption is therefore much broader than simply viewing corruption as an economic issue involving individual impropriety. Friedrich notes that this broader historic notion of corruption has developed into the modern sense of corruption—the abuse of public power for private gain. 'Corruption, then, has become a particular form of political pathology rather than a global degeneration' (Friedrich 1989:21). The current economic focus of corruption has possibly become more prominent due to the increased importance of economic activities in society and in international discourse, and also due to the increased notions of individuality in society. However, it is proposed that a reversion to these classical notions of corruption as being a broader societal problem may be useful for an alternative approach to anti-corruption efforts.

Corruption and violations of human rights

The difficulties encountered in answering the question as to whether corruption can lead to human rights violations may well be one of the reasons why it has not been adequately addressed in the past. Indeed, due to the limited empirical evidence establishing a link between corruption and breaches of human rights, it is difficult to present a clear case. This is not due to the absence of information regarding the status of human rights within a country, as this is fairly readily available, often in the form of UN reports, particularly annual reports such as the UNDP Human Development Report. The difficulty lies in linking breaches of these rights with incidences of corruption. This is the crucial work that remains to be done. There is some anecdotal evidence in the literature which can be drawn upon to demonstrate how corruption can run counter to states' obligations to respect, protect, and fulfil human rights, therefore leading to breaches. While these data are far from perfect, they nevertheless provide examples of how corrupt behaviour can lead to human rights violations and, therefore, provide a starting point for discussion.

Rights to affiliation. This category is proposed to include the right to self-determination (ICCPR, Article 1; ICESCR, Article 1), the right to freedom of association (ICCPR, Article 22; ICESCR, Article 8), the right to freedom of cultural belief and practice (ICCPR, Article 27; ICESCR, Article 15), and the right to freedom of religion (ICCPR, Article 18). An example of a possible violation of these rights, based on case law and recent reported events, is of corrupt behaviour on the part of a government official regarding leasing territory to private companies for mining or forestry. Where there is a group of indigenous people living and subsisting within the territory, extensive logging or mining may lead to the violation of the right of the group not to be deprived of their means of subsistence, a part of the right to self-determination under both Covenants (Jayawickrama 1998; Cockcroft 1998). In addition, this could also be construed as a violation of the right of the group to freedom of their cultural beliefs and practices guaranteed under both Covenants, if the change in the environment so drastically alters their way of life. Larmour points to several examples reported in two South Pacific countries where government officials were engaging in corruption in relation to the timber industry, to the detriment of traditional communities (Larmour 1997:6–8). Rose-Ackerman also notes the deleterious effects of widespread inefficient and environmentally destructive practices on traditional communities, many of the causes of which can be linked with corrupt practices in allocation and exploitation of natural resources (Rose-Ackerman 1999:19, 33). For example, corruption is often associated with decisions to undertake development projects, such as large-scale dams, which invariably cause the displacement of people from traditional lands, with violations of rights, including the right to self-determination and to a means of subsistence (HRCA 1995; Alatas 1999:94). As many as 90 million people may have lost their homes to make way for dams, roads and other development projects over the course of the last decade (Brown 1997:124).

Rights to life, bodily health and integrity. The general category of rights to life, bodily health and integrity is proposed to include the right to freedom from torture (ICCPR, Article 7), the right to life (ICCPR, Article 6), liberty (ICCPR, Articles 9–13), security of person (ICCPR, Article 9), the right to an adequate standard of living (ICESCR, Article 11), and the right to health and wellbeing (ICESCR, Article 12). One example of a violation of these rights is corrupt officials allowing the dumping of toxic waste into an area which is planned for residential purposes. There are also instances documented where the payment of bribes is thought to have influenced public officials' decisions in a Southeast Asian nation to allow the illegal importation of toxic waste from other countries (BAN website). Resulting ill health of the community caused by exposure to the toxic waste may mean that human rights—particularly the right to life, and the right to health and wellbeing—may be violated (Jayawickrama 1998).

Violations of the right to health and wellbeing are also linked with corruption through the distortion of government expenditure by corrupt officials. One study sets out preliminary findings that corruption reduces government spending on health, as a result of money going to large-scale projects, where the misuse of funds is easier to hide and presents more opportunities for corruption (Mauro 1998:265). It would be generally accepted that reduced spending on health is likely to lead to a decrease in the quality of healthcare available, and therefore a violation of people's right to health and wellbeing. It is also suggested that this can lead to corrupt behaviour on the part of medical professionals who must be bribed in order to obtain healthcare, further violating these rights (Alatas 1999; Cockcroft 1998).

High levels of corruption in governments and the resulting violations of human rights—especially the right to freedom from torture, right to life, liberty, and security of person—have often been linked. The Human Rights Committee—the UN treaty committee monitoring the ICCPR—has implied several times in its Annual Reports recognition of a link between corruption and violations of the right to life and the right to freedom from torture. In its 1998 Report, it noted in relation to one West Asian country

> The Committee is deeply concerned that all government power...is concentrated in the hands of an executive which is not subject to scrutiny or accountability, either politically or otherwise...the Committee notes with grave concern reports from many sources concerning the high incidence of summary executions, arbitrary arrests and detention, torture and ill-treatment by members of security and military forces, disappearance of many named individuals and of thousands of people...and forced relocations. In this respect, the Committee expresses its regret at the lack of transparency on the part of the Government in responding to these concerns (Human Rights Committee Report A/53/40 1998, paras 96–7).

Rights to political participation. This category is proposed to include the right to freedom of expression (ICCPR, Article 19) and the right to vote (ICCPR, Article 25). Freedom of expression includes the freedom to seek, receive and impart information and ideas of any kind. Violations of this right can occur on all three fronts as a result of corruption. Freedom of the press is essential to promote government accountability and transparency and there are several ways in which a corrupt government can stifle this freedom and control the media, which therefore may violate the right of freedom of expression (Rose-Ackerman 1999:165–7). Rose-Ackerman also notes the negative effect on freedom of expression by strong libel laws protective of public officials, pointing out that several North American, European, Middle Eastern, Asian and Latin American states have laws protecting public officials. These sorts of provisions often prevent or delay the publishing of matters that are of public interest—of which corruption by public official is certainly one—which may lead to a violation of the right to freedom of expression (Rose-Ackerman 1999:166–7). The CESCR noted in its 1998 Annual Report, in relation to the situation in one Middle Eastern state that 'the ability of people to defend their economic, social and cultural rights depends significantly on the availability of public information. Efforts to ensure accountability and to combat corruption also require such information in order to be effective' (CESCR Report on the 16th and 17th Sessions E/1998/22, para 346).

The Human Rights Committee noted in 1995, in relation to a North African state

> The Committee is…concerned that present laws are overly protective of government officials, particularly those concerned with security matters, it is particularly concerned that those government officials who have been found guilty of wrongdoing remain anonymous to the general public, becoming immune from effective scrutiny (Human Rights Committee Annual Report A/50/40, Vol.I, 1995, para 86).

And again in relation to the same state

> The Committee is concerned that dissent and criticism of the Government are not fully tolerated…and that, as a result, a number of fundamental freedoms guaranteed by the Covenant are not fully enjoyed in practice. In particular, it regrets the ban on the publication of certain foreign newspapers. The Committee is concerned that those sections of the Press Code dealing with defamation, insult and false information unduly limit the exercise of freedom of opinion and expression as provided for under article 19 of the Covenant. In this connection, the Committee is concerned that those offences carry particularly severe penalties when criticism is directed against official bodies as well as the army or the administration, a situation which inevitably results in self-censorship by the media when reporting on public affairs (Human Rights Committee Annual Report A/50/40Vol.I, 1995, para 89).

The right to vote and to be elected at genuine periodic elections—an aspect of the right to participation in public affairs—consists of two elements: the requirement of universal and equal suffrage and secrecy of ballot, and the guarantee that the vote must reflect the free expression of the will of the electors. This right can be violated by corrupt behaviour on the part of public officials, which is designed to interfere with the integrity of the electoral process, either through the bribery of electors to induce them to vote or to refrain from voting, or through the bribery of election officials to induce them to interfere more directly with the electoral process (Jayawickrama 1998). Such corrupt behaviour has occurred in some North American, European and Asian states (Rose-Ackerman 1999:137–8). Not only does corruption affect the voting process, but also the campaigning; politicians' political campaigns are often funded by wealthy interests concerned with influencing legislative outcomes and government policy. Examples of this occur in some North American, European and Asian states (Rose-Ackerman 1999:132–5). This represents further interference in the integrity of the electoral process and a possible violation of rights to vote and participate in public affairs.

Rights to non-discrimination and the rule of law. This category includes the rights to a fair trial and recognition as an equal person before the law (ICCPR, Articles 9–15). The main violation of these rights discussed in the literature is the right to a fair and public hearing by a competent, independent and impartial tribunal established by law. Corruption can affect the judicial process in several ways so that rights to a fair trial are violated.

> A corrupt or politically dependent judiciary can facilitate high-level corruption, undermine reforms, and override legal norms. When the judiciary is part of the corrupt system, the wealthy and the corrupt operate with impunity, confident that a well-placed payoff will deal with any legal problems (Rose-Ackerman 1999:151).

If one party has engaged in bribery of a judge, court official, or through bribery has access to documents the other party does not, then the trial will hardly be impartial, independent or fair (Jayawickrama 1998). In addition, where corruption of the entire government system is prevalent, the judiciary may not be impartial towards the state, so an individual attempting to take action against the state may not receive a fair trial. Rose-Ackerman notes that this has been the case in some Latin American and Asian countries, due to the lack of constraint by the judiciary of the executive (Rose-Ackerman 1999:147–8). For this reason, even where the judiciary is independent and impartial, it is necessary to conduct deeper reforms of the political system where corruption is prevalent in the state (Rose-Ackerman 1999). However, an honest, independent judiciary can be helpful in reforming the system and in protecting human rights, as has previously been the case in some European, Latin American and Asian states (Rose-Ackerman 1999:151–2). The CESCR has noted the importance of judicial independence in protection of human rights, commenting with concern in 1997 in relation to a Caribbean country

> that, according to the information received from various sources, that there is no mechanism for lodging complaints against the arbitrariness or corruption of some judges and that there is no appellate procedure for challenging the discriminatory application of the law, an executive degree or a decree of a court (CESCR Annual Report on the 14th and 15th Sessions E/1997/22, para 227).

The following year, however, the Committee noted with appreciation in relation to the same country that

> the measures taken to combat the problem of corruption of public officials, including judges, and in particular the increase in the salaries of government officials and judges. Furthermore, the Committee notes that the procedure for nominating judges to the new Supreme Court has been made public and transparent, with the objective of guaranteeing the impartiality of the judiciary and its independence from the executive…The Committee recommends that measures to combat the arbitrariness and corruption of some judges and public officials be pursued. In particular, the Committee recommends that information on the means available, if any, to challenge the discriminatory, arbitrary and unjust application of a law, an executive decree or a court decree be provided in the State party's next periodic report (CESCR Annual Report on the 16th and 17th Sessions, E/1998/22, paras 203, 228).

The CESCR also noted in 1998, in relation to one Middle Eastern state

> The Committee stresses the importance of an independent judiciary, ensured not only by constitutional declaration, but in fact by guarantees accorded to magistrates, in order to ensure the exercise of all human rights, in particular economic, social and cultural rights, and the availability of effective remedies in case of violation (CESCR Annual Report on the 16th and 17th Sessions, E/1998/22, para 332).

And in relation to a North African state, the Human Rights Committee noted in 1995 that,

> [a]lthough there is now in place an impressive array of State organs for the promotion and protection of human rights at various levels, the Committee notes that they have been concentrated exclusively within the executive branch of the Government. Consequently, it is not clear whether there are sufficiently independent mechanisms within the public administration and the judiciary to effectively monitor and enforce the implementation of existing human rights standards, including the investigation of abuses…The Committee is concerned about the independence of the judiciary. It is also concerned by the reports on harassment of lawyers who have represented clients accused of having committed political offences and of the wives and families of suspects (Human Rights Committee Annual Report A/50/40Vol.I, 1995, paras 85, 87).

Rights to social and economic development. This category includes the right to just and favourable conditions of work (ICESCR, Articles 6–9) and the right to education (ICESCR, Articles 13–14). Both of these rights can be violated through distortion of government expenditure due to corruption. Large-scale, capital-intensive projects which provide more opportunities for corrupt behaviour may be preferred by corrupt officials to labour-intensive projects providing work or spending on essential public services, such as education (Jayawickrama 1998). Indeed, a recent empirical study has shown a negative correlation between corruption and government expenditure on education. Mauro examines the relationship between corruption and the composition of government expenditure, using corruption indices produced by a private firm, for a cross-section of countries. The hypothesis he tests is that corrupt governments will spend more public resources on items which provide more opportunities for corrupt behaviour and for which bribes can be efficiently collected and secrecy maintained (Mauro 1998). Mauro's findings confirm the hypothesis that corruption alters the composition of government expenditure. Specifically, the study shows that government spending on education is reduced. Mauro's paper presents 'evidence of a negative, significant, and robust relationship between corruption and government expenditure on education' (Mauro 1998:277). Mauro comments that

> a possible interpretation of the observed correlation between corruption and government expenditure composition is that corrupt governments find it easier to collect bribes on some expenditure items than on others. Education stands out as a particularly unattractive target for rent-seekers, presumably in large part because its provision typically does not require high-technology inputs to be provided by oligopolistic suppliers (Mauro 1998:277–8).

When government expenditure on education is decreased, there are increased opportunities for violations of the right to education. In addition to the ICESCR, rights to education for children are protected under the Convention on the Rights of the Child. Where there is lack of resources to provide basic conditions for education, such as school buildings, textbooks and teachers, the access to and quality of education suffers and the right to education may be violated. Even where resources are provided, corrupt officials may divert these, and therefore the resources supplied will be inadequate or substandard. An example is provided by a project to extend primary schooling in a South Pacific nation which was affected by a corrupt official's misuse of some of the funds (Larmour 1997:9). UNICEF notes that the lack of basic education 'remains the most important single factor in protecting children from such hazards as exploitative child labour and sexual exploitation', which are violations of other human rights (UNICEF 1999:9). Decreased expenditure on education is a reason for concern, as previous literature has shown that educational achievement is an important determinant of economic growth (Mauro 1998), which is likely to be important for the protection of other human rights. Mauro notes that

> [t]he question whether corruption affects the composition of government expenditure may have important implications. First, while the empirical literature has so far yielded mixed results on the effects of government expenditure and, in particular, its composition, on economic growth, most economists seem to think that the level and type of spending undertaken by governments do matter for economic performance. For example, even though cross-country regression work has not conclusively shown the existence of a relationship between government spending on education and economic growth, it has gathered robust evidence that school enrolment rates and educational attainment play a considerable role in determining economic growth (Mauro 1998:264–5).

The CESCR has noted the deleterious effects that corruption can have, *inter alia*, on the right to education and work, through distortion of government expenditure. It noted in 1999 in relation to a West African state that 'economic, social and cultural rights were hindered by the negative effects of widespread corruption on the functioning of government institutions' (CESCR Report on the 18th and 19th Sessions, E/1999/22, para 97). It also commented in 1998 with regard to a transition state

> The Committee notes with apprehension that the process of transition to a democratic country with a market-based economy is being undermined by corruption, organized crime, tax evasion and bureaucratic inefficiency, resulting in inadequate funding for social welfare expenditure and for the payment of wages in the State sector (CESCR Report on the 16th and 17th Sessions E/1998/22, para 99).

The Committee noted that rights to food, health, nutrition, education and jobs were all affected due to the undermining of the social, economic and political structure in the transition state by, amongst other forces, corruption. Furthermore, in relation to a Middle Eastern state: '[t]he Committee notes with concern that a large proportion of resources necessary to finance social programs is diverted by corruption, which is pervading State organs and the sectors of the economy that are still under State control' (CESCR Report on the 16th and 17th Sessions E/1998/22, para 327).

Summary. This analysis indicates that, in many circumstances, corruption on the part of the state can lead to breaches of human rights. The analysis has sought only to give examples of how corruption can affect human rights and has attempted to provide supporting evidence where it is available. One of the difficulties mentioned above is linking corrupt behaviour with actual breaches of human rights. While this direct causal approach is useful for highlighting breaches, it should also be noted that breaches of human rights can also occur through indirect actions or omissions. It must also be recognised that corruption can have long-term effects which may not be as easily identifiable as being linked with resulting human rights violations, as well as short-term effects that are immediately recognised as breaches of human rights.

Conclusion: possibilities of a human rights approach

Taking a human rights approach to corruption highlights the fact that corruption is more than just misappropriation of money or abuse of power; corruption also has deleterious effects on people, which can lead to breaches of human rights. It acknowledges that corruption is a global problem, requiring global action and solutions. Giving corruption a 'human face' may lead to increased efficiency of anti-corruption efforts through better awareness of the effects of corrupt behaviour, increased calls for improved accountability and transparency in governments, and increased varieties of strategies that are available to combat corruption. The involvement of international organisations and institutions and non-governmental organisations in the process—many of whom already participate in human rights issues—may result in a strengthening of efforts towards human rights protection and anti-corruption, as these organisations put pressure on states to reform. Recognition of the effects of corruption as breaches of human rights as provided for under the ICCPR and the ICESCR may also lead to further attention being given to corruption within states by the respective Covenant Committees, which may be useful to highlight more explicitly the effects of corruption on human rights. Highlighting the human rights effects of corruption may serve to stimulate international concern and facilitate anti-corruption action. An element of this must be increased empirical study on the effects of corruption on human rights, which can only serve to stimulate further interest and action.

This chapter has highlighted that, while corruption is widely discussed in the literature and increasingly addressed in the international arena, a fundamental aspect of corruption has been left out of the discussion. The effect that corruption has on the fundamental human rights of people has been largely ignored, referred to only in the vague terms of 'development' and 'democracy'. The human rights discourse is an integral part of international law and needs to be incorporated into the international discussion and action against corruption. This chapter has highlighted instances where corruption has had, or may have, a deleterious effect on the rights of people. In examining the role and responsibility of states to respect, protect and fulfil human rights as guaranteed under the ICCPR and the ICESCR, the actions or omissions of states must be examined in regard to corrupt behaviour, as it has been argued that the tolerance of corruption by states through action or omission can result in breaches of human rights. States should be held accountable for this toleration. Utilising existing human rights discourse and mechanisms may be useful in the efforts to combat corruption to ensure human rights protection and accountability and transparency on the part of governments. The international community has an obligation to extend its anti-corruption efforts to the protection of human rights.

Notes

*   The author acknowledges the Centre for Democratic Institutions, The Australian National University, for its financial support, Roland Rich and Hilary Charlesworth for extensive discussions on the ideas and content of this chapter and for reading early drafts, and Peter Larmour and Barry Hindess for providing feedback on drafts and ideas.

1   OAS members which have ratified the Convention are: Argentina, Bolivia, Chile, Colombia, Costa Rica, Dominican Republic, Ecuador, El Salvador, Honduras, Mexico, Nicaragua, Panama, Paraguay, Peru, Trinidad and Tobago, Uruguay, Venezuela. OAS members who have yet to ratify the Convention are: the United States, Suriname, Jamaica, Guatemala, Guyana, Haiti, Brazil, Canada, Bahamas (<http://www.OAS.org/juridico/english/Sigs/b-58.html>).

2   The OECD countries which have signed the OECD Convention are: Australia, Austria, Belgium, Canada, Czech Republic, Denmark, Finland, France, Germany, Greece, Hungary, Iceland, Ireland, Italy, Japan, Korea, Luxembourg, Mexico, the Netherlands, New Zealand, Norway, Poland, Portugal, Spain, Sweden, Switzerland, Turkey, the United Kingdom, the United States. The non-OECD countries who have signed the OECD Convention are: Argentina, Brazil, Bulgaria, Chile, and the Slovak Republic. The following countries have deposited their instruments of ratification/acceptance of the Convention with the Secretary-General of the OECD: Australia, Austria, Belgium, Bulgaria, Canada, Germany, Greece, Finland, Hungary, Iceland, Japan, Korea, Mexico, Norway, Slovakia, Sweden, the United Kingdom, the United States (<http://www.oecd.org/daf/nocorruption/annex2.htm>, information correct up to 21 October 1999).

3   These countries were India, Argentina, Hungary, Morocco, Indonesia, Brazil, Poland, Nigeria, Philippines, Colombia, Russia, South Africa, South Korea, and Thailand (TI website).

4   The participants for the Limburg Principles came from Australia, the Federal Republic of Germany, Hungary, Ireland, Mexico, the Netherlands, Norway, Senegal, Spain, the United Kingdom, the United States, Yugoslavia, the United Nations Centre for Human Rights, the International Labour Organisation, the United Nations Educational, Scientific and Cultural Organisation, the World Health Organisation, the Commonwealth Secretariat, the sponsoring organisations, and four participants were members of the ECOSOC Committee on Economic, Social and Cultural Rights (Introduction, Limburg Principles, *HRQ* 9 (1987) 121; 285). The participants for the Maastricht Guidelines were

from Austria, Canada, Germany, Ghana, Italy, the Netherlands, Norway, the Philippines, Poland, Sri Lanka, Switzerland, the United Kingdom, the United States, the International Commission of Jurists, the Commission on Human Rights, the International Labour Office, Habitat International Coalition, and the sponsoring organisations (Appendix A, Maastricht Guidelines, *HRQ* 20 (1998) 702–4; Dankwa et al. 1998).

[5] The Limburg Principles on the Implementation of the International Covenant on Economic, Social and Cultural rights, adopted 8 January 1987, UN ESCOR, Comm'n on Hum. Rts., 43rd Sess., Agenda Item 8, UN Doc E/CN.4/1987/17/ Annex (1987).

4

Regulating virtue

formulating, engendering and enforcing corporate ethical codes

Andrew Brien

Amongst the most popular instruments used when attempting to inject ethics into organisational life is the code of ethics (or code of practice—I use the expressions synonymously). In fact, such codes are often the first formal structure to be established when the attempt is made to raise the ethical profile of an organisation. The popularity of codes stems from the fact that they are very adaptable; they are used in all types of regulatory environments, from external regulatory regimes to self-regulatory and enforced self-regulatory regimes. As well, all sorts of organisations— government departments and agencies, universities, along with many professions—have codes of ethics, as do many businesses (Abbott 1983:857). For example, one global study of business organisations found that 76 per cent of respondents had codes (Brooks 1989:120), while over 90 per cent of Fortune 500 firms and almost half of US companies have codes, mission statements or practice statements (Centre for Business Ethics 1992:863–7; Hoffman 1990:630; Murphy 1988:908).

The rapid growth in the number of ethical codes is a phenomenon characteristic of the past two decades. It is largely a result of widely-publicised ethical failures that have affected many people and have caused disquiet within the government and the professional, business and civic community about the behaviour of powerful sectors within the societies concerned. Writing in 1989, L.J. Brooks reported that 60 per cent of codes were less than ten years old. Six years earlier, Cressey and Moore (1983:55) reported that 43 per cent of their sample of codes in the United States 'were either drafted or revised in 1976, the year following the first nationwide publicity about corporate bribery', and almost two-thirds were written or revised between 1975 and 1977. Codes of ethics are also popular amongst academic theorists, many of whom consider them to have an important role to play in institutionalising ethics (see Purcell 1978; Mathews 1988:79; Snoeyenbos and Jewell 1983:129; Ferrell and Gardiner 1991; Weber 1983:534; Hoffman 1990; Maitland 1990:513–14).

Despite the popularity of codes, there is no evidence that they actually improve ethical standards. Violations are frequent, and compliance is a major practical problem (Brooks 1989:123; Snoeyenbos and Jewell 1983:103). The reasons why compliance is a problem are well known and fall into two categories—internal factors and external factors. Internal factors are those features of the code itself that predispose the code's constituents to violate it. The most common internal problem of codes is that they are poorly formulated (Starr 1983:104). They may contain inconsistencies, ambiguities, confusions or provisions that invite non-compliance and the development of cynical attitudes towards the code. For example, the code may be directed only at employees while management may be exempted, or the code may be self-serving and ignore the interests of other stakeholders, as many codes seem to do (Arthur 1987; Cressey and Moore 1983; Mathews 1988; Starr 1983). Thus, codes may lack an integral authority, and organisational actors will thus be encouraged to develop a disposition to ignore them or evade their provisions.

Codes may also possess inadequate external authority. This can be of two sorts. First, the ethical culture of the organisation may be weak. This sort of weakness is manifested in two areas.

- The leaders of the organisation may not fully support the code or affirm the importance of ethics in organisational life. Yet, enthusiastic support for codes, as well as ethics in general, by the leaders of an organisation is crucial to a code's success and, more generally, to the project of injecting ethics into organisational life. Without such support, a code is unlikely to be observed. The problem, however, is that since high-level executives have been frequently implicated in (or are the perpetrators of) much of the ethical misbehaviour that many of the codes have been formulated to correct, their support is unlikely to be forthcoming (Cressey and Moore 1983).
- The code may not have been internalised by its constituency. Often this means that the members of the organisation may not believe that the code embodies values that are important to their activities as members of the organisation. For example, actors may not respect a code because they have not been encouraged to see that the values embodied in the code are important in the daily functioning of the organisation.

Consequently, they will not be disposed to follow it, or, in ethically ambiguous situations, they may defect from it. Internalisation is important for the success of a code since people are more likely to behave in compliance with a norm if they hold the norm themselves. Therefore, such internalisation is essential to maintaining high levels of voluntary compliance.

Second, the code may not be adequately institutionalised. For example, the code may not be part of the organisational infrastructure, the mechanisms that promote the code may not exist or may not be used effectively, or there may be no systematic attempt to use the code, even if the infrastructure exists. Thus, codes may fail because the structure and culture of the organisation is not conducive to ethical action. Actors may be presented with mixed and confusing messages. Ethical ideals and an ambivalent or confusing organisational infrastructure for codes (for example, interpretation and adjudication mechanisms that are poorly coordinated, empowered, or which are not serious or clear about their respective roles) are often reinforced by pious affirmations from management and other organisational leaders within an ongoing organisational climate that is in fact antagonistic to ethics. The lack of institutions such as an ethics committee, an adjudication and interpretation committee, and an appropriate organisational climate are well known problems that undermine the success of ethical codes. This is widely recognised in the literature where it is often noted that such institutions are essential to the success of a code and its successful implementation, and it has been the absence of these bodies (or inactivity on their part) that has been a primary cause of their failure (Barber 1983:145, 151–2; Tomasic and Bottomley 1993:94–6). Surprisingly, while the drafters of codes seem to be aware of the importance of promoting compliance, judging by the fact that many codes include compliance procedures, few codes have compliance institutions, such as ombudsmen, ethics or watchdog committees, or well-developed, systematic and routine compliance programs (Cressey and Moore 1983:71).

The upshot is that while there is clear evidence that the organisational climate and institutionalisation of codes often have a more profound effect in promoting ethical action than behaviour modification and enforcement, which is usually at the heart of the project of implementing ethical codes, appropriate measures are seldom taken (Cressey and Moore 1983:71). In practical terms, this means that there must be effective and authoritative institutions within the organisation that interpret the code, clarify it, apply it to quandaries, resolve ambiguities and contradictions, communicate it, conduct ethical audits and enforce the code by adjudicating on alleged violations and responding to those found to have violated it.

The internalisation and institutionalisation problems include difficulties with grounding a code's external authority in the behaviour patterns of organisational actors. Clearly these are problems of implementation. How can the promulgator of a code encourage it to be internalised so that it becomes part of the culture of the organisation? How can it be made a part of the fabric of the organisation—a 'cultural artifact'—by establishing it as part of the stable institutions of the organisation? How can this be enforced most effectively?

While there are many suggestions for implementing and enforcing codes, there is surprisingly no discussion of the theory that grounds the formulation of codes or their implementation, nor does there seem to be any discussion of the criteria to be used to distinguish a good code from a bad one. There is, to be sure, an air of '*ad hocery*' in this entire area. It is this lack of a theoretical discussion that I want (at least to start) to make good here. I shall begin by developing an account of the nature of ethical codes. Using this, I shall then discuss the *desiderata* that determine the nature of a well-formed code. These *desiderata* are necessary conditions for the development of a code's internal authority. The nature of the implementation mechanism—a code's external authority—will then be discussed.

A code of ethics is, ideally, a statement of the organisational norms against which the actual or proposed actions of an actor—as a member of an organisation—are evaluated. Codes embody these norms in a variety of different forms as rules, principles, tenets, credos and ideals They in effect express the criteria for good and bad, right and wrong action, within an organisational setting.

Codes can be used in two ways—reactively and proactively. Reactively, an ethical code may be used as a basis upon which to regulate the behaviour of organisational actors because it provides the criteria for the evaluation of (performed) action. In that way, an ethical code may constitute the basis for discipline and deterrence. Proactively, an ethical code may be used as a standard to resolve ethical quandaries or, more simply, it may serve as a standard to which action must conform. In these ways, it guides the proposed behavior of organisational actors and educates and nurtures their ethical awareness.

Given this analysis of the nature of codes, *prime facie*, there seem to be both similarities to, and differences from, the institution of law that society has. To be sure, codes do differ from the laws of a society in that they are not typically punitive in orientation, nor do they expressly stipulate the result of non-compliance (Cressey and Moore 1983:69). Nevertheless, they do have a number of fundamental similarities to law. Like law, an ethical code operates on a one-way projection of power, from those who create and enforce the code, to those whom it regulates, guides and educates. And, like the law, a code relies for its success upon the voluntary cooperation of the code's constituency and acceptance by it of the code.

Such cooperation and acceptance will occur and be nurtured only if the code is seen to possess some inherent moral authority and legitimacy. In order that this aura of authority and legitimacy may develop, a code, like the law, must be framed so as to foster voluntary cooperation by the code's constituency. It will do this by taking account of the constituency's capacity to obey, by being, and being seen to be, 'reasonable', by taking into account the views of the constituency during the formulation and periodic reformulation processes and by being adopted through discussion and consent. This occurs in civil society with law, for example, when interested parties are invited to make submissions on a proposed law to a select committee of parliament and through the conduct of regular, free and fair general elections. Therefore, a code—like law—relies upon a projection of influence by its intended constituents, upon the drafters of the code when it is formulated, as well as a sensitivity on the part of the legislators to the needs, desires, aspirations and capacities of the governed.

This points directly to the similarities between codes and law—codes operate in an environment similar to that of law, and serve a similar function. First, they are the private laws of a private state; their efficacy is grounded ultimately upon the consent and support of the governed. On this analysis, a code's makers have a role in the formulation of the code that is analogous to that of the law's makers (Cressey and Moore 1983:67–8). Second, codes have a similar function to the law in society—they embody criteria that are used within the institutional context to guide and evaluate conduct, proactively and persuasively, and sometimes reactively and coercively. They have the capacity to provide the basis for discipline and a foundation upon which one member of the organisation may be empowered to behave in a certain way towards another, when in the ordinary course of events such behaviour would not be permitted. In this way, codes, like the law, may enjoin certain actions and prohibit others. In their general outlook, however, codes embody the values and ideals of the organisation in the same way that the law as a body of practice and knowledge embodies the values and ideals of society.

These similarities to law are important. Just as there can be well or poorly-drafted laws, there can be well or poorly-drafted codes of ethics, and it seems that given the extensive similarities, codes (like laws) may be well-drafted or poorly-drafted for the same sorts of reasons. The question then is what criteria should be used to distinguish well-drafted from poorly-drafted laws? One influential account of such criteria has been given by Lon Fuller. According to Fuller (1969:96), these criteria 'are like the natural laws of carpentry, or at least those laws respected by a carpenter who wants the house he builds to remain standing and serve the purpose of those who live in it'. Just as the natural laws of carpentry—the rules that a carpenter must obey in order to attain his purpose—are determined by the purpose he has, the natural laws or criteria governing the nature of well-drafted law—the rules that a lawmaker must obey in order to attain her purpose—are determined by the purpose she has in making laws.

This leads to another question. Do the criteria that a law must meet in order to be considered well-drafted also apply to codes of ethics? Clearly they must. The activity of lawmaking is, according to Fuller (1969:106, 122), 'the enterprise of subjecting human conduct to the governance of rules'. The activity of code-making is similar, since the aim is to regulate human conduct by using criteria for right and wrong conduct.

Moreover, according to Fuller (1969:205), the purpose of law is to provide a 'firm base-line for human interaction' in order to secure the good life. In order that they fulfil this purpose (that is, are effective), laws must be such that they are capable of being obeyed and of guiding action, and laws that do this are considered well-drafted. Codes share the same purpose. They are designed to provide a baseline against which behaviour can be evaluated and regulated and consequently to promote the flourishing of the organisation. This in turn promotes the wellbeing of the stakeholders. In order for this purpose to be fulfilled, codes must, like the law and individual laws, be capable of being obeyed and guiding action, and (like laws) codes that do this are well-drafted. Since the activity and the purpose of the law and codes are identical and the contexts of their operation analogous, it is reasonable to conclude that the properties the law must have in order to be capable of attaining its purpose must also be possessed by ethical codes.

What properties does a well-drafted law (or, as I have been arguing, a code of ethics) possess? Fuller's (1969:39, 46–91) answer to this question consists of eight necessary criteria

- there must be rules or laws that ground evaluation of action rather than *ad hoc* evaluation
- laws must be publicised
- laws cannot be made retroactively
- laws must be understandable
- laws should not be contradictory
- laws must be within the power of the citizens to obey them
- laws must maintain a degree of stability through time
- laws as announced must be in agreement with their actual administration.

Fuller claims that a total failure in any one of these eight *desiderata* does not simply result in a 'bad legal system'. He claims that it 'results in something that is not properly called a legal system at all, except perhaps in the Pickwickian sense in which a void contract can still be said to be some kind of contract' (Fuller 1969:38). Fuller's point is that what makes a putative legal system a genuine legal system is its capacity to fulfil the purpose that legal systems have in societies. The proximate purpose of the legal system is to 'subject human conduct to the governance of rules' in order to procure the ultimate purpose of promoting human wellbeing. A total failure in any one of these *desiderata* will result in a lack of general rules that can be used to regulate human conduct; consequently, the proximate and ultimate purposes will be prevented from being realised. In virtue of this, the system will fail to be a legal system. Similarly, a putative code of ethics would fail to be a 'code of ethics', since it would fail to embody (in a useful manner), the norms of the organisation that are used to guide, regulate and evaluate action in order to promote the flourishing and wellbeing of the organisation's stakeholders. It would be unable to fulfil its purpose and would, for this reason, fail to be a code of ethics.

Fuller's justification for each of the *desiderata* is based upon the capacities that human agents possess: that actors are rational, that there must be a point to action, that actors require guarantees that the laws will not be used against them capriciously or whimsically and certainty as to outcomes.

> Certainly there can be no rational ground for asserting that a man can have a moral obligation to obey a legal rule that does not exist, or is kept secret from him, or that came into existence only after he acted, or was unintelligible or was contradicted by another rule of the same system, or commanded the impossible, or changed every minute. It may not be impossible for a man to obey a rule that is disregarded by those charged with its administration, but at some point obedience becomes futile—as futile, in fact, as casting a vote that will never be counted (Fuller 1969:39).

Such reasons apply also to codes of ethics, since the nature of human agency within organisations is substantially similar, and the role of a code of ethics in civil society is analogous to that of the law.

Are there only eight *desiderata*? It would seem not. Actors must be able to trust the code, have confidence in it and see that it is not an instrument of repression, but one of protection, which promotes the good of the organisation and its stakeholders. Fuller's eight *desiderata* fail to do this completely, since by themselves they fail to deliver adequately the wellbeing of the code's stakeholders and the subjective sense of security that is essential if a code is to be capable of being effectively implemented and adhered to. They fail to provide grounds upon which to base trust in the code.

Such trust is based ultimately upon an agreement between the organisation's governors and governed, and the capacity of the governed to be certain that the agreement is being honoured. In other words, a culture of trust must be cultivated (see Brien 1998). Fuller's eight *desiderata* do not, however, provide an adequate means whereby the code's constituents can see that the agreement legitimising the code is being honoured. To be sure, the moral and rational basis of a code is the same as it is for law. Like the law, a code rests upon a contract between the code-makers and the code's constituents. The contract embodies the interlocking responsibilities of the governors of the (corporate) state and its citizens. These responsibilities arise from the same source, an offer which must be made by the organisation's governors if the code is to be effective: 'These are the rules we ask you to follow. If you will obey them, you have our promise that they are the rules we will apply to your conduct.' (Fuller 1969:216–17). Once accepted, the code attains legitimacy and the contract at the basis of the code's legitimacy embodies a bond of reciprocity; a person, in virtue of being a member of the organisation with this code, has an obligation to obey the code and the organisation's governors have an obligation to abide by the rules they have made.

To be effective, however, contracts must be nurtured by appropriate institutions and practices (something that Fuller seems merely to assume). That is, unless the constituents can see that it is being honoured, the code, like the law, will be ineffective. It will not be trusted and it will not attain the purpose set for it. To be effective, a code must have a form that promotes trust, that does not discourage voluntary compliance but rather promotes it, and which provides a means whereby the constituents can see and be assured that the contract that is the foundation of the code is being honoured. For these reasons codes must offer their constituents clear guarantees as to their application and use. These guarantees provide clear grounds upon which to trust the code and trust that it will not be used against them without justification. Ultimately, such guarantees provide a basis upon which to evaluate whether the contract is being honoured and a criterion for continued compliance and acceptance. To Fuller's eight *desiderata* must be added: due process, procedural justice, and substantive morality and justice. In other words, the code must contain explicit provisions stating that

- the implementation and enforcement will be carried out in a particular, known and settled way, rather than secretly or haphazardly
- the code will be applied to all members of the organisation, from the CEO down

- the code and its use rests upon legitimate authority, typically the consent of the governed
- people will be treated in accordance with their culpability, in the case of wrongdoing, or praiseworthiness in the case of exemplary service.

However, this is not all. Two further conditions concern the nature that the provisions themselves should have. The provisions must be general. However, provisions can be general in two quite different senses, both of which are important here—provisions must be general in the sense that they must refer to types or classes of actions, and provisions must be general in the sense that laws must not be directed at one individual but at classes of individuals. Why should the provisions of a code be general in any of these senses? Provisions directed at individuals, rather than individuals occupying a certain role, will smack of victimisation. And even if such a provision is initially benign, it may provide a precedent upon which an organisation may base future victimisation of individuals. It is best to avoid mention of individuals altogether and talk instead of 'role duties' and ideals.

Moreover, provisions should be directed at classes of actions since it is impossible to construct a workable code that will specify in advance all the vagaries and nuances of human action. Provisions must refer to general rules or principles in order to remain a code of ethics, rather than a code of directions, as one might find in an instruction manual.

Codes should be general so that the organisation's governors will not have to expend enormous energy formulating precise ordinances, and monitoring and enforcing compliance with individual ordinances. It is more sensible to have general rules or principles aimed at all, bolstered by organisational ideals where possible, and to leave the observance, interpretation and implementation to the commonsense of individuals, stepping in only when justified—in much the same way that the law does.

In addition to these extra *desiderata*, codes must be seen to address real issues and not be merely another mechanism for social control. A code which did that would destroy the trust between the organisation's governors and citizens. This would not only erode support for the code, but would also weaken the morale of the organisation. Therefore, there must be a point to having the code and any particular precept in it.

Moreover, the precepts of the code must not be outside the capacity of the organisation to implement. Just as a law that is never enforced because the state lacks the capacity to do so, or because it is too complex, quickly becomes a sham, so too a code or any provision in it. So, like a law, a code and its provisions must be practical and useable from the point of view of the code-maker.

Finally, there is a general requirement that any guide to behaviour must actually improve matters. If the ultimate purpose of a code is to promote the wellbeing of the organisation, and in that way its stakeholders, a code that fails to do so lacks moral justification. Hence, a code or an individual provision must not leave an organisation worse off than it would be if it did not have the code or the individual ordinance.

These *desiderata* work together to constitute an ideal against which any code (or element of a code) can be evaluated as 'well-drafted'. They determine whether a code will have an effective and credible internal authority—one of the areas that must be strong if a code is to succeed. Given that an organisation has developed a well-drafted code, how does it then go about implementing it so as to promote compliance—that is, how does it develop an effective and credible external authority?

No matter how well formulated a code may be, compliance will not result naturally or from haphazard efforts which implement the code in an uncoordinated manner. Effective compliance requires a compliance mechanism, that is, a structured approach that takes into account the capacities and features of the code's constituency. It is well known that an effective compliance mechanism would contain various elements—or institutions—that implement, interpret and enforce the code. It would operate within a sympathetic organisational culture. It would enjoy unequivocal support from the management and leadership of the organisation. As well, the code would be developed and promoted in such a way as to encourage 'ownership' of it by the organisational community. However, the question remains: what structure would the compliance mechanism have? To answer this, we must look at the nature and foundation of compliance.

As a matter of stipulation, I shall define 'compliance' in the following way: an actor A is acting in compliance with a standard X if, and only if, that actor knowingly, consciously and deliberately selects and performs an action precisely because it conforms (reflects, honours, instantiates) with standard X. Under this analysis, a compliance mechanism would be a group of settled institutions that work together to motivate the selection and performance of the appropriate act-option. How can actors be motivated to select the appropriate option? Acts of compliance rest primarily upon two, often mixed, motives. An actor may be motivated to comply because she believes some standard is right and ought to be obeyed, or she may be motivated to comply out of fear of the consequences for failing to do so. Since the motivational sources of compliance are, by and large, limited to these sorts of motivation, a successful compliance mechanism will consist of measures that create in actors one or another, or some mixture of both. How can these two types of motivation be developed?

These motives rest upon certain beliefs—belief in the rightness of values or belief that certain unwanted consequences will follow certain actions. In the former case, the aim of the compliance mechanism is to encourage the actor to internalise the code—that is, to have the actor develop a strong belief that the code of ethics embodies values that are (in an organisational context) good and right and which ought to be obeyed. Such values are engendered in each actor, become part of their belief system and become part of the organisational culture.

Compliance produced through the fear of the consequences also rests upon beliefs—the actor believing that non-compliance will be discovered and that certain unwanted consequences will follow. This is a deterrence theory—actors are deterred from wrongdoing by the likelihood of discovery and fear of the consequences. There is no change in the actor's beliefs about the merits of the code, whether it is right or wrong, good or bad. The code exists and actors must comply or face the consequences. Thus, actors are coerced into complying. The coercive approach attempts to enforce the code through credible sanctions and by inducing actors to believe that discovery will be highly likely.

Creating compliance-inducing motivation on this analysis rests upon beliefs generated by two different sorts of mechanism—engendering mechanisms based upon persuasion, discussion, affirmation and demonstration; and enforcement mechanisms based upon surveillance, coercion, threats and sanctions, leading to deterrence. What is the relationship between these two approaches? Is one preferable to the other?

Enforcement is a very blunt instrument, but it seems to be the approach favoured by some of the most influential writers and business leaders. For example, they speak of 'vigorous', 'savage' or 'routine' enforcement, '(credible) sanctions' and codes imitating the deterrence (and even retributive) nature of the criminal law.

Such an approach is mistaken. Empirical evidence from the study of the regulation of business suggests that persuasion and trust (reinforced by firm action only if persuasion and trust fail) are more effective and less costly regulatory approaches than enforcement through the use of surveillance and sanctions alone (Fisse and Braithwaite 1993). There are good reasons to infer that such findings would be replicated within any organisation, since agents are similar in all organisations, and similar sorts of relationships and causes of unethical behavior are at work. For example, most agents prefer to be trusted, given responsibilities, and left to act autonomously, rather than work under intense supervision and surveillance. They prefer to be assessed by known, reasonable and transparent procedures. Further, in business corporations as well as other organisations, the regulator and the regulated are individual people within whose responsibility wrongdoing and rightdoing reside. Corporate wrongdoers often face a tradeoff between corporate goals, customs, mores and ethics (which are often perceived not to be paramount corporate goals), while organisational wrongdoers face a similar trade-off between organisational goals, customs, mores and ethics.

Additionally, the effectiveness of any enforcement program relies upon adequate levels of detection of code violators. Few organisations possess the capacity to marshal resources for the high levels of surveillance and detection necessary to make an enforcement program credible. It is simply too costly, and in many different ways: in the use of time, financial and material resources; in the maintenance of an extensive and formal adjudication system and other institutions that ensure due process in what is effectively a private justice system; distractions from the purpose of the organisation, and employee goodwill and trust, since the organisation may become like a mini police-state (Cressey and Moore 1983:70–1). The very act of enforcement may lead to a cure far worse than the disease.

In general, the enforcement approach assumes that the members of an organisation cannot be trusted. It also fails to respect individuals, their autonomy and integrity, and their capacity to assume personal responsibility for actions they perform. Respecting these things has been identified as a major factor in an organisation having a strong ethical culture (Pastin 1986:221–5; Peters and Waterman 1982:55–88 cited in Newton 1986:253; Kotter and Heskett 1992:60–7). The enforcement approach, relying upon the blunt use of power, fails to affirm, promote and encourage the engendering of the very values at the heart of a strong ethical culture—the feature of an organisation that is essential if a code of ethics is to be successful (Ayres and Braithwaite (1992b:49). Used alone, enforcement fails to develop the motivation base for reliable compliance and is ultimately self-defeating.

Moreover, the enforcement approach is focused upon decontextualised individuals. It addresses only the violation and the possibility of repetition, while ignoring the causes of non-compliance, such as a poor ethical culture, an unsupportive organisational culture, and alienation from the organisational community and its values (Cressey and Moore 1983:68). However, an ethics program that makes pious pronouncements about the importance of ethics but does nothing to remove the causes of unethical behaviour is simply not credible and therefore unlikely to serve a regulatory role. Further, since it is concerned with results only, there is the possibility that it will license victimisation, the use of 'scapegoats' and impose solutions that are inappropriate and perceived to be so.

Since such an approach maintains alienation from the ethical culture of the organisation (because it uses power to deter and is unconcerned with what an actor believes is valuable), it fails to promote organisational 'citizenship', inclusion and ownership of the values that drive the organisation. Essentially, such an approach fails to foster organisational virtue. This has unwanted consequences—people who are alienated from their community, who feel that they have no investment in it, and who have not developed and cultivated organisational virtue, are more likely to offend when the opportunity presents itself (this, it is worth pointing out, is as true of society in general as it is of organisations, where the analogue for organisational virtue is civic virtue, and the analogue for code-compliance is lawfulness or law abidingness).

Finally, if the enforcement strategy is to succeed, the penalties for violations must be set at a level that is credible; that is, at a level that deters the majority of potential miscreants. In the majority of cases—if not all—this level is likely to be higher than the level that seems appropriate given the intrinsic wrongness of the violation. Thus, an effective enforcement strategy would violate one of the principles of retributive justice, namely, that a person should be punished only in proportion to the gravity of the wrongdoing. Such a principle is important for the citizens of any community, since it plays an important role in grounding their confidence in the system. In addition, the level may be so high that it paralyses decisionmaking within the organisation—actors become fearful of acting lest they breach the code. This engenders a 'better do nothing than risk everything' policy.

These problems are all paradoxes of deterrent-orientated enforcement programs. Should they arise, they lead to cynicism about, and disenchantment with, the compliance mechanism amongst the members of the organisation. That such paradoxes would arise is highly likely, given the nature of the system and because the sanction levels must be high if the system is to be credible and deter would-be wrongdoers.

The alternative to enforcing a code of ethics is engendering one. This approach is attractive for a number of reasons. It tends to produce ethically reliable actors. Most agents prefer, other things being equal, to do what they believe to be right and good—that is, to act in a way that seems ethical to them. Engendering involves getting actors to believe in something, or believe that it is right. If the code of ethics has been engendered, it will be perceived to be an ethical reference point, and actors will believe that it embodies relevant ethical values. They will be disposed, other things being equal, to ensure that their acts comply with it. Since the code means something to the actors because it has been engendered, the rate of compliance will be higher.

There are many ways to foster such beliefs. They may be promoted through demonstration, such as by the upper-echelon managers and leaders of the organisation behaving ethically. They may be affirmed through ethics education programs within the organisation which explain the code and the values in it, or by creating institutions that encourage ethical action— for example, employee involvement in the formulation and administration of the code, as well as ethics 'hotlines' or advisers who will clarify, interpret, or apply the code and resolve a quandary, or provide ethics counselling. All of these measures serve to educate the code's constituents, persuade them of its merits, and generally foster belief in the code and, in that way, promote ethical motivation.

Moreover, engendering ethics involves fostering values and traits of character—such as autonomy and integrity—that are at the heart of a strong ethical culture and organisational virtue. This is likely to be a more effective regulatory approach than enforcement since it is more likely to result in higher rates of compliance. The reason is simply that people prefer to act in ways that accord with their values, and people are more likely to do what they want to do (which in this ease is to act ethically) than what they have been coerced to do. Consequently, there are sound motivational reasons to select engendering programs over enforcement programs.

Apart from the motivational advantages that engendering offers, such an approach avoids many of the costs associated with enforcement. Unlike the enforcement strategy, it does not require as much intrusive surveillance or monitoring of actors, with the consequent loss of employee goodwill and trust. Engendering mechanisms address causes (since to fail to do so would undermine the credibility of the mechanism). Consequently, an engendering approach addresses matters of concern or potential concern, specific problems, and so on. It is for this reason that it provides a more honest way for actors to interact with each other, since reasons are given, the motivation underlying decisions and directives is clear, and problems are dealt with. This encourages confidence in the system and the organisation, fosters citizenship (a reduction of alienation) and ultimately compliance with organisational norms. It fosters organisational virtue.

Furthermore, in the special case of miscreants, the engendering process reincorporates them into the life of the organisation, offering them a chance of 'redemption' and forgiveness (that is, an actor's wrongdoing is not held against her). They have the opportunity of once again exercising full membership of the organisation. This process strengthens and repairs the relationships between actors, and tailors the response to violation of the code to the causes of the wrongdoing and the needs and situation of the perpetrator. This has the effect of reducing alienation from the life of the organisation on the part of all organisational citizens. They can develop a sense of involvement and ownership in the process of ethical action. This can be heightened if they are incorporated into the process of developing and administering the code. This in turn fosters compliance since actors are reluctant to destroy those things in which they have a personal investment or which they value.

Finally, engendering ethics is a more ethically-sound approach than enforcement. Unlike enforcement strategies, which treat actors as self-interested players and a means to an end, engendering ethics assumes that actors are rational (since it attempts to persuade them), that they are autonomous and deserving of respect for no other reason than they are rational human beings. Such moral defences of engendering should not be discounted. Actors evaluate in moral terms what they do to others and how they are treated themselves. A program that seems ethically suspect will not obtain and maintain the support of a group of people. The capacity of such a program to promote compliance will be diminished.

Such an approach does not abandon entirely some level of enforcement through the use of coercive programs. In any community there will be wilful wrongdoers displaying all levels of culpability, from trivial offenders against organisational norms to egregious actors who play the system but who never believe in it—so-called 'organisational sociopaths'. Enforcement should focus only on those actors who cannot be reformed through engendering programs alone. The type of response to an actor's particular wrongdoing should be determined by her level of culpability and capacity for reform. For some code violators, it may mean a period of supervised work and education about the values of the organisation; for others, a warning or demotion; for yet others, some combination of these.

This approach keeps coercive programs in the background, as an avenue of last resort to be used only against wanton and negligent actors. The organisation does not develop the thorough, far-reaching and intrusive programs to detect wrongdoers that enforcement programs assume. This approach uses targeted audits aimed at known weak spots and reported problem areas, rather than constant, general surveillance. The organisation encourages reporting and disclosure—that is, proactive behaviour on the part of corporate citizens. Once wrongdoing is discovered, however, the coercive programs become an option, if warranted—that is, if education and reform fail. This sends a clear message to organisational citizens, that they are trusted but that their actions are subject to assessment, as in civil society.

Such a system operates on a similar basis to ordinary, non-organisational life—something with which actors are comfortable and familiar. Such familiarity encourages support. In this way, the autonomy of the individual is promoted and respected, while the organisation demonstrates clearly that it possesses the capacity and the willingness to deal with egregious miscreants. Actors know that only wilful wrongdoing will attract institutional sanctions and that inexperience, ignorance and mistakes will not be held against them. Such a system further promotes the engendering of the code, and compliance with it, since it reinforces the grounds upon which such engendering occurs. For example, it appears to be a reasonable and fair system. As such, it fosters feelings of security and trust, rather than feelings of vulnerability.

From this, it is clear that the aim of any compliance mechanism should not initially be merely to deter. Deterrence rests on nothing more than a threat and is power at its crudest and most unimaginative. It obtains its credibility from the capacity of the powerful agent to induce the vulnerable agent to believe that she is willing and able to use her power. Such flaunting of power breeds resentment, mistrust and fear. A more imaginative use of power is to use the threat of deterrence and coercion as a last resort in a program of ethical education. The threat of power (albeit veiled) focuses attention on wrongdoers; having done that, education can begin. The problem, of course, is finding a balance between enforcement programs and engendering programs. This will be determined largely by the local conditions, such as the nature of the organisation, the state of its ethical and organisational culture, and the behaviour of its citizens.

In the model sketched here, engendering the values of the organisation is the first option and enforcement is a last resort. In all events, the compliance mechanism should be internal to the organisation. There is good reason for this. It is cheaper, tailored to the needs and circumstances of the organisation, and, because it comes from within the organisation, the members feel that

Figure 4.1   Code of ethics compliance mechanism

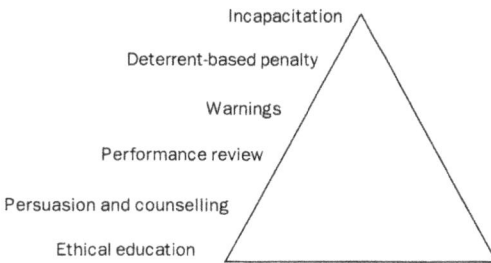

Source: Derived from Ayres and Braithwaite (1992a:45). See also Ayres and Braithwaite (1992b:35ff) and Fisse and Braithwaite (1993:142ff).

they own it. Furthermore, studies have shown that keeping discipline within the organisation may in fact promote compliance (Fisse and Braithwaite 1993:170).

What emerges is a compliance mechanism that consists of an ordering of compliance programs based upon the level of coercion involved. Engendering programs and enforcement programs are organised so as to form a unified, progressive compliance mechanism. It begins with engendering programs such as education, affirmation, persuasion, information, counselling, and so on, which involve no coercion It then moves to programs designed less to engender and more to deter and educate from a position of power, each with increasing levels of coercion, moving finally to pure deterrence. The levels should not be seen as exclusive, and practices from one level may be mixed with those from another. This code of ethics compliance mechanism is illustrated in Figure 4.1.

The amount of effort invested in engendering ethics decreases as one ascends the triangle, while the amount of coercion increases. At the top of the pyramid only the most blatant, obvious and egregious actors are dealt with—those who are unable to be convinced of the relevance of organisational norms. Often they will be re-offenders for whom the best engendering efforts were unable to nurture allegiance. They effectively become a self-selecting group that does not require the expenditure of vast amounts of resources to detect. As a result, the organisation has to expend fewer resources in dealing with them and is exposed to fewer of the risks and costs associated with suveillance and punitive enforcement measures. There is, for the organisation, an economy of effort.

Resources can be reallocated and the organisation can use proactive programs, such as targeted ethical audits (which can often be quite effective since internal auditors often know 'where the bodies are buried') to identify problem areas, to provide opportunity for confession, and to encourage actors to seek help, guidance and the clarification of ethics policies. As a result, actors will not be caught in a web of perpetuating unethical behavior, but will have clear exits, and fewer cases will go so far as to require the most drastic coercive responses—the sorts of responses that may easily use enormous resources compared to the returns generated, and which often end up being resolved in the civil courts. Throughout this process, the coercive level of the response must be limited by the culpability of the actor and the seriousness of the offence, rather than by the harshness required to attain some desired level of deterrence. In this way, the enforcement paradoxes will be avoided, but the lessons that can be learned from deterrence programs will be communicated to the citizens of the organisation, without the costs.

This strategy seeks to educate all and redeem those who can be redeemed, while providing a mechanism to incapacitate the most dangerous offenders. It rests upon the assumptions that agents are rational actors who are capable of choosing and weighing reasons, that most of them care about ethical concerns and that they desire to 'do the right thing'. Such a mechanism promotes and fosters the engendering of ethics in the organisation since it nurtures the ethically confused or ignorant as well as the virtuous; it reforms the ethically wayward; it deters the ethically uncommitted and venal actor. Ultimately, it may be used to incapacitate the ethical rogue. It does all these things while minimising enforcement costs and redirecting resources into the most important part of any organisation—its people.

This structure sends the message to the members of the organisation that they are valued and trusted by the organisation as individuals, and not merely as recipients of coercive treatment. This is reinforced by the fact that at all stages, agents are respected as autonomous, rational and responsible for their own decisions. In this way, this structure promotes participation in the life of the organisation and a reduction of alienation from it and organisational goals. It enfranchises (and re-enfranchises) them as members of the organisational community; as well, it promotes confidence and trust in the overcall compliance system, further promoting the engendering of ethical attitudes. This is particularly important. Trust encourages ethical action and ethical action further encourages trust, in a self-reinforcing circle (Braithwaite 1993; Brien 1998). This structure provides the foundation for that trust and, in that way, grounds the trust necessary for actors to internalise the code and live by it.

Finally, embodied in the structure of this mechanism (as opposed to being merely stated in the code) are three guarantees that actors in vulnerable positions value highly and which underpin the credibility of any ethics program. First, this system embodies a due process. There is a definite, known, public and agreed-upon process that must be worked through, and a progression through a system of steadily escalating responses towards actors who violate the code. They know that organisational power cannot be wielded capriciously, that they do not live at the whim of their superiors, and that the possibility of victimisation—one of the criticisms of codes—is minimised. This further engenders trust in the organisation and the ethics program, and fosters ethical action.

Second, there is procedural justice. In other words, the due process and the substantive elements of the code are applied to all institutional actors alike. This is because without procedural justice there would be no guarantee that the compliance mechanism would be applied to all similar cases. This would tend to encourage cynicism about the mechanism and the motives of its proponents, thus weakening support for it. If it is not to be self-defeating, the compliance process must assume and utilise procedural justice.

Third, there is substantive justice or fairness. It would be unfair to hold accountable a person who violates the code accidentally, through ignorance, or because of pressure from her superiors, if she cannot access appropriate mechanisms that allow her to ignore such pressure with impunity. On the compliance mechanism developed here, an actor's individual circumstances are taken into account, the causes of a violation are determined and an appropriate response is developed. Again, so that it is not self-defeating the compliance process must assume and deliver substantive justice or fairness.

Moreover, opportunities are given whereby actors can seek assistance and guidance, as well as be given it before violations occur This accords with received opinion of what counts as fair and just. Such received opinion is important. Fairness and justice (along with reasonableness) are principles that actors prize highly in all sorts of circumstances. No system can long maintain the support of citizens and be as successful as it has the capacity to be unless it makes some effort to abide by at least the principles of fairness and justice. Organisations as mini-communities are no different in this respect from general society (Kotter and Heskett 1992:52; Pastin 1986:222). Such principles serve as criteria that actors use to evaluate the organisation, and in grounding any commitment to the organisation and appropriation or internalisation of organisational values. For this reason, if a compliance mechanism is to be successful, it and its constituent elements must operate on the basis of substantive justice and fairness.

This chapter has examined the theory that underlies ethical codes and which grounds the development of a code's internal and external authority—the features which determine whether a code will be successful or not. I have attempted to set out the *desiderata* that an ethical code must satisfy in order to be well formed, and so be capable of fulfilling the purpose that was intended for it. I have also attempted to set out the structure of the compliance mechanism that well formed codes must use in order to be effective. This structure, along with the *desiderata*, is determined by the role that codes of ethics play in organisational life—to guide human conduct, raise the ethical profile of an organisation, and in that way promote the wellbeing of stakeholders.

It is surprising that more research has not been done on the theory underlying ethical codes. Over the past few years the citizens of the Western democracies have shown an increased intolerance of those who, holding various sorts of positions of power, abuse the trust placed in them. Such intolerance has been directed not only at legislators, but also at the paradigm professions, such as law and medicine, and professionals, such as business people, public servants and even university lecturers and school teachers. 'Accountability' has become the 'buzz-word' of the 1990s. Apart from various pieces of legislation, ethical codes are often an integral part of the attempt to ensure accountability and exert some measure of control by the community over people who live largely without constraint. Such codes, however, need to be well formulated and adequately implemented. The theory expounded here provides a basis for assessing codes and their implementation mechanisms. It remains to be seen whether this approach to reining-in the power of influential sectional interests will be successful.

Notes

This is a longer version of a paper originally presented at the Ethics in Business and the Professions conference, Massey University, Palmerston North, New Zealand in June 1993. My thanks to conference participants for their very helpful comments and to Jim Battye and Peter Schouls for reading the penultimate version. This chapter previously appeared in the the *Business and Professional Ethics Journal*, 15(1), 1996. The author thanks the journal for allowing the chapter to be reproduced here.

5

Building organisational integrity

Catherine Boardman and Vicki Klum

An organisation's leaders are the key to its operational effectiveness. They are its principal motivators. They provide focus, direction and inspiration. They set its ethical tone.

Why is ethical tone important?

Every public sector agency, from local councils to government trading enterprises, is established for a specific purpose. That purpose might be to provide municipal services to the local community or health services to regional areas, coordinate education services for the state, or ensure an adequate water supply to the capital. Whatever an organisation's purpose, it has a public duty to optimise the value of its services to the community.

Corruption and other unethical behaviour compromise the value of those services. Apart from affecting the cost, quality and availability of services, unethical behaviour can lead to a loss of public trust. Loss of public trust can further undermine the ability of public sector agencies to provide effective and equitable services, especially to those most in need.

Therefore, public sector agencies also have a public duty to reduce corruption risks and promote high ethical standards of performance. Furthermore, as major purchasers, as well as providers, of services in the community, they have the power to influence the behaviour of those they deal with. Therefore they have both the opportunity and responsibility to lead by example.

In New South Wales, the importance of ethical tone is acknowledged by the explicit requirement that state public sector leaders behave ethically and maintain high ethical standards in their agencies.[1]

This chapter emphasises the ethical dimension of good management and its links to corruption prevention. Its focus is on building organisational integrity or completeness. Organisational integrity can be said to exist when an organisation's operational systems, corruption prevention strategies, and ethical standards are fully integrated to achieve its purpose.

Background

The benefits of maintaining high ethical standards

High ethical standards are not simply an end in themselves. There are significant benefits to be gained from raising the ethical tone of an organisation. Zipparo (1998) established that sound ethical practices contribute not only to an organisation's integrity, but also to its operational effectiveness. Zipparo demonstrated that the ethical tone of an organisation can affect
- efficiency and effectiveness
- decisionmaking processes
- staff commitment and job satisfaction
- staff stress
- staff turnover.

Given these findings, organisations that optimise their ethical performance will not only protect the public interest and improve their resistance to corruption, but are also likely to enhance
- their reputation
- their competitiveness
- their ability to attract and retain quality staff
- the career prospects of their staff
- their ability to meet new challenges
- their ability to serve the community well.

These are persuasive reasons for giving attention to the ethical dimension of good management.

The causes of unethical behaviour

In deciding how to promote and maintain high standards of ethical behaviour and corruption resistance it is worth looking at some of the causes of unethical behaviour.

Gorta (1998b) has shown that unethical behaviour, such as corruption, is likely to occur where there is

- opportunity—for example, through poor systems
- little fear of exposure or likelihood of detection—for example, lack of organisational reporting mechanisms, or an organisation's poor history in dealing with reports of corruption
- lack of ethical leadership and support—for example, unclear messages about what is acceptable, setting poor examples, failure to reinforce ethical behaviour
- cultural acceptance of aberrant behaviour, both within the organisation and the wider community (including self-excusing rationalisations—for example, 'it didn't hurt anyone', 'it's standard business practice', 'it's not illegal').

It also concludes that examining the context in which corruption and other unethical behaviour occurs (organisational culture) can aid corruption prevention.

Zipparo (1998) suggests that the ability to behave ethically in a workplace may be related more to aspects of the organisation than to attributes of the individual. It establishes that an organisation's ethical culture has a powerful influence over an individual's behaviour and, specifically, that people are more likely to behave unethically where

- their managers behave unethically
- organisational values are unclear
- ethical behaviour is not rewarded
- sanctions for unethical behaviour are not clear
- there is no practical ethics training.

These findings highlight the need for a multifaceted approach to reducing corruption risks and enhancing ethical performance. In fact, they point to the crucial importance of building organisational integrity to create a corruption resistant organisation.

Building organisational integrity

An organisation's systems, policies and procedures indicate what its leaders say they want done, but an organisation's culture determines what is actually done. An organisation's culture is strongly influenced by the ethical tone set by its leaders.

An organisation's leaders play the key role in building and maintaining a strong ethical culture. A strong ethical culture is a prerequisite to organisational integrity. Many of the management initiatives leaders introduce to ensure operational effectiveness also contribute to their organisation's culture. The focus of this section is simply to provide guidance on strategies to integrate the ethical dimensions of good management into overall management objectives and practices. Many CEOs and senior managers will already be doing some or all of these things.

What does a strong ethical culture look like?

An organisation's culture evolves from a complex web of influences, and a strong ethical culture certainly doesn't just happen nor is it necessarily instantly recognisable.

However, ICAC research and experience suggests there are certain signs that an organisation has a strong ethical culture. These signs include

- a sense of common purpose
- wide recognition of the importance of individuals' contributions to achieving the common purpose
- a high level of trust amongst all staff and especially between management and others
- a strong sense of public duty and a natural tendency to use agreed values to guide actions and decisions
- a willingness to share responsibility for ethical performance
- a high level of willingness by staff to participate in decisionmaking, discuss concerns, seek advice about ethical dilemmas, suggest improvements, attend training, contribute to corporate activities and so on
- wide understanding of, and support for, mechanisms for handling complaints, grievances and reports of corrupt conduct
- a focus on how best to achieve desired outcomes rather than on unquestioning acceptance of 'this is the way we do it round here'.

Clearly, these signs have a lot in common with those a CEO or senior manager would be looking for to confirm their organisation's operational effectiveness.

What are the prerequisites of an ethical culture?

While there is no one-size-fits-all version of an ethical culture, an organisation's culture is determined by the underlying values and attitudes shared by its members. In turn, those shared values and attitudes are shaped by features of the organisation such as its functions, its structure, the quality of its systems and procedures, its staff profile, its history and, most importantly, the values of its leaders.

Do you know your organisation's existing culture?

Leaders seeking to build organisational integrity need to know what their organisation's existing culture looks like so that they can tailor the broad strategies suggested in the next section to the needs of their particular organisation.

One way to find out about your organisation's culture is to carry out a survey. The ICAC has developed a survey, *Perceptions of Your Workplace*, for this purpose and has piloted the survey with a random selection of public sector agencies and local councils, with positive results. An *Ethical Culture Survey Kit* is available to NSW public sector agencies. It contains the survey, tips on conducting a successful survey, a report of results of the pilot, and practical guidance to assist organisations respond to survey outcomes.

Strategies for leaders

Obviously, a CEO or senior manager seeking to enhance the ethical performance and therefore corruption resistance of his or her organisation will need to acknowledge the particular features of the organisation that may have contributed to its existing culture.

For example, if an organisation has a history of failing to deal appropriately with allegations of corruption or hostility between management and other staff, strategies for building an ethical culture will need to acknowledge these issues through open and honest discussion about

- the fact that they occurred
- why they might have occurred
- what the organisation might do to overcome these problems.

This chapter does not propose to consider every possible obstacle a leader may face. Rather, its focus is on promoting broad strategies that can be adopted by all public sector leaders.

Leaders can demonstrate their commitment to creating and/or maintaining a sound ethical culture by adopting five key strategies.

- Identifying appropriate organisational values.
- Acting in accordance with those values.
- Promoting the values to others.
- Ensuring the values are built into every decision and action of an organisation.
- Striving for excellence.

Identifying appropriate values

Everyone has a personal set of ethical values and the vast majority of public officials have positive ethics. The focus here, however, is on organisational rather than personal values.

A set of values, whether stated or not, is implicit in the way each public sector organisation aims to operate. But the ICAC has found that the absence of an explicit set of common ethical values or principles and a shared understanding of how they may be applied to an organisation's work can lead to inconsistent decisionmaking and poor resolution of ethical dilemmas. In the worst cases it can lead to corrupt conduct.

At the heart of public sector ethics lies the concept of public duty, of serving the public interest above all else. Public duty underpins the public sector's reason for being. It remains a principal objective of all public sector organisations—ranging from local councils and government departments to public sector boards and government trading enterprises—regardless of their purpose.

A range of values and principles already feature, in one form or another, as probity principles in ICAC publications and are implicit in the *Model Code of Conduct for NSW Public Agencies*. Both the Ombudsman's Office and the ICAC have provided guidance on values. The Ombudsman's Office has published *Principles of Administrative Good Conduct* and the ICAC has developed a Model of Public Duty that was published in its 1998–99 Annual Report (Independent Commission Against Corruption 1999b).

The ICAC model aims to identify a set of key ethical standards, give them some structure and provide a reference point for guiding public sector actions and decision making. The key ethical standards include

- serving the public interest
- acting with integrity by being honest, open, accountable, objective and courageous
- demonstrating leadership.

Identification of key values or principles is just a starting point. More important is the expression of those values, which is found in the quality of leadership, communication and support for staff and in the systems, policies and procedures an organisation chooses to adopt.

In NSW, the ICAC encourages all CEOs and senior managers to take the lead by adopting and promoting the values contained in the model both within their organisations and in dealing with clients, contractors and the wider community.

Acting in accordance with agreed values

People in organisations are far more likely to be influenced by what their CEO and senior managers do than simply by what they say. Therefore, CEOs and senior managers need to lead by example. Acting in accordance with your words is crucial to creating trust. A breakdown in trust will undermine the best efforts to build an ethical and effective organisation. Consider the effect on trust of the following examples.

- A CEO discusses budget cuts with staff and emphasises the need to trim costs, but makes no concessions himself, and continues to claim his full entitlements (such as first class air travel).
- A manager talks to staff about conflicts of interest that can arise from inappropriate relations with contractors, but regularly lunches with contractors herself.

Consider the following examples of leaders' actions that might flow from adopting the values outlined in the Model of Public Duty.

Public interest. Leaders should always put the public interest first by

- guarding against making decisions and taking actions that put their own or their organisation's interests above the public interest—for example, they should not form strategic alliances or accept speaking engagements simply on the basis that they may enhance future employment opportunities.
- always fully disclosing conflicts of interest promptly.
- acting to minimise the impact of perceived conflicts of interest.

Honesty. Leaders should be honest. In this respect, they should

- always comply, and be seen to comply, with an organisation's code of conduct, policies and procedures—for example, declare gifts and benefits without being asked.
- ensure their decisions are consistent with government policy and guidelines.
- examine their actions in the context of what they are asking others to do and make sure they are consistent—for example, leaders should always apply the same rigour to the recruitment of their own staff as they expect of other managers when they are recruiting.

Openness. Leaders should seek to be open; they should try to

- communicate openly, honestly and consistently with staff and those who deal with the organisation (words should always match actions).
- ensure they communicate with clarity and sensitivity.
- encourage staff to have an active part in an organisation's decisionmaking processes and acknowledge and consider diverse views, ideas and concerns—for example, leaders should involve staff early in corruption prevention planning initiatives (such as in identifying corruption risks and suggesting ways to minimise them) otherwise they may consider suspicion is being cast on them and therefore resist change.

- maintain a high profile and build informal opportunities for interacting with staff.

Accountability. Leaders should strive to be accountable, which involves

- practising ethical decisionmaking and being prepared to give reasons for decisions.
- Attempting not to hide actions and decisions from scrutiny or appearing to do so.

Objectivity. Leaders must always be objective. Thus, they must

- examine their decisions for consistency with agreed values or principles.
- consider only relevant issues and guard against the appearance of favouritism.
- ensure their decisions are fully informed.

Courage. Leaders must always demonstrate courage, by

- applying public duty principles consistently, regardless of pressure to do otherwise.
- providing frank and fearless advice.
- supporting staff even in the face of adversity (they must avoid making scapegoats).
- dealing properly with reports of suspected wrongdoing.

Of course, appropriate actions and decisions will reflect decisionmaking that has involved weighing up each of the relevant values. For example,

- brutal honesty in dealing with a staff error could inhibit future openness and accountability and should therefore be tempered with sensitive communication
- in dealing with disclosure of personal information, openness would be tempered with the need to protect confidentiality (where disclosure is not in the public interest).

Promoting the values to others

Acting in accordance with an organisation's values or principles is one way of promoting them to others. There are, however, other strategies that a leader can adopt to enhance understanding about the importance and relevance of the values.

Leaders can reinforce what they practice by

- translating abstract values into practical ethical issues that are relevant to the workplace and communicating these at every opportunity—for example, discussing the risk to the public interest and objectivity of accepting hospitality from a would-be contractor

- telling and retelling stories about appropriate and inappropriate ethical action until they become part of the organisation's history and signal the type of behaviour that is valued by the organisation
- ensuring the organisation has in place practical, relevant ethical awareness programs and that all staff have access to them
- ensuring that all training and development, whatever its focus (from computer or leadership skills to procurement best practice), covers relevant ethical issues
- ensuring the organisation effectively communicates the principles by which it operates and its expectations of its clients, contractors and suppliers.

Leaders can encourage others to share responsibility for maintaining high ethical standards by creating a culture founded on trust. Trust is confidence that an individual or organisation will do the right thing. Individuals are more likely to accept responsibility where

- they trust an organisation and its leaders
- they feel trust is placed in them
- breaches of trust by others in the organisation are swiftly addressed.

Trust does not exist in a vacuum. Leaders can help create an environment of trust, respect and cooperation by communicating with honesty, clarity and sensitivity.

Trust must have boundaries. Even the most trustworthy employee should be prepared to be subject to scrutiny. Unlimited trust can provide opportunities for corruption—for example, the ICAC's investigation into the conduct of a former purchasing officer at a Sydney council uncovered an example of excessive trust. In that instance, the officer was able to subvert the policy of obtaining three quotations, by creating false quotes or calling in favours from other contractors to submit excessive quotes, to ensure that particular suppliers were awarded contracts. There was unquestioning reliance on the officer's recommendations and, in the absence of reasonable limits on his discretionary powers (such as regular review of the purchasing process), the officer was able to act corruptly.

Leaders need to establish boundaries within which values can guide acceptable behaviour. Codes of conduct, systems (including reward and disciplinary systems) and appropriate policies and procedures provide such boundaries. For example,

- measuring an applicant's apparent suitability for a job against referees' comments
- checking the probity of new recruits

- requiring passwords for computer access
- having more than one person involved in tendering processes
- implementing performance measures that can test the degree to which staff carry out their responsibilities efficiently, effectively and ethically.

Appropriate boundaries that ensure public accountability enable an organisation to trust its staff to exercise reasonable discretion and to reduce its reliance on prescriptive rules.

Ensuring the values are built into every decision and action of an organisation

Identifying the right values, acting in accordance with them and promoting them to others goes some way towards establishing a culture of trust. But leaders should also examine other aspects of their organisation to ensure they reflect the values if they are going to build a sound ethical culture.

Policies, procedures, training programs, organisational structures and so on can be analysed in terms of the values they express. How consistent they are with the right values is likely to coincide with how resistant they are to corruption and how effective they are operationally.

An analysis of an effective corruption resistant tendering process would, for example, have integrity and the public interest as its guiding principles. **Public interest.** To the serve the public interest, the process would be competitive, selectors would be suitably qualified, conflicts of interest would be well managed, and the best value achieved.

A number of factors contribute to maintaining the integrity of a tendering process. These include

- openness—a corruption resistant tendering process involves advertising for tenders, disclosing selection criteria, and publishing decisions (key details of winning tender).
- honesty—the process complies with the letter and spirit of the law and relevant policies and participants disclose conflicts of interest promptly.
- accountability—the decisionmaking process is recorded appropriately (avoids hiding detail behind unjustified 'commercial in confidence' clauses), and tenderers are given reasons for decisions.
- objectivity—the tendering process establishes relevant selection criteria and engages independent participation in the selection process.

- courage—the process maintains probity even if stakeholders push for improper outcomes; the process refuses to take short cuts for the sake of expediency.
- leadership—the process promotes values to suppliers/ contractors and indicates expectation that they will uphold them; it also strives for best practice.

However, individual policies or procedures, no matter how well they respond to corruption risks and reflect appropriate values, do not function in isolation. For example, public sector organisations are strongly encouraged by the NSW Protected Disclosures Act to have in place an internal reporting system to enable staff to report corruption and other unethical behaviour without fear of reprisals. A good CEO or senior manager, however, understands that the existence of a reporting system alone will not encourage reports. People will make reports only if they know about the system, understand what constitutes corruption and why it is important to expose it and, importantly, only if they are confident their report will be dealt with appropriately and that they will be protected from retaliation.

In other words, a good system depends on the support of

- leaders and managers (who clearly communicate a strong commitment to it)
- appropriate training and raising of awareness for both potential users and administrators of the system
- clear administrative and responsibility structures.

The same is true for any of the key corruption-prevention tools that the ICAC considers essential to enhancing an organisation's resistance to corruption. These include

- corruption prevention and corruption risk management plans
- a code of conduct
- internal reporting, grievance handling, complaints handling, recruitment, performance management, disciplinary, rewards, internal auditing and internal investigation systems
- gifts and benefits, conflicts of interest, secondary employment, procurement and disposal policies and procedures
- leadership and ethical awareness programs.

Their effectiveness is dependent on their content, the extent to which they are understood and used and the outcomes that they deliver, which are largely determined by the quality of leadership and organisational culture.

An organisation's leaders should be used to looking at the organisation as a whole and to determining the components necessary to enable the whole to perform effectively. It is worth looking at ethical culture the same way.

Mapping ethical culture

An ethical culture can be represented as a dynamic system of interdependent elements (illustrated in Figure 5.1).

Figure 5.1 takes the key elements identified in the ICAC research as critical to an ethical culture (values, communication and leadership) and sets them in an organisational context.

Corruption resistance depends on the key elements being supported by management tools, reflected in organisational structures and strategies and utilised to manage an organisation's external environment.

These key elements include

1   Ethical values, which underpin everything organisations do (the right values are a prerequisite to organisational integrity).
2   Leadership, which drives the development and integration of the values.
3   Communication, which ensures shared knowledge and understanding of the values and their impact on the organisation's operations.

Encircling this core are the tools and structures which support and reflect the key elements. By expressing an organisation's values in practical terms, they guide behaviour which will help an organisation achieve its goals.

Management tools should incorporate

1   Codes of conduct, which help communicate values and provide benchmarks for behaviour.
2   Systems, policies and procedures, which assist in maintaining shared values and translate them into practical, flexible and effective actions and decisions.
3   Training and development, which enable individuals to apply values effectively to their work.

Organisational structures and strategies should encompass

1   Corporate strategies, which translate values into 'big picture' plans of action.
2   Administrative structures, which contribute to the effectiveness of management based on values.
3   Resources, which ensure services are provided in accordance with values.

The external environment can include the government of the day, clients, contractors and the wider community, which can influence an organisation's ethical performance and exposure to corruption risks.

The ICAC encourages CEOs and senior managers to consider the interdependencies that exist in their own organisations—how changing a

Figure 5.1 Ethical culture

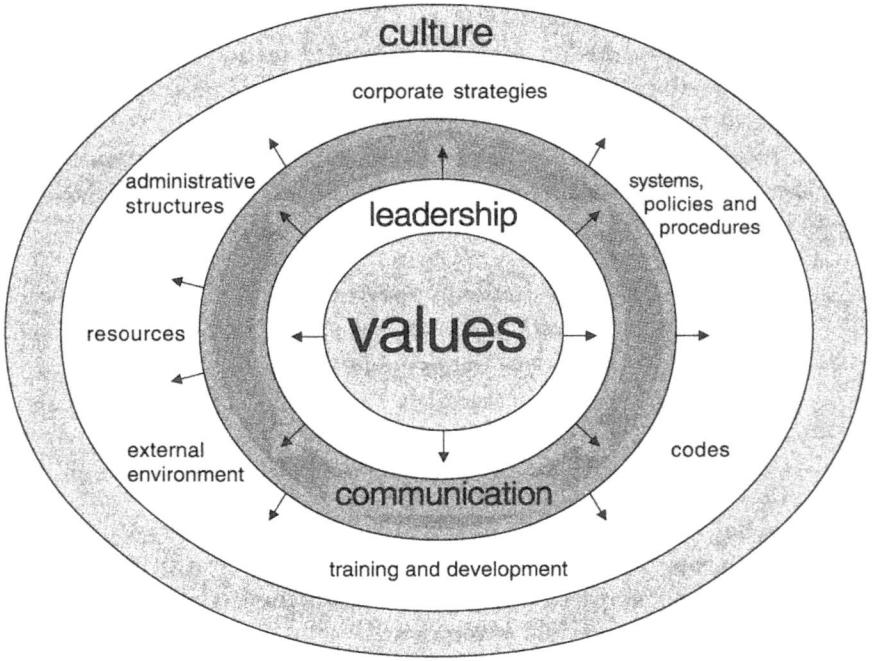

part will affect the whole. If the right values are to underpin everything an organisation does, there may be a need to change relevant systems and procedures and the way staff are managed, trained and supported.

For example, this may involve one or a number of the following activities.

- Reviewing the code of conduct for continued relevance.
- Updating corruption risk management strategies and corruption prevention plans.
- Changing the way the organisation communicates its values to, and manages the expectations of, its clients and contractors.
- Revising leadership training, induction, and general ethical awareness programs.
- Restructuring workgroups and functional areas.
- Reviewing job descriptions and duty statements.
- Revising policies and procedures such as those on auditing, conflicts of interest, gifts and benefits, and reporting wrong doing as well as those guiding operational tasks.

- Reviewing recruitment, performance management and disciplinary systems.
- Introducing new technology.

Striving for excellence

The final key to organisational integrity is a leader's commitment to the pursuit of excellence. This means aiming for best practice, especially as it applies to public duty and the obligations it imposes, and applying it consistently. As research has shown, strong ethical leadership will create an ethical organisational culture that has a positive impact on:
- efficiency and effectiveness
- decisionmaking processes
- staff commitment and job satisfaction
- staff stress and turnover
- organisational reputation and competitiveness.

Organisational integrity checklist

As a leader,
- do you know your organisation's culture or cultures? How?
- can you identify your organisation's values?
- do those values include, or are they consistent with, public duty principles?
- do you act in accordance with those values?
- do you promote those values to others? How?
- do those values underpin decisions and actions of the organisation? How do you know?

Have you ensured the organisation has
- sound corruption prevention and risk management plans?
- a clearly stated and understood code of conduct?
- sound corporate, strategic and business plans that are consistent with the organisation's purpose and values?
- clearly stated and understood roles and responsibilities?
- a commitment to, and strategies in place for, open and honest communication?
- effective awareness programs for staff, clients, contractors, suppliers and the community (including practical ethics training for staff, guarantees of service for clients, publicity on rights and responsibilities for clients, contractors and suppliers)?

- rewards for those who act ethically and punishments for those who act unethically?
- clearly stated and understood policies, systems and procedures that enable individual staff, clients, community members to have their concerns resolved without reprisals or detriment to themselves (including internal/ external reporting, grievance handling, complaints handling)?
- a commitment to recruiting the right people (those that most closely share the values of the organisation) and developing them so that they continue to provide high quality, ethical contributions and services (for example, recruitment policy and procedures, individual performance management, ongoing training and development)?
- sound internal boundaries to behaviour which reflect core ethical values (policies and procedures for organisation's operations such as gifts and benefits, conflicts of interest, procurement, contracting out, revenue collection) and that are conducive to high ethical performance (flexible and efficient, not rigid and overly bureaucratic)?
- sound audit processes?
- a commitment to and policies and procedures that encourage learning and enable continual improvements to the organisation's corruption resistance and ethical performance (monitoring and evaluation, participative decision making, training and development)?

How do you know that

- the messages you are sending about ethical behaviour are being received and accepted by staff, contractors, suppliers or clients?
- the strategies your organisation decides to use to promote ethical behaviour and enhance corruption resistance are effective?

Acknowledgements

The authors would like to acknowledge the assistance of Melissa Dryden, Peter Gifford, Lisa Zipparo, Peter Stathis, Carolyn Grenville, and Arianne Van der Meer in helping prepare this chapter.

Note

[1] Executive Service Model Contract of Employment (Premier's Memorandum No 98 – 37) specifically requires CEOs to behave ethically and maintain high ethical standards. Therefore CEOs' performance agreements are likely to make them accountable for carrying out this responsibility effectively.

6

Controlling corruption by heads of government and political élites

David A. Chaikin

Grand corruption

The fraudulent enrichment and corruption of heads of states and senior government officials is a problem which has only recently begun to interest international lawyers. The organised and systematic plundering of national treasuries or spoliation of assets by political and military élites has ravaged many developing countries, exacerbating poverty and undermining economic and social development.

When a greedy authoritarian leader or despot is in power, there are few (if any) opportunities for taking legal action to prevent or interdict stolen monies or the proceeds of corruption. If, however, the authoritarian leader is deposed, the new government may seek the assistance of foreign governments and courts to investigate and recover stolen assets which are located abroad.

Although grand corruption is not a new problem, it has more serious consequences when practised by modern dictators. First, even if the dictator is overthrown, this does mean that the stolen money will be recovered, for the mobility of wealth has had the consequence that money may be deposited outside the country. Another consideration is the sheer size of the theft. The following examples are worth considering.

- The former Shah of Iran misappropriated an estimated US$35 billion over 25 years of his reign, largely using various foundations and charities to conceal his illegal acts. No monies were recovered by the new Islamic regime of Ayatollah Khomenei.
- Ferdinand Marcos abused his position as President of the Philippines from 1965 to 1986 to acquire vast amounts of

property and wealth—including gold—belonging to the people. The Guinness Book of Records states that Marcos is one of the biggest thieves in history. But Switzerland only 'discovered' a mere US$340 million of Marcos money, and after ten years of litigation those millions plus interest were repatriated from Switzerland to the Philippines.

- Papa Doc Duvalier and his son, as Presidents of Haiti from 1957–86, used the entire machinery of the state to extract between US$500 million and US$2 billion. It is estimated that during 1960–67, 877 per cent of government expenditure was paid directly or indirectly to Duvalier and his supporters. Only a relatively small amount of money was ever recovered by the Government of Haiti. The case was handicapped by a lack of a criminal conviction against Duvalier.

- Manuel Antonio Noriega, convicted cocaine trafficker and former commander of the Panamanian Defence Forces, transferred nearly US$20 million of his fortune to banks in Europe in 1988. A significant part of this fortune was obtained through bribes from Colombian drug traffickers, but the fact that the US intelligence service also provided large amounts of finance to Noriega complicated the question as to whether his monies were licit or illicit.

- Mobutu Sese Seko of Zaire stole billions of dollars from one of the poorest countries in the world, and yet the Swiss authorities and banks have only found US$3.4 million in Switzerland. Mobutu's untimely death while in exile, and the international legitimacy of the new government have complicated the recovery process.

- The former communist leader of Romania, Nicholas Ceausescu, acted as a feudal lord over his estate—he treated it as a resource to be plundered at will. During his more than twenty years in power, Ceausescu stole millions of dollars for the benefit of his family, while Romanians suffered abject poverty. An investigation by a Canadian team of investigators in 1990 traced significant assets corruptly diverted by Ceausescu, but a lack of political will in Romania meant that there was no effective follow-up action.

- The self-proclaimed Emperor Bokassa of the Central African Republic looted his country to the point of starvation. President Siaka Stevens of Sierra Leone, President Ahidjo of

Cameroon, and former President Amin of Uganda are all
accused of looting the treasuries of their respective countries.

It has been often stated that corruption by the political élite is perhaps
the most important obstacle to economic development. There is plenty of
evidence that corruption may render a country bankrupt.

Criminality of political élites

The case of Ferdinand Marcos provides a useful illustration of grand
corruption. Marcos was President of the Philippines from November 1965
until his flight from the Republic in February 1986. In an act of infamy,
on 21 September 1972, Marcos declared martial law in the Philippines
and then imposed an unjust dictatorship.

For various geopolitical reasons, the Marcos regime was strongly
supported by the United States and its allies. For example, between 1962
and 1983 the United States provided US$3 billion in economic and military
aid. During this same period the World Bank lent US$4 billion to the
Philippines government. The large-scale borrowing from official lenders
and foreign banks was seen as a major source of economic development.

Unfortunately, a substantial part of the Philippines' external borrowing
was redirected out of the country via capital flight, which for the most part
was in violation of Philippines law. Former-President Marcos must take the
lion's share of responsibility for this capital flight. By 1985, the Philippines
had the heaviest external debt burden (measured by the external debt to
national income ratio) of any country in East and Southeast Asia. An
important new feature was that, while the external debt was largely public,
the external assets were strictly private.

The Marcos rule was undoubtedly economically disastrous for the
Philippines. The causes were varied but greatly facilitated by the criminality
of the former President, his family, friends and cronies. Evidence of their
predatory criminality is found in various published materials. A Racketeering
Influenced Corrupt Organization (RICO) claim brought in 1989 in
California sets out in some 100 pages the details of how Ferdinand Marcos,
Imelda Marcos, and others conspired to loot, divert and launder public
assets for their personal use and benefit. The RICO claim estimated that
US$5 billion in ill-gotten wealth was taken by the Marcos family, their
associates and accomplices.

The illicit wealth was gleaned by looting of money and property owned
by the Philippines government and the central bank; diversion of
entitlements to foreign economic assistance, including assistance from the
United States and Japan; and extortion of and/or soliciting of bribes and

commissions in exchange for the granting of government employment, government contracts, licenses, concessions, permits, franchises and monopolies.

It is difficult to believe that the United States was unaware of the looting of the property of the Republic of Philippines for the benefit of the Marcos/Romualdez family and their associates. The display of public indifference by the US government to the Marcos family's predatory criminal activities may be justified as *realpolitik*. It had the side-effect, however, of giving comfort to Swiss banks and other financial institutions who were assisting the Marcos family in investing and disguising their illicit wealth.

The meaning of illicit wealth

The distinction between illicit assets and property lawfully belonging to a dictator or authoritarian leader is by no means clear in countries that suffer appalling regimes—for example, that imposed by Saddam Hussein in Iraq. Where the authoritarian leader takes control of all the institutions of government, where there is no distinction between the head of state and the state itself, and the law is changed to 'legitimise' if not justify the economic plunder, then the law of the dictator authorises economic crimes. Moreover, where there is no legal distinction between the funds of the state and those of the ruling class, it is problematic to define 'illicit assets'. Abuse of political power for economic ends is thereby sanctioned by the state.

Furthermore, if the authoritarian leader is deposed and the state brings into play a new constitution and laws which retrospectively criminalise acts of spoliation by the former leader, then the question arises as to whether courts in other countries will recognise retrospective criminal acts. Under the laws of most countries, the answer to this question is no.

Intelligence and investigatory techniques

The significance of practical investigatory and legal problems in tracing and recovering of assets in an offshore setting cannot be underestimated. Even well-resourced international banks write off billions of dollars each year in bad debts which are sourced through fraud. The usual procedures for tracing of assets, liquidators and official receivers often do not result in adequate recovery.

The problems are extensive. First, the illicit assets must be located and shown to be owned or controlled by the target—for example, a deposed dictator. The tracing of assets is an extremely complex task, which has been made more difficult in a world where wealth is mobile and money laundering more sophisticated. The facilities of tax havens and the instruments of bank secrecy must be overcome. Second, the recovery of illicit monies may take a considerable period of time because of procedural and substantive laws in the requested country. Where third parties make claims on the same assets, the recovery process is complicated.

Few international investigations are supported by adequate intelligence and surveillance systems. The traditional passive methods of obtaining information are often unsuitable in the context of detecting serious economic crime. The difficult and often time-consuming task of penetrating the target— especially one that is protected by organised crime or powerful elements in the government—suggests a need for alternative mechanisms. Such mechanisms will not be elaborated on here. A key part of any recovery strategy is secrecy.

Net worth analysis

A simple method of determining whether a political leader has accumulated illicit wealth is to carry out a net worth analysis test. A person's net worth is the amount by which one's assets exceed one's liabilities. A political leader's net worth should increase during his period of public office only to the extent that he has legitimate savings from his income and/or capital appreciation. Any increase in net worth that cannot be explained should be treated with suspicion. Indeed, in some countries such as Hong Kong and India, any unexplained increase in wealth by a public official constitutes a *prima facie* criminal offence.

Net worth analysis is a valuable investigatory tool in circumstances where there is no direct link between the political leader and the alleged illegal activity, for example, where money has been effectively laundered. It is also useful when the target has acquired many assets, or where the records or documents showing the financial activities of the political leader are missing, destroyed or are unreliable.

The Marcos family are a prime example of people with political power who failed the 'net worth test'. A financial analysis based on the Marcos family's income tax returns for the financial years 1966–85 are revealed in Table 6.1. It is interesting to note that Ferdinand Marcos was barred from practising as a professional lawyer during his entire twenty-year presidency, but Marcos claimed that his legal fees represented 'receivables from prior years'—that is, prior to the period 1967–84.

When Ferdinand and Imelda Marcos became the First Couple in 1965, their net worth was only P120,000 (US$7,000). When they were thrown out of the Philippines in 1986, their estimated assets amounted to more than US$5 billion. Indeed, the Swiss accounts of the Marcos family which were frozen in 1986 amounted to approximately US$357 million. This sum far exceeded the Marcos family's legitimate increase in net worth.

Money laundering and offshore financial secrecy

A major obstacle in the recovery of the hidden wealth of the Marcos family is that the former President was a master manipulator of financial transactions and used an extensive and complex system of laundering monies through Swiss and offshore banks. Marcos did not generally use his own name in illegal transactions; instead he used nominees such as friends, cronies and layers of foundations and companies to conceal his activities. The Marcos family thrived on the idea of secret names. For example, in a letter dated 18 October 1968, Marcos informed his Swiss bank that the 'word John Lewis will have the same value as our own personal signatures'. Later President Marcos chose the pseudonym 'William Saunders' while Imelda Marcos chose the name 'Jane Ryan' in transacting business with their Swiss banks. The Marcoses used every laundering scheme available to conceal their investments. At the same time his Swiss banks offered him various instruments of bank secrecy to protect his interests, such as numbered accounts, Liechtenstein Foundations, and attorneys with professional secrecy obligations.

Much has been written about Swiss bank secrecy. It is well known that it is not only based on a contractual relationship between banker and client, but is also backed by criminal sanctions. Swiss Bank Corporation explains Swiss bank secrecy in the following way

> …that no one working in a bank, be he an officer, employee, authorised agent or auditor, may divulge any information whatsoever about any matters dealt with in the course of his job. This even includes knowledge of whether someone is a client, no matter whether temporarily or permanently, whether the client is Swiss or a foreigner, whether he resides in Switzerland or abroad and whether the bank transacts business for him only in Switzerland or abroad as well (Schutze 1983).

Swiss bank secrecy has gained a formidable reputation because the Swiss authorities take breaches of bank secrecy (which amount to a criminal offence) very seriously, and because Swiss bankers fiercely protect the privacy of their customers through various practices and technological systems. For

---

Table 6.1   Income tax returns for Marcos family, 1966–85

Reportable income	P 16, 408.442 (US$2,414,484.91)
Official salaries	P 2,627,581
Legal practice	P 11,109,836
Property income	P 149,700
Others	P 2,521,325

Source: Republic of the Philippines v Ferdinand E. Marcos and Imelda R. Marcos, Case No 0141, Sandiganbayan, 17 December, 1991.

example, accounts of VIPs are usually listed by numbers or codes which are known only to a limited number of bank employees, and not to all employees dealing with the account. The secrecy principle used by government intelligence agencies, that is the 'need to know' principle is diligently applied by Swiss banks for the benefit of their clients.

The Swiss banks also offered Ferdinand Marcos the use of corporate vehicles to protect his interests. For example, the Swiss bank accounts which were originally in his own name were replaced by Swiss bank accounts in the name of various Liechtenstein Foundations. Thus Marcos did not appear as the account-holder. The advantages of a foundation is that the identity of the beneficial owner is concealed in a private fiduciary agreement and the existence of a Liechtenstein Foundation does not appear in a publicly available record.

Extreme secrecy was facilitated in Switzerland by the use of lawyers or notaries in setting up Swiss bank accounts. Ordinarily, a Swiss bank was required to identify its customers so as to prevent the anonymous and illicit investment of assets. Indeed, since 1977 the Due Diligence Agreement of the Swiss Banking Association set out specific rules on proper identification of accounts, the breach of which could lead to a fine of up to SFr. 10 million. The Agreement had a serious flaw, however, in that clients could conceal their identity by using lawyers who would front for their clients. The banks required the lawyers to sign the notorious Form B in which they declared that they were familiar with the beneficial owner of the account and that they were unaware of any improper business of the owner. Form B allowed lawyers to vouch for their client's good standing and in effect also allowed the banks to claim that they did not know the true owner of the account.

There is evidence that the Swiss financial intermediaries used Form B as a vehicle to assist President Marcos in hiding his assets. For example, one of the documents found at the Malacanang Palace in Manila following Marcos' flight was a letter dated 19 May 1983 from a Senior Vice President of a major Swiss bank to President Marcos, informing him that due to changes in Swiss banking law, the attorneys of his Liechtenstein Foundation, who were also bank employees, had resigned and had been replaced by new attorneys from a prominent Geneva law firm. The advantage of this change was that 'the independent lawyer (can offer)...the additional secrecy of his professional privilege'.

The significance of the above transactions is that none of the Swiss banks acknowledged that Marcos used Swiss lawyers as a front to conceal Marcos assets. Indeed, in 1986, when the Philippine government requested the Swiss authorities to freeze Marcos family accounts, there was complete silence about the nature of the Marcos family interests. Furthermore, even after the Swiss Supreme Court ruled that the banks must disclose all the bank documents concerning the Marcos accounts to the Philippine government, the Swiss authorities failed to provide comprehensive information about the accounts. Not one Form B document in the name of Swiss lawyer was disclosed. The documents disclosed by the Swiss merely confirmed what the Philippine government already knew about the Swiss bank accounts.

In theory, the extent of the problems in the Marcos case would not be seen again because Switzerland has abolished Form B accounts and introduced a new stringent money laundering law. Indeed, it has been claimed that the effects of these changes to Swiss law is that Switzerland is no longer as attractive a place for secreting illicit assets. However, the facts suggest that the Swiss banks continue to be attractive to foreign dictators and politicians.

Operation Big Bird and Philippine mutual assistance requests

Operation Big Bird was a plan devised by a Filipino banker, Michael de Guzman, to 'recover' a part of the Marcos fortune in Switzerland. It was hatched shortly after the revolution in 1986 when Ferdinand Marcos and his family were forced to flee the Philippines. De Guzman, who knew the son of Marcos' security chief, flew to Hawaii and obtained powers of attorney from both Ferdinand and Imelda Marcos. He then flew to Zurich and, on 24 March, requested Credit Suisse to transfer the money and assets of eleven of Marcos' Liechtenstein Foundations to an Austrian bank in Vienna. The bank officers stonewalled de Guzman and told him to return the next day. Credit Suisse then informed the Swiss authorities that a Marcos agent was seeking to withdraw US$213 million. Later that evening the Swiss Federal Council imposed an emergency freeze order on the Marcos assets.

Evidence suggests that, at that stage, de Guzman was acting on behalf of the Marcos family and not on behalf of the new Philippines government. Only de Guzman knows whether he had a secret agenda to double-cross Marcos and steal the money for the Philippines people. What is interesting is that Credit Suisse did not act immediately on the instructions of Marcos agent, even after its bank officers telephoned Marcos, who confirmed that the had issued a power of attorney to de Guzman. One of the reasons for Credit Suisse's caution was that the Swiss Banking Commission had ordered all banking institutions to report their holdings in Switzerland or their management from Switzerland of any assets of the Marcos family, or of persons or legal entities connected with them.

The Federal Council's unilateral freeze order was unprecedented in Swiss banking history. Some Swiss bankers claimed that 'it would compromise Switzerland's reputation as a haven of banking secrecy'. Its legal justification was said to be the external affairs power of the Swiss Constitution. The freeze order was made in anticipation of a claim by the Philippines government for Marcos' money.

The Philippines government welcomed the freeze order. At this time, it was confident that the Swiss legal system would provide an expeditious mechanism to recover the ill-gotten fortune of the Marcos family. The Philippines government hired three politically well-connected and highly competent lawyers from Zurich, Geneva and Lugano to handle their case.

An official request by the Solicitor General of the Philippines to continue the freeze was made on 7 April 1986. This was followed by the filing of a formal mutual assistance request with a detailed brief, setting out the criminal charges which were being investigated in relation to Marcos and the evidence of the Marcos family's Swiss bank accounts. The Swiss Federal Department of Justice then issued a freeze order in substitution for the exceptional freeze order by the Federal Council. This freeze order was later confirmed by the Swiss Supreme Court and is still in force today.

Meanwhile, de Guzman had joined forces with Colonel Jose Almonte, a distinguished army officer, in order to recover the Marcos monies. De Guzman tried again to withdraw the Marcos money at Credit Suisse but without success. He then sought the assistance of the Presidential Commission for Good Government (PCGG) and the Solicitor-General. On 4 July Solicitor General Ordonez filed a request with the Swiss Federal Office for Justice and Police asking Credit Suisse to transfer monies in eleven Foundations to an Austrian bank account controlled by de Guzman. The request was signed by the Solicitor General and Colonel Almonte on behalf of the Philippines Government, and de Guzman as the duly authorised representative of the Marcos family. It was supported by Swiss government officials who promised to arrange for the defreezing of the Swiss accounts.

However, the money was never sent to the Vienna bank. Solicitor General Ordonez had became disillusioned with Operation Big Bird and was concerned about a possible diversion of the funds. His concerns were supported by PCGG's Swiss lawyers who received information that the Vienna bank was in financial trouble. On the instructions of Ordonez, and without informing Almonte or de Guzman, the Swiss lawyers requested Credit Suisse to transfer the Marcos monies to a new destination, namely an account of the Philippines government to be opened at Credit Suisse. Before complying with this request, the Swiss bankers contacted Marcos, who now said that the powers of attorney were fake and that his only representative in Switzerland was his lawyer, de Preux. Subsequently, the Swiss authorities rescinded the defreeze order. The monies thus stayed in Credit Suisse under the name of the Marcos Foundations, and were subject to a freeze order.

The Philippines government did not recover any money from Operation Big Bird. The failure of this operation has been the subject of a report by a Special Committee on Public Accountability by Representative Victorico Chaves, as well as a report by Senator Salonga, the first chairman of the PCGG. The Chaves report blamed Salonga, Ordonez and the Swiss lawyers for aborting what it described as the best chance for recovering some of the Marcos money. On the other hand, Salonga says that Ordonez saved the Philippines government from a massive theft.

This is not the place to comment on whether Operation Big Bird was an ingenious operation to double-cross Marcos for the benefit of the Philippines people or whether it was an operation controlled by a Marcos agent to secure money for the former President. I do not wish to add to the rumours, speculation and political backstabbing concerning this affair. However, I make three observations. First, Swiss lawyers representing the PCGG—the body tasked by the Philippine President to trace and recover the Marcos assets—have asserted that Marcos must have been sure that if and when the money was transferred to Vienna, it would be available to him. That is, Marcos would have only agreed to the transfer to Vienna if he was sure that he would be the beneficiary. This assertion fails to take into account how vulnerable Marcos was in Hawaii and that he was just as dependent on de Guzman as was the Philippines government. Second, it has been suggested that de Guzman intended to steal the money for himself. But for de Guzman to steal money so openly would be stupid. Moreover, de Guzman was entitled to over 540 million pesos (that is, a 20 per cent commission on the US$213 million) if it was recovered. It is likely that de Guzman did not trust Philippines officials to pay him a commission, and that is why he wished to keep control over the account. Third, one of the beneficial effects of Operation Big Bird was that the information gathered by de Guzman, together with the documentation found at Malacanang Palace, formed the basis of the Philippines government's claim on the Marcos fortune.

International legal cooperation and asset recovery

In the Marcos case, Swiss cooperation with the Philippines was based on the 1981 Swiss federal law on international criminal assistance, the 1982 implementing ordinance, and various procedural and enforcement provisions in the laws of the cantons of Switzerland. Not surprisingly, a team of attorneys for the Marcos family waged a vigorous battle against the Philippines government's recovery efforts. It is interesting to note that the Marcos family have never given an adequate explanation as to how they could fund this expensive litigation, given that their assets in the Philippines, United States and Switzerland were frozen in early 1986. It is estimated that tens of millions of dollars in legal fees have been expended by the Marcos family in protecting their overseas assets.

The Swiss litigation has essentially involved three stages. First, the Marcos family opposed the provisional freeze order, as well as the order that their banks hand over to the Swiss authorities information concerning the accounts. This stage of litigation proceeded through various cantonial supreme courts and was ultimately heard by the federal (Supreme) court in Lausanne, which ruled in favour of the Philippines government on 1 July 1987.

The second stage concerned whether and when the information and details concerning the bank accounts would be transmitted to the Philippines government. It took another three years before the Swiss courts reached a decision. On 21 December 1990, the Swiss Federal Supreme Court ruled that the Swiss authorities were entitled to hand over to the Philippines government the information concerning the Marcos family's Swiss bank accounts. In particular, the court noted that although no charges had been brought against the Marcoses or their accomplices, the Philippines government had expressed a clear desire to institute criminal proceedings before the Sandiganbayan (anti-corruption) court. The court also observed that the Philippines government had delayed opening a criminal proceeding against the Marcos family until it received the banking information from Switzerland.

The third and final stage of the litigation concerns whether and when the assets in the Swiss bank accounts will be returned to the Philippines. The Swiss Supreme Court, in its decision of 21 December 1990, accepted that in principle the assets should be returned to the Philippines. But the Court set out certain preconditions for the transfer of the frozen assets to the Philippines. First, the Philippines government had to file a criminal charge and/or bring a forfeiture proceeding against Mrs Marcos in the Philippines by 21 December 1991. If a criminal prosecution or forfeiture proceeding was not instituted within this period, not only would the assets not be returned to the Philippines but the freezing order would be lifted. Second, the assets would only be repatriated to the Philippines when the Sandiganbayan or another Philippines court competent in criminal matters made a final decision concerning the criminal prosecution and/or forfeiture. That is, the Filipino courts had to render a final judgment that the assets were stolen property and were to be forfeited and returned to their original owner, the Philippines government. Thirdly, the criminal prosecution and/ or the forfeiture proceeding were required to comply with the procedural requirements of due process and rights of the accused under the Swiss Constitution and the European Convention on Human Rights.

No Philippines government official would have predicted that the Swiss courts would impose such strict conditions before repatriating the illicit Marcos assets. This led Mr Gunigundo, former chairman of the PCGG, to voice considerable reservations about the utility of IMAC (International Mutual Assistance in Criminal Matters), the Swiss law on judicial assistance. In 1996, Mr Gunigundo made the following comment

> I believe that IMAC has really been conceptualised to make it more difficult for the requesting state to secure the release of any frozen account given so many conditionalities which are involved, and given our experience with the Marcos accounts since 1986 which have been frozen for 10 years.[1]

Despite these comments, the Swiss authorities made a deal with the Philippines government for the repatriation of the monies to the Philippines prior to the satisfaction of the conditions imposed by the Swiss Supreme Court. Under this deal, the Office of the District Attorney of Zurich ordered the restitution of the now US$570 million frozen in Switzerland to the Philippines National Bank, to be held in escrow pending the satisfaction of the various conditions. The decision of the District Attorney of Zurich was challenged by the Swiss banks and various Marcos foundations. But, in a series of decisions in December 1998 and January 1999, the Swiss Supreme Court upheld the order of the District Attorney of Zurich. In reaching its decision, the Swiss court said

> Today's state of knowledge does not allow serious doubt about the illegal provenance of the seized monies. The incompleteness of the records makes it impossible to attribute the individual assets to specific offences, and it is possible therefore that also legal assets of the Marcos family were deposited with the foundations. However, such legal assets could, as established correctly by the claimant, only be minor sums compared to the total amount of the assets seized. With respect to the overwhelming majority of the assets seized, the facts are sufficiently clear to allow the assumption of an obvious illegal provenance. Under these circumstances an early restitution of the assets is possible in principle if there are sufficient guarantees that the decisions regarding seizure or restitution, respectively, will be rendered in proceedings according to law and order. The decision whether to seize or restitute monies seized must be taken in the Philippines where the criminal actions were committed.[2]

The court also recognised that 'Switzerland has a considerable interest in an early restitution of (the frozen) monies'.[3] In essence, the court said that the money should be returned to the Philippines where the local court(s) would make the final decision as to the lawful ownership of the alleged Marcos monies.

Limits to international assistance

The political dimensions in cases of recovery of grand corruption should never be underestimated. The Marcos case is a leading example of how different interest groups have sought to prevent recovery. The Swiss banks have been singled out because they have been the prime beneficiary of grand corruption and state theft. There is now considerable evidence that the Swiss banks have not fully cooperated with Philippine government pleas for assistance in retrieving the illicit assets of former dictator Ferdinand Marcos. The evidence of non-cooperation can be found in the following material.[4]

- Operation Domino—an undercover operation of the Philippine government to trace the gold and cash assets of the Marcos family which was sabotaged by the Swiss authorities resulting in the laying of criminal charges for economic espionage against Reiner Jacobi, an agent of the Philippine Presidential Commission on Good Government. In 1991, the German courts rejected a Swiss request to extradite Jacobi on the grounds that the Swiss charges were of a political nature.
- The 1994 documentary film on Operation Domino including a filmed confession by the Director of Communications of a leading Swiss bank admitting to a Marcos account.
- Failure of the Swiss authorities to respond adequately to Philippine government requests in 1998 to freeze the assets of Irene Araneta Marcos which were allegedly held at the abovementioned Swiss bank.
- A criminal complaint made by Attorney Francisco Chavez, the former Solicitor General of the Philippines, concerning the conduct of various Swiss banks, Swiss and Liechtenstein fiduciaries, and Swiss public servants. The criminal complaint was made in 1999 to the then Swiss Attorney General Carle de Ponte.
- The evidence submitted to the Philippine Senate Blue Ribbon Committee, which conducted hearings in 1999 and 2000 into an alleged conspiracy between the Swiss banks and the PCGG to divert and hide the assets of the Marcos family.
- German Goverment Intelligence Reports on the 'Money Laundering Community in Liechtenstein' which specifically identified five Liechtenstein financial advisors to the Marcos family and pointed to the intimate links between Liechtenstein and Switzerland (1999, 2000). Subsequently, Liechtenstein

was named as an un-cooperative country by the Financial
Action Task Force into Money Laundering (FATF).

In February 2001, Irene Marcos Araneta, the youngest daughter of former
Philippine President Marcos, visited Germany and unsuccessfully attempted
to transfer the Marcos family monies out of secret accounts in a Swiss bank.
The failure of the Marcos family to get access to their illicit funds suggest
that after the death of Ferdinand Marcos, the Marcos family may have lost
control of the funds vis-á-vis the Swiss banks and Swiss fiduciaries.

Criminal sanctions against political élites: extradition and prosecution

In many cases, the bringing of criminal charges against a former dictator
will be a vital part of the process of recovering the proceeds of corruption.
However, the bringing of criminal charges against a deposed dictator raises
difficult issues, including the following.

- Criminal trials are usually heard in the presence of the
  defendant. For example, under the Bill of Rights chapter of the
  1987 Constitution of the Republic of the Philippines, the
  accused is entitled to meet the witnesses face to face and no
  trial may take place in the absence of the accused except after
  arraignment, provided the accused has been duly notified and
  his failure to appear is unjustifiable.
- A criminal trial would require that the deposed dictator be
  extradited from a third country. It is rare for a dictator to be
  returned to his home country, usually because he has been
  given sanctuary or asylum.
- Even if there was an extradition treaty or arrangement with a
  third country, it is unlikely that that country would consent to
  extradition. Further, the defendant may seek to rely on various
  exceptions to extradition, such as the 'political offence' exception,
  or to rely on doctrines such as 'act of sovereign immunity'.
- Extradition is not usually granted where there is a substantial
  risk that the accused will not obtain a fair trial in the requesting
  state. It is difficult for a deposed dictator to get a fair trial,
  especially because of the problem of selecting an impartial jury.

In most cases, the new government will not wish to extradite a deposed
dictator because of concerns about national security. For example, the
government of Corazon Aquino considered that the return of former President
Marcos to the Philippines would provide a rallying point to Marcos loyalists
and set the stage for a *coup d'etat*. There is evidence to show that Marcos
was conspiring in 1987 to invade the Philippines with a military force and

seize power. Indeed, US State Department officials, after learning of Marcos's covert schemes, confined him to Oahu Island in Hawaii.

Another possibility is to arrange for the trial to be heard in a third country or the so-called country of asylum. For example, President Aquino of the Philippines signed an executive order authorising Sandiganbayan (anti-corruption) court to try cases outside Philippines territory and Solicitor General Chavez asked US officials whether the tribunal could be convened in Hawaii. But the United States would not permit a foreign court to conduct a criminal trial within US jurisdiction.

The remaining option in the case of former President Marcos, was a criminal trial in the United States for US offences. Grand juries in New York and Virginia were already investigating the Marcos family. Any future trial might be heavily politicised, given that Marcos had been a 'staunch ally of the United States' and that President Reagan still considered Marcos a friend. The US Attorney-General offered a plea bargain to the Marcos family whereby if they pled guilty and surrendered certain assets they would not be imprisoned. Marcos refused. Consequently, on 21 October 1988, the Marcos family was indicted by a federal grand jury in New York for RICO offences, including mail and wire fraud, fraudulent misappropriation of property, and obstruction of justice.

Marcos was too sick to attend the arraignment and on 28 September 1989 he died. On 20 March 1990, Imelda Marcos was arraigned and put on trial. On 2 July 1990, Imelda Marcos was acquitted on all counts. A number of reasons have been given for the acquittal, but the major weakness was the difficulty of linking Imelda to the criminal conduct of her husband. Jurors interviewed after the trial told some reporters that they could not hold the widow responsible for the crimes of her husband. The Philippines government explained the loss in the following terms

> Imelda Marcos (Imelda, for short) was acquitted in New York. There was a failure of evidence, an illusion of innocence. The American prosecutor waited for the transmittal from Switzerland of documents that would have established Imelda's direct participation in the illegal deposits in Swiss banks of money belonging to the Filipino people. The Swiss documents never came. Her defence that she had neither knowledge nor participation in the illegal dollar deposits in Swiss banks by her late husband, was consequentially sustained. Somehow, she had hypnotised herself into believing her own lies. After all, she got the American judge and jurors to believe her.[5]

In the Philippines, more than 100 criminal and civil cases have been brought against Mrs Marcos. For example, more than 26 criminal cases were filed in the Sandiganbayan, 37 criminal cases were brought in the Manila Regional Court and 16 criminal cases were brought in the Quezon

City Regional Trial Court. The criminal cases concerned, among other things, Mrs Imelda Marcos' involvement with various Liechtenstein Foundations, the looting of the Central Bank of the Philippines by the sale of US$125 million treasury notes to various foundations. Mrs Marcos was accused of violating the anti-graft law, and of tax fraud and misappropriation of public funds. Most of these cases were filed within the time limits imposed by the Swiss court. The filing of the criminal cases was made on the basis of the approval of the Ombudsman, who certified that the accused was probably guilty of the offences.

A significant problem in resolving the cases against Mrs Marcos is that under the judicial system of the Philippines, long and interminable delays are commonplace and the judiciary is inclined to postpone hearings at the request of the defense or prosecution. Mrs Marcos' lawyers have successfully exploited the Philippines judicial system and made a mockery of the notion of timely justice by, for example, filing no less than seven motions for the dismissal/quashing of the charges against her, all of which were refused by the courts. Mrs Marcos' lawyers also sought to delay the hearing of the cases by filing numerous postponements.

Nevertheless, following a trial of twenty months, Mrs Marcos was convicted in 1993 by the First Division of the Sandiganbayan. Mrs Marcos was sentenced to prison for 18–24 years, with a minimum of 9–12 years, and was perpetually disqualified from public office. Mrs Marcos' motion for the consideration of her conviction and sentence was subsequently dismissed. Her appeal to the Supreme Court was initially unsuccessful, but a differently reconstituted Supreme Court reheard her case *en banc* and she was acquitted. Mrs Marcos faces numerous other criminal charges, however, which may take years before a hearing and final conclusion is reached. Finally, the Sandiganbayan (the anti-corruption court) in Manila has held that the Marcos family must forfeit the secret deposits in Swiss banks. The civil forfeiture decision is now subject to appeal.

Defences in civil recovery proceedings

There are a number of defences which may be available in civil recovery proceedings involving former dictators. The relevant doctrines include the act of state doctrine, the doctrine of *forum non conveniens*, and the doctrine of head of state immunity.

Act of State doctrine

Under the 'act of state' doctrine, a court will not conduct a hearing in a case which involves it making decisions concerning the conduct of a foreign government under the law of a foreign sovereign. But does this doctrine apply to spoliation cases against former dictators of a country?

In the United States, the act of state doctrine was a significant part of the defence of former President Marcos in claims brought by the Republic of the Philippines for the recovery of substantial property and assets in New York and California. In New York, the Republic of the Philippines sought to recover five substantial properties, including a 71-storey office building on Wall Street which was held by, and through, corporations in Panama, the Netherlands Antilles and the British Virgin Islands, which were allegedly puppets of the Marcos family.

In New York, the Court of Appeals upheld a preliminary injunction restraining the transfer of the properties pending trial, and rejected the Marcos defence of act of state. The Court said that a distinction had to be drawn between private acts and official acts of a foreign head of state; that official acts were not reviewable to US courts, even if they were in violation of international law; but acts committed in a private capacity did not fall within this exclusion. The court noted and considered significant the fact that the Plaintiff in the case was the foreign state which the former head of state had controlled. Although the court initially refused an injunction, it later reheard the case and decided that the act of state doctrine would not be a barrier to the suit and granted worldwide injunctions.

In contrast to the Marcos case is the decision of the French courts in the Duvalier litigation. In 1986, the Republic of Haiti sued the Duvalier family in France, claiming that the family had embezzled over US$120 million from the Republic during the Presidency of Baby Doc Duvalier from 1971 to 1986. The French Court de Cassation ruled that it would not exercise jurisdiction in order to enforce claims of the Republic which were not founded upon public law—that is, their purpose was related to the exercise of governmental power.

Court of convenience/ *Forum non conveniens*

Under US practice, a court may decline to hear a case, even if it falls within the jurisdiction of the court, in circumstances where the court has decided that the case could be more conveniently and appropriately heard in another jurisdiction.

After the fall of the Shah Pahlavi of Iran, the new Islamic Republic sued the former Shah in New York and the principal money laundering deposit vehicle, the Pahlavi Foundation. It was alleged that the defendants had accepted bribes, misappropriated or embezzled many billion dollars in Iranian funds. The Court of Appeals of New York upheld the dismissal of the suit based on the doctrine of forum *non conveniens*. The case ostensibly failed because the Islamic Republic had not established a substantial nexus or connection between the acts complained of, and the forum where the action was brought. The court reached this decision even though the record did not establish that there was an alternative forum where the action could be maintained.

Head of State immunity

The head of state doctrine was considered in the Noriega case (see United States v Noriega 117 F 3d. 1206 (1997)). Manuel Antonio Noriega was convicted in the US Federal Court of multiple counts of involvement in cocaine trafficking. He appealed against his conviction on a number of grounds, including his claimed status as a head of state. The relevant facts pertaining to Noriega's political status were as follows. At the time of his indictment in March 1988, Noriega was the commander of the Panamanian Defence Forces in the Republic of Panama. The Panamanian President, Eric Arturo Delvalle, dismissed Noriega from his military position, but Noriega refused to accept the dismissal. Panama's legislature then sacked Delvalle, but the US government continued to recognise Delvalle as the constitutional head of Panama. A presidential election was held but the results were hotly contested, with allegations of vote rigging and corruption. The US government recognised Guillermo Endara as Panama's President and thus head of state. On 15 December 1989, Noriega publicly declared that a state of war existed between Panama and the United States. The United States, on the orders of President Bush, invaded Panama and seized Noriega (see United States v Noriega, 746 F. Supp. 1506, 1511 (S.D. Fla. 1990)).

The District Court, and on appeal the Court of Appeals in the United States, rejected Noriega's claim for head of state immunity. On the assumption that the head of state immunity is operative, the court looked at the Executive Branch for direction on the propriety of a claim for head of state immunity (Kadic v Karadzic, 70 F. 3d 232, 248 (2d Cir. 1995)—holding that Executive Branch had not recognised defendant as head of state). It had been suggested that in the absence of a formal determination by the Executive that the defendant was to be treated as a head of state, no immunity should be granted by the courts (In re Doe, 860 F. 2d 40, 45 (2d. Cir)). And prior to the enactment of the Foreign Sovereign Immunity Act the former Fifth Circuit had held that where the Executive Branch does not convey clearly its position on an immunity question, the judiciary should make an independent ruling on that issue (Spacil v Crowie, 489 F 2d 614, 618–619 (5th Cir 1978)). In the Noriega case, the Court of Appeal considered that Noriega's community claim failed under either the Doe or the Special standard. It went on to conclude that

[t]he Executive Branch has not merely refrained from taking a position on the matter: to the contrary, by pursuing Noriega's capture and this prosecution, the Executive Branch has manifested its clear sentiment that Noriega should be denied head-of-state-immunity. Moreover given that the record indicated that Noriega never served as the constitutional leader of Panama, and that Panama has not sought immunity for Noriega and that the charged acts relate to Noriega's private pursuit of personal enrichment, Noriega likely would not prevail even if this court had to make an independent determination regarding the propriety of immunity in this case (p. 121).

Indeed, in re Doe the court noted at 45 that 'there is respectable authority for denying head-of-state (immunity) for private or criminal acts'.

Turning to the question of act of state doctrine, the District Court said

In order for the act of state doctrine to apply the defendant must establish that his activities are 'acts of state', that is, that they were taken on behalf of the state and not, as private acts, on behalf of the actor himself...That the acts must be public acts of the sovereign has been repeatedly affirmed... Though the distinction between public and private acts of government officials may prove elusive, this difficulty has not prevented the courts from scrutinising the character of the conduct in question (pp. 1521–2).

The court concluded that acts of drug trafficking could not conceivably constitute public acts on behalf of the Panamanian state. See also Hilao v Estate of Marcos (1994) 25 F.3d 1467, where the claim for immunity by the Estate of former President Marcos of the Philippines Government failed in circumstances where the Philippines government filed a brief in which they asserted that foreign relations with the United States would not be adversely affected if claims against former President Marcos and his estate were litigated in US courts.

Head of state immunity was raised in a criminal context in the Pinochet case. In December 1998, the British House of Lords was faced with one of the most important international human rights legal questions since World War II. Was Augustus Pinochet Ugarte entitled to immunity as a former head of state from arrest and extradition proceedings in the United Kingdom in respect of acts alleged to have been committed whilst he was head of state? According to the Chilean authorities, Pinochet had been President of the Government Junta of Chile and then Head of State for the Republic of Chile from 1973 to 1990. Pinochet had assumed power in 1973 after a military coup in Chile against the democratically elected government of Salvador Allende. His military regime was recognised by the government of the United Kingdom and the United States. Pinochet continued in power until after democratic elections, whereupon he handed over his power to the newly-elected President Aylwin in March 1990.

It was not Chile, the country where Pinochet resided, that sought Pinochet's arrest and extradition. It was Spanish prosecutors who sought the extradition of the former Chilean leader on the basis that he had procured and ordered the most serious of crimes—genocide, murder on a grand scale, torture and the taking of hostages—against Spanish citizens in Chile. The Government of Chile lodged a formal protest with the British government over Pinochet's arrest, pointing out that Pinochet was entitled to immunity as a former head of state and visiting diplomat to the United Kingdom.

The House of Lords held that the crimes of torture and hostage-taking fell outside what international law would regard as functions of a head of state and therefore General Pinochet was not entitled to immunity from criminal process, including extradition. This decision was set aside by the House of Lords because of claim of appearance of bias of one of the Law Lords.

Rights of third parties

One problem facing governments in the recovery of assets from a former head of state is competing claims made by third parties. In the case of the Marcos assets, claims were made by third party creditors, including unpaid lawyers, suspected bogus claimants, and by various torture victims of the Marcos regime.

The most significant non-government claimants are the victims of Marcos' human rights abuses. During Marcos' rule, the political opposition was suppressed and massive human rights abuses were inflicted on a large number of—mainly poor—Filipinos. In Hawaii, a class action suit was brought by nearly 10,000 victims and/or their relatives for summary execution, torture, disappearance and arbitrary detention. The class actions suit was brought under a unique US federal law, the Alien Tort Claims Act, 28 USC #1350. This statutory provision authorises US Federal Court jurisdiction over 'any civil action by an alien for a tort committed in violation of the law of nations or a treaty of the United States'. Former President Marcos, who lived in Hawaii, sought unsuccessfully to dismiss the suit on the grounds of head of state immunity, lack of personal jurisdiction, and lack of subject matter jurisdiction under the Alien Tort Claims Act. After ten years of litigation, a judgment of nearly US$2 billion was obtained by the Plaintiff class of nearly 10,000 Filipino victims of torture, summary execution and disappearance. This judgment has been upheld on appeal to the US Court of Appeals for the Ninth Circuit. But as at today the human rights victims have collected an insignificant portion of monies on their US judgment. All efforts to collect the judgment have been frustrated.

Conclusion

There is increasing international concern as to the devastating effect of grand corruption on developing countries. An important international measure to deal with grand corruption is the Convention on Combating Bribery of Foreign Public Officials in International Business Transactions which was adopted by 28 of the 29 OECD countries on 17 December 1997. The OECD Bribery Convention requires each signatory to introduce into domestic law a criminal prohibition for bribery of foreign public officials, effective sanctions against such bribery, and accounting and auditing laws so as to 'prohibit the establishment of the off-the-book accounts, for the purpose of bribing foreign public officials or of hiding such bribery' (OECD 1997).

A related and equally important development is the introduction of new and more comprehensive money laundering rules. In many countries, officers and employees of financial institutions render themselves liable to prosecution for money laundering if they accept, deposit, invest or transfer assets stemming from crime and corruption. For example, since May 2000, Swiss banks which intentionally accept funds belonging to foreign holders of office and which stem from corruption may be prosecuted for money laundering.

A useful preventative measure is the increased due diligence standards adopted by international banks. For example, in 1987 as a direct consequence of the Marcos case, the Swiss Federal Banking Commission developed a practice requiring Swiss banks to enter into business relationships with high-ranking public officials, such as heads of state of members of government, only with the approval of senior management.

Unfortunately, there is considerable evidence that Swiss banks continue to accept foreign political leaders as customers. For example, in November 1999 the Swiss Federal Banking initiated an investigation into nine Swiss banks which had accepted and handled funds (of over US$670 million) from the entourage of the President of Nigeria, Sanni Abacha. The Commission publicly condemned six banks for not handling the customer relationship with the necessary due diligence.

Finally, the case of former Philippine dictator Ferdinand Marcos provides a prime example of the obstacles faced by a successor government in tracking and recovering corrupt and stolen assets. This chapter has detailed the wide-ranging legal, political and institutional problems beset by developing countries in retrieving such assets. It is time to consider whether the proposed International Criminal Court should extend its jurisdiction to include cases of grand corruption and economic plunder since such criminal activity can have as great an economic and social impact as war crimes.

Notes

[1] Letter from PCGG Chairman M Gunigundo to Dr D Chaikin, 11 June 1996.

[2] Republic of the Philippines v Estate of Ferdinand Marcos, Swiss Federal Supreme Court, 1st Public Legal Department, 1A.103/1997/kls, 7 January 1998:10.

[3] Republic of the Philippines v Estate of Ferdinand Marcos, Swiss Federal Supreme Court, 1st Public Legal Department, 1A.103/1997/kls, 7 January 1998:11.

[4] See the website of Reiner Jacobi, www.marcosbillions.com.

[5] See petition for forfeiture of assets under RA 1379 in the case of Republic of the Philippines v Ferdinand Marcos (represented by his Estate and Heirs) and Imelda Marcos, Case SB No. 0141, Sandiganbayan, Republic of The Philippines, 17 December 1991:1.

7

The microeconomics of corruption

the classical approach

Flavio M. Menezes

This chapter reviews the classical approach to the microeconomics of corruption. Based on the pioneer work of Gary Becker (1968) and George Stigler (1970) on the economics of crime, Becker and Stigler (1974), Rose-Ackerman (1975, 1978) and Banfield (1975), among others, have applied standard economic tools to analyse corruption.

In particular, this chapter focuses on a principal-agent model of corruption: the relationship between the principal—the top level of government—and the agent—an official, susceptible to taking bribes from private firms interested in supplying the government with a particular good or service. This chapter provides a simplified version of Rose-Ackerman (1975, 1978) to explore the relationship between market structure, government preferences and the likelihood of corruption. As a corollary, it considers the extent to which corruption can be reduced by revising contracting procedures and reorganising market structures.

Although no formal training in economics is required to understand this chapter, knowledge of economic principles such as demand, supply and market equilibrium is useful.[1] The only analytical tools used are simple algebra and diagrams. There are three types of agents in the stylised economy examined; namely, a policymaker, a lower-level bureaucrat, and firms. The policymaker is assumed to be an honest individual who establishes the government's preferences over goods and services that will be procured by the government. The lower-level bureaucrat, who is responsible for the purchasing decisions, chooses his actions in order to maximise his expected gains from any dealings—which may include bribes. However, the policymaker monitors the purchasing decisions. The firms also choose their actions to maximise profits. This may include, for example, deciding whether or not to offer a bribe to the official and if so the size of the bribe.

Throughout the chapter we consider the case where the goods the government wishes to buy may be potentially provided by many sellers.

Government with well-defined preferences

This section assumes that the government has well-defined preferences—it knows what it wants. For example, the government will accept a less preferred alternative only if the price is lower. The likelihood of corruption will depend on the homogeneity of the goods and on the existence of private markets where these goods are traded.

Homogenous goods

Suppose private markets exist and goods are homogeneous. Examples include office supplies, computers, furniture and cleaning services. In this case corruption is unlikely to occur for at least two reasons. First, sellers have no incentive to bribe government officials to sell a good that otherwise would be sold in the market. Second, corruption can be easily detected as it will be apparent that the government paid more than the market price.

Now suppose private markets do not exist but goods are still homogeneous. Examples include the construction of a children's playground or a bridge. These goods are homogenous in the sense that they will be built according to a given specification. As the bridge specification is unique, however, there is no universally-known pre-existing price. The government cannot buy this good in the marketplace and therefore bribery may occur. Firms may try to bribe the government official so that he chooses to buy their goods or services. Bribery may be eliminated, however, if the government uses a tender process in which sealed bids are submitted, the winner is the seller with the lowest bid, and bids are made public after the winner is selected.[2]

Differentiated goods

Now suppose each seller provides a somewhat differentiated good. Examples include the provision of accounting or word-processing software, or the design and production of military aircraft or nuclear submarines. If these differentiated goods are available in the marketplace, as is the case with word-processing software, then corruption is unlikely to occur. The reason is that the prices of word processors are known to all economic agents and the government is able to rank the products in terms of their desirability. Therefore, the existence of bribery is easily detectible by observing whether more has been paid than the price of a preferred product. Under these circumstances, corruption can only persist if there are special advantages to the briber in doing business with the government, such as reputation-building or if the government is a large buyer. Again corruption of this type can be eliminated by using a sealed-bid tender process.

If private markets do not exist, then corruption is likely to occur. For example, although there are general accounting software packages available in the marketplace, they may not be suitable for use by the government, which requires instead the development of a customised package. In this case, it is still reasonable to assume that the government has well-defined preferences over distinct features of the software. That is, it is prepared to pay more for more preferred options.[3]

The assumption has been that an honest policymaker establishes the government's preferences and reviews purchasing decisions, but a lower-level bureaucrat makes the purchasing decisions. There are many potential sellers who offer a spectrum of price and quality packages. These goods or services are not available in the marketplace.

Given that firms have perfect knowledge of the government's preferences, all sellers' offers should appear equally desirable to the government. If one producer clearly dominated the others at the initial offering price, then the other sellers could be expected to lower price and raise quality to bring themselves into line with the dominant seller (if this can be done without causing financial losses).

Once sellers have equalised their price-quality offerings, the contracting official can satisfy the policymaker by purchasing from any of the competitors because there are no private markets. Thus, firms may attempt to win the contract through bribery. The contracting official is assumed to organise the bribery market by truthfully informing each corrupt firm of the size of the bribe offers he has received.

Denote the size of the total bribe offered by seller i to the official as b^i, and the expected penalty to the official as

$$P^0(b^i) = \frac{b^i}{2}$$

The expected penalty is simply the penalty if caught multiplied by the probability of being caught. One possible interpretation of the given expected penalty is that the entire bribe is confiscated if the official is caught and the probability of this event is equal to 50 per cent. Note that this expected penalty increases with the bribe.[4]

Thus, the expected gain to the official from engaging in corruption, denoted by π^0 is given by

$$\pi^0(b^i) = b^i - P^0(b^i) = \frac{b^i}{2}$$

The official will accept a bribe if, and only if, the expected gain from doing so is greater than or equal to zero. Thus, the official will accept any non-negative bribe.

Let p denote the price per unit offered in equilibrium, q the quantity demanded by the government, T^i i's total cost of producing q units, and $P^S(b^i) = b^i$ the expected penalty to seller i. One possible interpretation of the given expected penalty is that the seller has to pay a fine equal to twice the value of the bribe if caught and the probability of this event is equal to 50 per cent. Note that this expected penalty also increases with the bribe.

Seller i's expected profit, denoted by π^i, is given by the difference between total revenue from selling q units at price p and the total cost which includes both production costs and the cost of bribing the official (bribe plus expected penalty). That is

$$\pi^i(b^i) = pq - T^i - b^i - P^S(b^i) = pq - T^i - 2b^i$$

Seller i is willing to offer a bribe rather than lose the contract as long as i's expected profits from doing so are greater than or equal to zero

$$pq - T^i - 2b^i \geq 0$$

That is

$$b^i \leq \frac{pq - T^i}{2}$$

The maximum feasible bribe from seller i's point of view is

$$\frac{pq - T^i}{2}$$

Therefore, the firm with the lowest cost can offer the highest bribe and win the contract. But they will not usually have to offer as much as the maximum bribe; they can still win by offering a bribe just fractionally above the second firm's maximum. The actual size of the bribe is somewhere between the maximum feasible bribe for the winner and the maximum feasible bribe for the firm with the second lowest cost (Figure 7.1). Let firm 1 have the lowest cost and firm 2 the second lowest cost. The actual size of the bribe is somewhere between

$$\frac{pq - T^1}{2} \quad \text{and} \quad \frac{pq - T^2}{2}$$

and is determined by the relative bargaining power of the official *vis-à-vis* that of firm 1. Any bribe less than or equal to

$$\frac{pq - T^2}{2}$$

Figure 7.1   Corruption equilibrium with many sellers

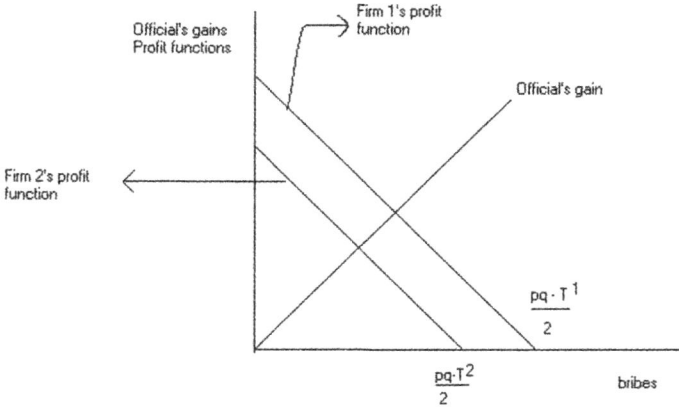

cannot be an equilibrium because at this level firm 2 will also be willing to bribe the official in order to win the contract.

For the bribery market to work as described above there must be at least two firms willing to participate. That is, we need $pq - T^2 \geq 0$. Moreover, the resulting allocation is efficient as the contract is won by the firm with the lowest cost.

Bribery when the government's preferences are unclear

Suppose now that the government is procuring a military training aircraft or the construction of a bridge. It is reasonable to assume that the government's preferences are not well-defined. Suspension bridges may be aesthetically more appealing than the alternative but it is unclear how much more the government should pay for such a bridge. A military training aircraft that can fly very low may be preferred to one that cannot. Again it is not clear how much more the government should be prepared to pay for such a feature.

As before, it is assumed that an honest policymaker establishes the government's preferences (which are now not well-specified) and reviews purchasing decisions. The purchasing decisions are made by a lower-level bureaucrat who can engage in corrupt dealings with firms. This official is again assumed to organise the bribery market by informing each seller truthfully of the bribe offers received from other firms. As before, there are many potential sellers.

In this stylised model, the quality level of the good provided by seller i, denoted by α^i, is fixed but the price charged by seller i, denoted by p^i, can vary. The parameter α^i is assumed to be a number between 0 and 1, where $\alpha^i = 0$ implies that the good is of the worst possible quality and $\alpha^i = 1$ means that the good is of the best possible quality. This parameter can also be interpreted as some feature of the good being procured by the government—in the example of a bridge, α^i could represent the number of lanes or the life expectancy of the bridge provided by firm i.

The expected penalty to the seller is assumed to be

$$P^S(b^i) = p^i(b^i + \frac{p^i}{\alpha^i})$$

That is, an increase in the price charged by firm i or a decrease in the quality provided increases the expected penalty. This increase can occur either because both low quality and expensive goods are more likely to attract the attention of the policymaker who reviews the purchasing decision, or because penalties may be more severe in the case of either lower quality or higher price. For example, an official who was proven to have received a bribe for the construction of a bridge that has collapsed because of low quality is likely to receive a harsher penalty than an official who was caught but whose corrupt dealings did not include procuring a bridge of low quality.

Suppose firm i produces q units of a good of quality α^i, and chooses to charge a price p^i and offer a bribe b^i. Then firm i's expected profit is given by

$$\pi^i(p^i,b^i) = p^i q - T^i - b^i - p^i(b^i + \frac{p^i}{\alpha^i})$$

Firm i's expected profit is equal to the revenue obtained from selling q units minus production costs and the costs of bribing the government official (bribe plus expected penalty). For a given price p^i, firm i is willing to offer a bribe b^i as long as

$$\pi^i(p^i,b^i) \geq 0$$

Let the function $(b_0^i, p_0^i)^S$ denote the price-bribe combination that yields zero profits for each firm where

$$b^i \leq \frac{p^i q - T^i - \frac{(p^i)^2}{\alpha^i}}{1 + p^i}$$

The shaded area in Figure 7.2 illustrates all combinations of price p^i and bribe b^i that yield positive profits for firm i. Note that, for prices below $\bar{p}^i$, an increase in the price has to be accompanied by an increase in the bribe in order to keep profits equal to zero. For prices above $\overline{p}^i$, an increase in prices has to be accompanied by a decrease in the bribe in order to keep profits equal to zero. The value of $\overline{p}^i$ can be obtained by deriving the right-hand side of the above expression, with respect to $\overline{p}^i$ and setting it equal to zero. This yields

$$\overline{p}^i = \sqrt{1+(\alpha^i)^2 + \alpha^i T^i} - 1$$

The official's expected penalty is also assumed to be an increasing function of the price charged by seller i and a decreasing function of the quality. The justification is the same as above. In particular, the expected penalty to the official is given by

$$P^0(b^i) = p^i \left(\frac{b^i + \dfrac{1}{\alpha^i}}{20} \right)$$

Given a price p^i charged by firm i, the official's expected gain from receiving a bribe b^i is equal to

$$\pi^0(b^i, p^i) = b^i - \frac{p^i}{20}(b^i + \frac{1}{\alpha^i})$$

For any price p^i, the official accepts a bribe b^i if

$$\pi^0(b^i, p^i) \geq 0$$

Figure 7.2 Firm i's price–bribe combination for $T = 5$, $q = 10$ and $\alpha^i = 0.7$

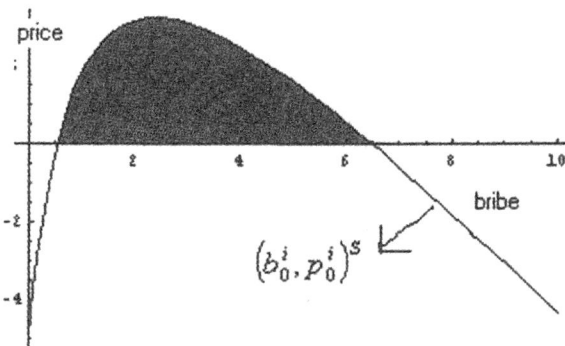

Denote by $(b_0^i, p_0^i)^0$ the price-bribe combination that yields at least zero gain for the official where

$$b^i \geq \frac{p^i}{(20 - p^i)\alpha^i}$$

The shaded area in Figure 7.3 indicates all combinations of price p^i and bribe b^i that yield positive profits for the official. Note that, for any given p^i, one can find the value of b^i that makes the official indifferent between accepting or rejecting the bribe.

If expected penalties are sufficiently high, bribery is deterred— $(b_0^i, p_0^i)^0$ lies above $(b_0^i, p_0^i)^S$, so mutual gain is impossible. Otherwise, any bribe–price combination satisfying these two inequalities simultaneously is feasible in that both the firm and the official can gain from the transaction. In this case, the firm that wins the contract is the one for which the official's net gain (measured by the distance between the two curves) is the highest. The equilibrium price and bribe combinations are displayed in Figure 7.4 for the case where firm i can offer the official the highest net gain and $T^i = 5$, $q = 10$ and $\alpha^i = 0.7$.

Policy implications

There are several important implications from the above analysis. First, the more efficient is the firm—that is, the lower its costs are—the more likely it is to win the contract by bribing the official. Second, firms can also

---

Figure 7.3 Official's price-bribe combination for $T' = 5$, $q = 10$ and $\alpha' = 0.7$

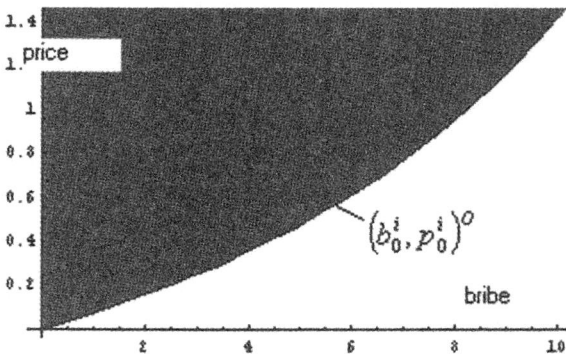

---

reduce their and the official's expected penalties by offering goods of higher quality. Third, political influences can also play a role. For example, firms may lobby lawmakers to introduce less severe penalties and reduce the likelihood of an audit. This could be accomplished by convincing lawmakers to reduce the appropriation to the government department that conducts the audits. Finally, perhaps the most important implication is that penalties may be ineffective in eliminating bribes unless they are sufficiently large.

The above models assume away several interesting possibilities. First, it was assumed that firms that lose a contract either do not learn of the bribe or fail to report the winning firm to law enforcement officials. If, however, a losing contractor does credibly threaten to expose corrupt practices, it is in the winner's interest to propose a cartel in which contractors share in the bribes and the benefits. Whistle-blowing legislation is typically designed to create the right incentives for members of the cartel to report other members' illegal activities. A more complete model would address such possibilities.

The above models also assume away informational issues. The official may not truthfully inform firms of the bribe offers he has received and may exaggerate their value. If firms think that this is possible, they may not believe the official's claims. Similarly, a firm's cost may not be known to other firms or the official, resulting in strategic behaviour by all agents. These information asymmetries may cause moral hazard (hidden actions) and adverse selection (hidden information) problems. One of the main contributions of economists over the last 20 years has been to try to

Figure 7.4 Equilibrium price-bribe combinations when firm _i_ offers the highest net gain to the official and _T'_ = 5, _q_ = 10 and _α'_ = 0.7

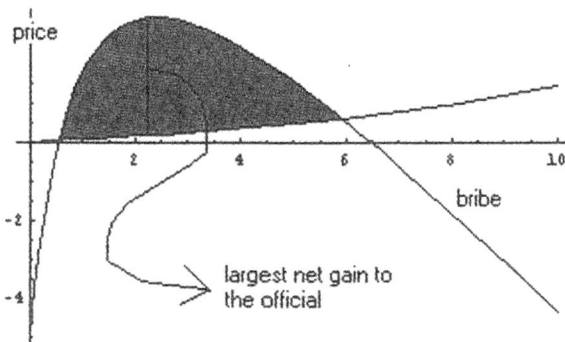

understand how information issues can affect outcomes. In particular, under information asymmetries, corruption may lead to inefficient outcomes—in contrast to the analysis above where the winning firm exhibited the lowest cost. Thus, the analysis above may underestimate the costs of corruption.[5]

Conclusion

The objective of this chapter was to introduce some of the insights from the classical microeconomic theory of corruption. The underlying message is that the rigorous analytical approach of economists may provide insights into the causes of corruption and assist in the design of anticorruption mechanisms. A simplified version of the work of Rose-Ackerman was provided to point out that the amount of corruption discovered is not a function only of the resources devoted to surveillance and law enforcement; there are other economic factors as work. In particular, if the market structure changes from one of the forms that are more prone to corruption to another in which the incentives for bribery are smaller, pre-existing corrupt relationships are more likely to be uncovered. For example, if a good that was produced exclusively for the government is now sold in private markets, bribery will be easily detected. Similar discoveries may occur when policymakers can specify their preferences more precisely. For example, by revealing the technical criteria used in the procurement of a certain good, it may become clear that officials paid more for a less preferred object.

This analysis also suggests the wisdom of considering more basic changes in the relationship between government and private sector. When there may be hidden corruption costs involved in buying goods for the specific use of the government, it may be better to purchase standard goods from the marketplace, despite possible quality loss. If this is not possible, policies should be designed to reduce vagueness in purchasing instructions given to officials and to increase monitoring of purchasing decisions. It should be stressed that although such policies may help to reduce corruption, they may not be able to completely eliminate it unless penalties are very large.

Appendix

Further reading

The economics literature[6] on corruption has grown substantially since the seminal work of Banfield, Rose-Ackerman, and Becker and Stigler. Instead of providing a complete list of recent contributions to the literature, I indicate below some representative papers from the different approaches taken by economists.

One issue that has attracted the attention of economists is the relationship between corruption and development. Mauro (1995) provides empirical evidence that corruption lowers investment and consequently lowers economic growth. His work is extended in Mauro (1998) to include cross-country evidence on the link between corruption and the composition of government expenditure. Bardhan (1997) provides an excellent survey of the theoretical research on the link between corruption and development. Gray and Kaufmann (1998) and Robinson (1998) provide a more interdisciplinary and policy-oriented view on this link.

A second strand of papers explores the link between market structure and corruption—as in Rose-Ackerman (1975, 1978). Examples of papers in this strand include Banerjee (1997), Bliss and Di Tella (1997) and Lui (1996). While Banerjee and Lui link the existence of corruption to the presence of market distortions, Bliss and Di Tella point out that competition may not necessarily lower corruption in certain industries.

A third stream follows Becker and Stigler (1974) and, for a given market structure, investigates compensation schemes for the bureaucrat that may reduce or eliminate corruption. For example, Mookherjee and Png (1995) propose an optimal compensation policy for a corruptible inspector, charged with monitoring pollution from a factory. Chand and Moene (1997) examine the issue of controlling fiscal corruption by providing incentives to officials. They conclude that simply providing bonuses is not enough.

Finally, there is a strand of the literature that examines corruption within an organisation. For example, Kofman and Lawarrée (1993) present a model of corruption in an organisation that suggests that external auditing can be better explained by its role in enhancing the independence of internal auditors. Mehmet (1998) examines the more specific problem of the existence of corruption in a public organisation. It is shown that there is a trade-off in the choice of the supervision procedure and penalties: the reduction of individual corruption results in higher risk of organised corruption.

Notes

The author thanks Robert Albon and Steve Dowrick for many useful comments.

1 There are many outstanding economics principles textbooks that may be helpful to the reader such as Gans, King and Mankiw (1999) and Taylor (1998).

2 One still has to determine the price to be paid by the government to the seller with the lowest bid. With an honest auctioneer (that is, the individual who conducts the tender process) and when the sellers' costs are represented by independent and identically distributed random variables, the pricing rule chosen does not matter. For example, the government's expected price is the same whether it pays the lowest or the second-lowest bid (Riley and Samuelson 1981). In particular, the government's expected price is equal to the second-lowest seller's cost. However, if the auctioneer is corrupt, then the particular mechanism does matter for the likelihood of bribery occurring (Jones and Menezes 1995). Moreover, sellers may still collude and force an (honest) government official to pay more than the second-lowest price (Mailath and Zemsky 1991).

3 This assumption may not be reasonable in the purchase of nuclear submarines or military aircraft where preferences over distinct features may be unclear or not even specified at the time of design. The next section examines the situation where the government does not have well-specified preferences.

4 One can argue that the likelihood of detecting bribery increases with the size of the bribe; larger bribes are easier to detect because the official may exhibit signs of wealth, or larger banking transactions may attract the attention of the taxation office. In addition, many legal systems impose penalties (fines and jail terms) for corruption that increase with the size of bribes.

5 Shleifer and Vishny (1993) explicitly investigate the effects of corruption on resource allocation.

6 The recent literature on corruption in the related fields of sociology and political science is not listed here. See, for example, the citations in Alam (1989). There is also a large related literature on tax evasion that is not referenced below. See Chander and Wilde (1992) and the references therein.

8

Transnational crime
corruption, crony capitalism and nepotism in the twenty-first century

John McFarlane

The 1990s saw some of the most dramatic developments in modern history. The collapse of the former Soviet Union and consequent conclusion of the Cold War has changed the entire security architecture developed over the last fifty years. Other substantial changes in the political map in those fifty years include the emergence of new political and economic alliances, such as the European Union (EU) and the Association of South East Asian Nations (ASEAN); the establishment of the World Trade Organization (WTO); the proposal to establish an International Criminal Court, and the return of Hong Kong to Chinese sovereignty. Many nations have come to the conclusion that by surrendering some sovereignty they may benefit from the collective security and prosperity offered by cooperative arrangements with other states.

Superimposed on recent political and economic developments have been a number of other important changes, mostly derived from the spectacular developments in technology over the last decade. There has been a revolution in the way we handle information and communicate it to others. The globalisation of banking and commerce has changed the way international business is transacted. The speed and efficiency of international travel have changed our way of thinking as we have become citizens of the 'global village'. Our capacity to transport cargoes and provide services at the international level would have been inconceivable a few decades ago.

It is clear that the social, political and criminal environment in the twenty-first century will be infinitely more complex than that of previous years. The end of the Cold War has marked the beginning of a period of dangerous chaos in many countries, where good governance has been replaced by anarchy (Russia and former Yugoslavia), apparent inter-communal harmony has deteriorated into inter-ethnic savagery and 'cleansing' (Rwanda and Bosnia), unemployment and poverty have increased dramatically (Indonesia and El Salvador), population disruption has reached serious proportions (Sierra Leone and China), religious and cultural schisms have given rise to extreme violence (Algeria and India), and many weak states have effectively failed (Somalia and Liberia). Other states, including some in the Asia Pacific region, have little chance of surviving without massive injections of aid, which they are unlikely to receive. Many of the pessimistic predictions made by Kaplan (1994), van Creveld (1996) and Huntington (1993) are proving to be accurate.

Developments to transnational crime

These changes have also opened up new opportunities for criminals operating at the transnational level. Trends such as easier travel, deregulated business transactions, and rapid technological change are likely to continue and become key causes of crime in the years ahead (Williams 1995a, 1995b). Crime, particularly at the transnational level, will become increasingly entrenched, widespread and complex. For example, Russia, which initially embraced the opportunity for change, was ill-prepared for the market economy and the social and political problems which followed the collapse of the previous system, so that the only people who appear to have benefited from the changes have been corrupt politicians and businessmen, regional warlords and the sophisticated and well-established *mafiya* groups. To say that Russia, a former 'superpower', is now on the verge of disintegration and collapse is not an exaggeration. Similarly, there is little doubt that greed, poor regulatory practices, corruption, crony capitalism, nepotism and criminal extortion were all significant contributors to the precipitation of the Asian financial crisis.

No country has been unaffected by these changes. The micro-states of the South Pacific have such limited resources that two small countries have generated, quite legally, up to 10 per cent of their national revenue from leasing facilities to the operators of international telephone sex lines. One South Pacific country, Tuvalu, with a population of only 9,500 people, is hoping to generate up to US$65 million per year from the sale of its internet domain name, 'tv' (*Pacific Islands Monthly*, January 1998). Some of these countries are also providing offshore banking facilities which appear to have been exploited by transnational criminal organisations (*Pacific Islands Report*, 15 February 1999)

As a result of these and other changes in the international criminal environment, some transnational organised crime groups now have the capabilities and enough resources to challenge nation-states. Furthermore, transnational crime in its various manifestations can have a significant impact on international stability and security. Indeed, transnational crime is now widely accepted as part of the new security agenda in an increasingly complex and unstable global milieu.

Transnational and cross-border crime

There is no internationally accepted definition of transnational or cross-border crime. André Bossard, Secretary-General of the International Criminal Police Organisation (INTERPOL) between 1978 and 1985, has written that elements constituting transnational crime are

- the crossing of a border either by people (criminals, fugitives on the way to commit a crime, or victims—such as in the case of traffic in human beings), or by things (firearms—such as when terrorists put arms on a plane before takeoff, techniques of money laundering). Objects used in the commission of a crime, such as drugs on carriers or in containers, or even criminal will may also cross borders (such as in computer fraud, when an order given from Country A is transmitted to Country B)
- international recognition of a crime. At national level, according to the principle *'nullum crimen, nulla poena sine lege'* (no offence, no sanction without law), antisocial conduct can be considered as a crime only if there is a legal text providing for it. At international level, the act must be considered a criminal offence by at least two states. This recognition may result from international conventions, extradition treaties or concordant national laws (Bossard 1990:5).

In describing transnational crime, W.F. McDonald (1995:2, 14) noted that, as with traditional criminology, the new field can be divided into two loosely linked sub-areas. First, there is transnational criminality, its causes, characteristics, social and geographic distributions, and effects. Second, new transnational and global institutions of crime control are being constructed. He added that

> [t]he international regime being constructed to deal with the new transnational criminality represents a post-modern crossing of borders and assertions of particular values as universals...The borders to be crossed are not just the political boundaries of nations but legal, cultural, religious, and organizational boundaries within states.

Williams (1995b:6) describes 'transnational criminal organisations' as '...organised crime groups that have a home base in one state, but operate in one or more host states where there are favourable market opportunities'.

The nature of transnational criminal activity

In recent years, transnational crime has encompassed a very large number of criminal activities, ranging, for example, from art theft, computer crime, and illegal immigration, to piracy and crimes involving tourists. It operates at both the national and transnational levels. Supporting these criminal activities are specialist accountants, lawyers, financial advisers, bankers and chemists, as well as corrupt or compliant politicians, judges, government officials, law enforcement officers, members of the military, businessmen and even priests. The underlying motive for criminality is often simple—power and money. Transnational criminal organisations are diverse in structure, outlook and membership, but they pose formidable challenges for law enforcement at both the national and regional levels. One reason for this is their contemporary emphasis on loose networks rather than excessively formal and structured hierarchies (Williams 1995a).

Future prospects for transnational crime in the Asia Pacific region

Most of the current forms of criminality will continue to be of concern in the years ahead. However, a number of trends will encourage both new areas for criminal exploitation and new criminal enterprises. Probably the most significant threats to regional security and stability are the developing sophistication and globalisation of organised crime groups. Such groups are likely to increase their cooperation in areas of mutual interest—all forms of fraud, money laundering, cybercrime and corruption—which will continue to have a significant impact on regional economies. There is likely to be an increase and diversification in regional drug production, abuse and trafficking, and it is likely that insurgency groups in the region will become more dependent on crime—particularly drug production and trafficking—to finance their political campaigns.

In spite of the predicted expansion and diversification in crime within the region, it is highly unlikely that manpower or financial resources will be available to increase law enforcement resources at the same rate. The only realistic way in which regional law enforcement agencies will be able to effectively address future trends will be to recruit or train specialists to address the new and more sophisticated criminal threats and to place a higher priority on regional cooperation and intelligence-sharing on criminal matters.

Corruption, crony capitalism and nepotism—the CCN factor

Currently, corruption—like terrorism—is not recognised in international law as a crime in itself, but rather a term that describes a set of activities or behaviours that can have a very serious impact on the way in which decisions are made at numerous levels. In particular, corruption facilitates crime (at both the national and transnational levels) because it protects the secrecy of criminal activities, it diverts or compromises law enforcement resources and distorts the decisionmaking process.

Williams (1995b) notes that corruption is used to create a congenial environment in which criminal organisations can carry on their activities with impunity. It can range from the bribery of low-level law enforcement officials to ignoring particular criminal activities, to the offering of inducements to high-ranking government officials to acquiesce in the group's activities and to provide information about countermeasures by the government. Corruption can be used to neutralise individuals and institutions and can have deleterious effects on political culture and the social fabric.

Lupsha (1996:35) describes corruption as 'the ability to acquire information, take actions, acquire influence, access to rule makers and rule enforcers, and to penetrate opponents and targets of interest'.

The Queensland Criminal Justice Commission (CJC) notes that corruption is often motivated by greed and flourishes in an atmosphere of management neglect or where there are inadequate controls, checks and balances (1993). Transparency International (TI), an international anti-corruption non-government organisation established in 1993, use the term 'grand corruption' which covers 'massive payments that feed greed, not need' (Transparency International Australia 1995:7).

Change and corruption

In a paper written in 1968, Huntington suggested four reasons why a state's modernisation process increases the incidence of corruption. First, in many pre-modern societies, patronage, favouritism and the appropriation of public funds for personal use were acceptable and legitimate forms of behaviour. In some countries undergoing 'modernisation' these traditional practices have persisted. Second, the process of modernisation actually increases the potential for corrupt practices due to confusion over the issue of public and private domain during the change process. Third, people with new wealth used that wealth to buy power, often through bribery, from the nobles, landlords or bureaucrats who dominated the old order. Corruption became a technique for 'new men' to overcome their alienation from the political process and achieve political participation equivalent to their wealth and economic power. Finally, the modernisation process in newly independent nations or in newly developing countries goes hand in hand with the expansion of the state apparatus in the economic and social spheres. This invariably leads to an increase in bureaucratic control over economic activities, which tends to increase costs and reduce the profitability of business undertakings. More controls means more corruption.

In the same article, Huntington traces the links between corruption and political stability. When politicians are seen to be using financial power to secure support or to control the behaviour of individuals, or when politicians are seen to be enriching themselves from public funds rather than executing the public projects which they have promised, the decline in public confidence can open the way for coups, revolts and other forms of violent change (Huntington 1968).

These analyses have some relevance to understanding the environment in which corruption operates in the Asia Pacific, particularly during periods of social or political instability.

Corruption and transnational crime

As Lupsha observes, transnational crime is not a new phenomenon, but

> [w]hat is new is the scale of activity and the fact that organised crime now possesses tools once reserved for nation states. It is the dispersion of technology access, global mobility, expertise for hire, cheap easily acquired weapons of mass lethality, and the vast illicit capital and financial resources of modern organised crime permit it to threaten, rival, and undermine the stability of nation states, and to corrupt civil society...(1996:23–4).

Lupsha believes that underlining transnational criminal activity is the scourge of corruption, without which the criminals undertaking these transnational criminal activities would be far less successful. Criminals have been able to subvert politicians, judges, local government officials, law enforcement officers, businessmen and other influential people through threats, extortion, and blackmail. Probably the greatest incentive is greed coupled with an assumption that they will not be discovered, or if discovered, that they will be protected by others in power.

Souheil El Zein, the Director of Legal Affairs for INTERPOL, recently wrote that '[c]orruption is becoming an increasingly international problem which needs to be addressed by the entire community...The need for international action against corruption may never have been more acute than today' (El Zein 1998:28). The link between organised crime (both national and transnational) and corruption is of considerable importance.

Financial resources to support corruption

It is not difficult for sophisticated criminals to play on the greed of politicians and government officials, if only due to the enormous amounts of money generated by criminal activities.

The United Nations has estimated that global organised crime earns US$1.1 trillion per year (Mosely 1995:4). According to the best estimates currently available, the annual value of the international illicit drugs trade exceeds US$400 billion per year which, according to the United Nations International Drug Control Programme, is '...equivalent to approximately eight percent of total international trade' (UNDCP 1997:124). In any event, the international drugs trade is reported to exceed the value of the international oil trade and is exceeded only by the value of the international arms trade (*The Economist* 1997:19–21; Kraar 1988:27–38). Journalist Philip Knightly recently wrote that 'drugs are now too big a part of the global economy and the US and Australia have found, to their cost, that they cannot buck the market' (Knightly 1999:3).

In the same article, Knightly quotes Nobel Prize winner, Professor Milton Friedman, and former US Secretary of State, George Schultz, agreeing at a conference at the Hoover Institution at Stanford University, that 'the war on drugs [had] not only failed miserably [but] did not even have a moral dimension'. Friedman asked '[c]an any policy, however high-minded, be moral if it leads to widespread corruption?' (Knightly 1999:6).

In 1996, an International Monetary Fund working paper assessed international money laundering at about US$500 billion, which represents 2 per cent of global GDP. Robinson (1996:13) claims that money laundering is 'the world's third-largest business'. A 1997 study by the Chulalongkorn University in Bangkok put the economic value of crime in Thailand during 1993–95 at between US$24–32 billion, equivalent to 14–19 per cent of Thailand's GDP (*Money Laundering Bulletin*, February 1997:3).

With these kinds of financial resources at their disposal, it is hardly surprising that there is such a strong link between corruption and transnational criminal activities. The Russian Prosecutor-General, Yuri Skuratov, recently wrote to the Duma (the Russian Parliament) alleging that that the Russian Central Bank had secreted US$50 billion (including IMF money) in the account of an offshore company established in Jersey, Channel Islands, apparently to hide Russian assets from creditors. Commenting on this matter, Dr Andrei Piontkovsky of the Russian Strategic Studies Centre was quoted as saying, '[i]t's not corruption. It's beyond corruption. It's complete collusion between money and power in Russia (Lewis 1999:20).

The regional impact of corruption

Recent revelations of high-level corruption in South Korea and Japan and alleged corruption in Indonesia and Papua New Guinea have emphasised the importance of international initiatives, such as those taken by the OECD. Clearly, such behaviour—most of which has international implications—constitutes a serious abuse of power. It bypasses the desirable standards of transparency and accountability in decision making and can lead to a substantial loss of confidence in the government of the day, and hence threats to the stability of the governing regime.

Since his fall from power, former President Suharto of Indonesia, and his family, have been under investigation for alleged corruption and nepotism. In 1996, a former President of the Republic of Korea, Chun Doo-wan, was convicted of corruption and his involvement in the 1980 Kwangju massacre. His successor, Roh Tae-woo, was also convicted of bribery allegedly amounting to some US$650 million.

Similar problems of serious corruption at the political level have occurred in recent years in Japan, Pakistan, China, Russia, Vietnam, Papua New Guinea and a number of other countries in the Asia Pacific region. This has led to popular movements against political corruption and nepotism, and against those who appear to have benefited accordingly (see Rashid and Islam 1997:18; Imbaruddin 1997:12–15; Tampipi 1997:16–18).

Pasuk attributes the 'wave of anti-corruption sentiment [which] has swept across Asia' to press publicity of corruption scandals, a new generation of politicians and lawyers who have spear-headed the attack on corruption, and the judiciary, for converting corruption charges into criminal convictions (Phongpaichit and Piriyarangsan 1966:iv, vi).

There have been major problems with crime and corruption in Australia. Over the last 30 years, there have been many Royal Commissions and other inquiries into organised crime, drug trafficking, paedophile activities and corruption, particularly at the police level. The best known of the recent inquiries in relation to police corruption were the Fitzgerald Inquiry in Queensland (Fitzgerald 1989) and the Wood Royal Commission in New South Wales (Wood 1997). Arising out of these Royal Commissions and Inquiries, several specialised agencies were established, such as the National Crime Authority (established in 1984), the New South Wales Independent Commission Against Corruption (1988) the Queensland Criminal Justice Commission (1990), the Western Australian Anti-Corruption Commission (1997) and the New South Wales Police Integrity Commission (1997). The Commonwealth Ombudsman exercises certain review responsibilities in relation to police corruption at the Commonwealth level.

Corruption in international organisations

On 16 March 1999, the European Union was plunged into crisis after the publication of a report into fraud and corruption forced the resignation of the President of the European Commission and all 19 Commissioners. The International Olympic Committee (IOC) has also been plagued by allegations of corruption and nepotism, resulting in serious damage to the reputation of the Olympic movement and recommendations of expulsion of several IOC members.

International anti-corruption efforts

On 16 December 1996, the United Nations General Assembly adopted a *Declaration Against Corruption and Bribery in International Commercial Transactions*. Although other international organisations, such as the OECD and the World Bank, have placed emphasis on combating bribery of foreign officials in business dealings, the impact of high-level corruption on good governance has only recently been acknowledged. Now corruption is of concern at the highest level of global policymaking (Walsh 1998:37–43).

In 1994, the OECD issued a set of 'Recommendations on Bribery in International Business Transactions' which called on member governments to take effective action to deter, prevent and combat the bribery of foreign business officials. Such measures include reviewing their criminal, civil, administrative, tax, business accounting and banking laws. In October 1995, the OECD took the matter further with specific recommendations on the tax treatment of illicit payments (Bosch 1997). An OECD convention incorporating these proposals was signed in Paris on 17 December 1997 by 34 countries, together accounting for 70 per cent of world trade and 90 per cent of foreign direct investment. The Convention obliges signatories to criminalise bribery of foreign public officials and to cooperate in mutual monitoring of implementation. The Convention entered into force on 15 February 1999 with ratification by Bulgaria, Canada, Finland, Germany, Greece, Hungary, Iceland, Japan, Korea, Norway, the United Kingdom, and the United States (USAid Center for Democracy and Governance 1999).

Good governance and anti-corruption

In recent years much emphasis has been placed by bodies such as the World Bank, the IMF (see IMF 1998), and the Asian Development Bank on the concept of 'good governance', which the Australian Foreign Minister, Hon. Alexander Downer, has described as 'the effective management of a country's resources in a manner that is open, transparent, equitable and responsive to people's needs' (Downer 1997).

Larmour notes that '"governance" [is] a polite way of raising awkward issues of corruption, incompetence, and abuse of power'.

> Good governance works by statistical comparison, the creation of league
> tables, visiting missions, international conferences and the emulation of best
> practice. It may be imposed by conditionality, but may also be self-imposed
> for fear of being left behind, or outside the club (1998:4).

Such institutions as parliamentary democracy, a free press, an independent judiciary and the role of ombudsmen all contribute to maintaining scrutiny over good governance by highlighting corrupt practices, incompetence and abuses of power. Where such institutions are either absent or weak, the opportunities for abuse are obviously greater.

Planning for the twenty-first century

In the rapidly changing environment previously described, transnational organised crime and corruption flourish. The efforts which Hong Kong has made to counter corruption, particularly since the establishment of the Independent Commission Against Corruption (ICAC) 25 years ago, have set an international standard for others to emulate. In recent years, the People's

Republic of China has also placed a much higher priority on anti-corruption measures, which have resulted in intervention at the highest levels. The fight against corruption is a high priority for Premier Zhu Rongji.

Dealing with the threats of transnational crime and corruption requires a set of carefully crafted action plans. The formulation of such plans depends on local circumstances and contemporary events. It is important that specific forms of corruption are identified and dealt with specifically, rather than attempting to fight corruption as if it were a homogeneous phenomenon. In this way, it is possible to identify the forms of corrupt behaviour which have the greatest impact on the security and stability of the state. To do this it will be necessary to collect and analyse information to better understand the dynamics and mechanics of the different types of corrupt conduct. Then, through a systematic and scientific study of corruption, appropriate countermeasures can be developed that are relevant to the circumstances in which the corruption is identified.

The response to transnational crime

With the growing awareness of the increasing threat of transnational crime in recent years, initiatives have been taken at the national, regional and international level to deal with this problem. The United Nations, particularly through the United Nations International Drug Control Program,[1] has been particularly active in counter-narcotics initiatives[2] and in anti-corruption measures.[3]

The United Nations Convention Against Transnational Organised Crime, which was opened for signing at an international conference in Palermo, Italy, between 12–15 December 2000, was the culmination of six years of intensive effort by the Vienna-based United Nations Office of Drug Control and Crime Prevention, under the leadership of Pino Arlacchi. This process began with the *Naples Political Declaration* and *Global Action Plan Against Organised Transnational Crime,* which the United Nations General Assembly adopted in 1994, to deal with the increasingly insidious threat of transnational crime. The Convention will become an instrument of international law when 40 countries have ratified it. Ratifying the treaty is done when each country brings the terms of the Convention into force within its own jurisdiction. The United Nations expects this to take about two years.

The Convention, and its accompanying Protocols, oblige countries which ratify them to take a series of measures against transnational organised crime. The Convention establishes four specific crimes: participation in organised criminal groups, money laundering, corruption and obstruction of justice. The Convention seeks to align national laws in criminalizing acts committed by organised criminal groups. Under the Convention, this behaviour includes organizing, directed or aiding serious offences committed by an organised criminal group. It entails agreeing with one or more persons to commit a serious crime for financial or other material gain. To combat money laundering countries would have to require their banks to keep accurate records and make them available for inspection by domestic law enforcement officials. Anonymous bank accounts would not be permitted and bank secrecy could not be used to shield criminal activities. Corruption must be criminalised where there is a link to transnational organised crime. This includes offering, giving, soliciting and accepting any form of bribe, undue advantage or other inducement, where the proposed recipient is a public official and the purpose of the bribe relates to his or her official functions. The Convention will attempt to make extradition easier. It will also be easier for investigators and law enforcement officials to obtain evidence, conduct searches, obtain bank or corporate documents and question suspects. The convention contains a general basis for conducting joint investigations and measures for cooperation in special investigative procedures, such as electronic surveillance.

Accompanying the Convention are three Protocols. The first, titled *Protocol Against the Smuggling of Migrants by Land, Sea and Air,* addresses the problem of human smuggling. The second, titled *Protocol to Prevent, Suppress and Punish Trafficking in Persons, Especially Women and Children,* is concerned with sex trafficking. The third, titled *Protocol Against the Illicit Manufacturing of and Trafficking in Firearms, Their Parts and Components, and Ammunition*, deals with the illicit trade in firearms. In addition to the Protocols, the UNODCCP is working on an implementation strategy for a *Global Program Against Corruption* and a *Global Program Assessing Transnational Organised Crime Groups: Dangerousness and Trends.*

Initiatives taken on a regional level include
- the expressed desire of Ministers at the 3rd ASEAN Regional Forum in Jakarta in July 1996 to consider 'the question of drug trafficking and related transnational issues, such as economic crimes, including money laundering, which could constitute threats to the security of the countries of the region'
- the ASEAN Ministers' Declaration on Transnational Crime, concluded in Manila on 20 December 1997
- the Manila Declaration on the Prevention and Control of Transnational Crime, concluded in Manila on 25 March 1998
- the Joint Communiqué of the 2nd ASEAN Ministerial Meeting on Transnational Crime, held in Yangon, Myanmar, on 23 June 1999, including the adoption of the ASEAN Plan of Action to Combat Transnational Crime
- the ongoing work of the Asia-Pacific Group on Money Laundering
- the ongoing work of the International Criminal Police Organisation (INTERPOL) in the Asia-Pacific region

- the ongoing work of regional police cooperation, through ASEANAPOL
- the establishment of the International Law Enforcement Academy in Bangkok in 1997[4]
- the establishment of the Philippine Centre on Transnational Crime in Manila in March 1999
- the proposal by ASEAN Ministers to consider establishing an ASEAN Centre for Combating Transnational Crime
- the establishment of an ASEAN Regional Forum Experts Group on Transnational Crime.

Finally, at the 'Second Track'[5] level, in December 1996, the Council for Security Cooperation in the Asia-Pacific (CSCAP)[6] decided to establish a Working Group on Transnational Crime, chaired jointly by Australia, the Philippines and Thailand. The Working Group has now met on eight occasions and has dealt with a very wide range of transnational criminal issues from the operational and policy perspectives, as well as assessing the relevance of such activities to regional security and stability.

In most circumstances, the capacity of a state to intervene operationally against transnational crime is limited to its own jurisdiction, nevertheless there are a number of strategies which can be employed at the national and regional levels to deal with this threat. The basic investigative tools apply transnationally, as they do nationally, but the emphasis is on sound liaison relationships, good information and intelligence exchanges, a sound understanding of the law enforcement systems in place in the other jurisdictions, a preparedness to consider mutual support and/or joint operational approaches, and professional trust.

There are a number of guidelines for dealing with transnational crime. These include the encouragement of greater legal and administrative compatability, accession to relevant conventions, and bilateral and regional cooperation.

The relationship between corruption and organised crime is the most dangerous, along with the illicit financing of political parties. Corruption is often the cornerstone of the activities of some criminal organisations. Its general effect on administrative departments (for example those delivering identity documents, customs services, tax offices) can facilitate all types of fraudulent activities including, particularly, international trafficking. It also protects criminals, since the officials who have been corrupted are frequently those who should be investigating the criminals' activities, or at least contributing to such investigations. Furthermore, the funds available to criminal organisations make it possible to offer bribes that are difficult to resist. It is their success in accumulating wealth that gives criminal organisations their power and makes them dangerous.

Conclusions

There is little doubt that transnational crime, in its various manifestations, is on the increase in the Asia Pacific region. Transnational crime is becoming far more sophisticated, wide-ranging and serious in its impact on national and regional security and stability. The East Asian financial crisis and the internal disruption faced by several states have created circumstances in which it will be even more difficult for states to allocate the appropriate resources and expertise to counter the increasing threat of transnational crime, particularly if police resources need to be diverted to undertake public order tasks.

There is a close nexus between corruption and the rise of transnational crime—drug trafficking, firearms trafficking, money laundering, sex slavery and paedophilia, and many other types of criminal activity. The massive funds generated by transnational crime—particularly drug trafficking—can corrupt or suborn almost any system. Undoubtedly, the money so generated can be, and is being used, to corrupt politicians, judges, officials, police, and other people responsible for maintaining good governance and the rule of law. Corruption provides the lubricant that enables transnational crime to flourish, both within the states immediately affected and across jurisdictional borders. Transnational crime will never be contained, let alone overcome, unless there is a major global assault on the citadels of corruption.

Corruption is a major threat to democracy, economic and social development and good governance. It has been described as 'a moral and financial gangrene which stops society from functioning normally' (Transparency International and Worldaware 1994:3). It is an economic as well as a moral problem in that it discourages good business practices and, by creating a barrier against trade and investment, acts as an impediment to development. It raises the cost of goods and services. It is gives rise to waste and inefficiency through diverting tenders away from the best and most suitable supplier. The losses caused by corruption by far exceed the sum of the individual profits derived from it, because it distorts the whole economy. Finally, it taints the international reputation of the country concerned, making it more difficult to attract foreign investment.

Even more importantly, corruption is damaging because it strikes at the core of integrity and trust in the state and the way it operates, through undermining fairness, stability and efficiency. As an African Head of State once observed, '[y]oung people in my country now have as their role models the leaders who have made money from corruption. Corruption is destroying the future of our society' (Olesegun Obasanjo, quoted in Transparency International and Worldaware 1994:3). President Jiang Zemin has repeatedly called the fight against corruption in China 'a matter of life and death for the party and the state' (Lawrence 1998:10).

In a corrupt environment, resources will be directed towards such non-productive areas as the police, armed forces and other organs of social control and repression as the élite move to protect themselves, their positions and their material wealth. Laws will be enacted and resources otherwise available for socioeconomic development will be diverted into security expenditure (Transparency International 1995b:5).

Although transnational crime and corruption continue to present considerable threats to the security and stability of the countries of the Asia Pacific region, there are some grounds for optimism. At both the United Nations and regional levels, there is now a much greater awareness of the dangers posed by transnational crime in its various manifestations, and practical legal, law enforcement and political measures are being taken to deal with this problem. The fight against transnational crime has gained momentum over the last two years and cooperation at both the international and regional levels has probably never been better. This cooperation transcends the national, political, cultural and other divisions which so often make international cooperation difficult.

Similarly, as a result of greater regional cooperation against transnational crime, shared concern over such issues as the Asian financial crisis, and the problems in particular countries, there is a much greater awareness of the serious implications of allowing corruption, crony capitalism and nepotism to flourish. Almost every government in the region is taking these problems much more seriously, and there is certainly a groundswell throughout the region against corrupt practices and those who benefit from them. Realistically, there is an increasing awareness that international capital and aid could be denied to those countries that allow corruption to thrive.

Perhaps one of the few rays of hope to emerge from the Asian financial crisis is that each nation in the region is seriously reviewing the way its economic and social systems have been operating. The financial crisis exposed not only the weaknesses in financial regulation and fiduciary responsibility, but also the corruption and nepotism which contributed to precipitating the crisis. The opportunity has now presented itself to address the problems of the past and, above all, to introduce the transparency, accountability and political changes necessary to ensure that the likelihood of such problems arising again is minimised. Failure to grasp this opportunity will not bode well for the future security and stability of the Asia Pacific region.

Notes

[1] See, for example, the United Nations International Drug Control Program *World Drug Report,* Oxford: Oxford University Press, 1997.

[2] The three principal initiatives taken by the UNDCP have been encompassed by three international Conventions: the *Single Convention on Narcotic Drugs, 1961,* whose purpose is to prevent and combat drug addiction by means of coordinated international action, using two complementary forms of intervention and control: prevention and repression; the *Convention on Psychotropic Substances, 1971,* which establishes an international control system for psychotropic substances which are generally produced by the pharmaceutical industry; and the *Convention Against Illicit Traffic in Narcotic Drugs and Psychotropic Substances, 1998,* which provides for comprehensive and innovative measures against drug trafficking, such as provisions against money laundering and against illicit activities related to precursor and essential chemicals and provisions for new methods of international cooperation such as transfer of proceedings, controlled deliveries and extradition of drug traffickers.

[3] The *United Nations Declaration Against Corruption and Bribery in International Commercial Transactions,* was concluded in New York in December 1996. This lead to the Organisation for Economic Cooperation and Development (OECD) *Convention on Combating Bribery of Foreign Officials in International Business Transactions,* which was concluded in Paris on 17 December 1997, and has since been the model for anti-corruption legislation in many countries, including Australia.

[4] The ILEA is sponsored by the United States Drug Enforcement Administration.

[5] The 'Second Track' is a dialogue process involving academic and other regional subject experts, as well as 'officials operating in their private capacities'.

[6] The current membership of CSCAP comprises Australia, Cambodia, Canada, China, European Union, Indonesia, India, Japan, Malaysia, Mongolia, New Zealand, North Korea, Papua New Guinea, Philippines, Russia, Singapore, South Korea, Thailand, Vietnam and the United States. It is likely that the Pacific Islands Forum, based in Fiji, will be granted observer status in CSCAP later this year.

9

The prevention and control of economic crime

Peter Grabosky

Economic crime, by which I refer generally to fraud in its various manifestations, is among the most costly of all criminal activities. Although it would be interesting to determine its cost with some precision, the total impact is unquantifiable. There are a number of reasons why attempts to estimate the costs of economic crime are bound to be futile. First, the most skilfully perpetrated offences are not even detected by victims. Even when an offence is detected, and the victim knows that he or she has sustained a loss, they may be reluctant to report. In the case of an individual, he or she may simply be too embarrassed, and the expectation of recovering lost assets may be remote or nonexistent. In the case of an organisation, they may be concerned about possible damage to their commercial reputation, and decide as a matter of business judgment not to disclose their vulnerability.

Statistics aside, the reasons for being concerned about economic crime should be obvious to many. The essence of fraud is a breach of trust. Trust is the very foundation of commerce and of civil society. Economic crime thus jeopardises basic interpersonal relations, economic development, and in some cases, even the stability of governments. One wonders, for example, what the economy of the former Zaire might have become had its corrupt leadership not plundered the nation's wealth. The collapse of the Albanian regime following massive losses sustained by thousands of citizens in an investment fraud constitutes another example. One could compile a long list of cases, but the purpose of this chapter is to discuss the risks of economic crime and the countermeasures which might be put in place to minimise them. This chapter places special emphasis on computer-related crime, because the convergence of computers and communications will become the dominant factor in commerce in the new millennium.

Crime is a changing phenomenon. Some activities, such as criminal exploitation of online commerce, which were inconceivable less than a decade ago, now pose significant risks to the economy and society of many nations.

Fraud is one general type of crime which, whilst as old as commerce itself, may be expected to take new forms as the twenty-first century progresses. In some cases, these forms have already begun to emerge. This chapter outlines a number of social, demographic and economic developments which may be expected to influence the shape of economic crime in years to come. It is of note that these trends, and the variety of economic crimes which may be expected to accompany them, are beyond the capacity of law enforcement agencies alone to control.

The environment of economic crime

It has become trite to suggest that the world is shrinking. The world is now characterised by unprecedented mobility of information, finance, goods and services, people, cultural artefacts, flora and fauna, even viruses—both those of the microbial variety as well as those which infect one's hard drive.

The globalisation of finance, where electronically mediated exchanges occur in nanoseconds, is far removed from the days where deals were sealed with a handshake, and a man's word was his bond. In recent times, the Barings and Sumitomo experiences have had significant global repercussions, with adverse effects on financial markets and commodity prices. In brief, the proliferation of anonymous financial transactions is accompanied by a commensurate proliferation of opportunities for betrayal of trust.

Varieties of economic crime

There are several major forms of economic crime which confront society in the new millenium. The following categories are not mutually exclusive, but are intended to illustrate the range and variety of economic crime.

Insurance fraud

Insurance is a most important institution, enabling us to spread risk and thereby engage in activities of tremendous commercial or individual benefit. With insurance, however, comes the opportunity for fraud. The fabrication of false insurance claims is as old as the institution of insurance itself. Whether at the hands of opportunistic individuals or criminal organisations, the cost of insurance fraud is substantial and often borne by honest and law-abiding policyholders.

Fraud against governments

Governments are at great risk of fraud. They dispense benefits, and many citizens are not beyond obtaining these benefits fraudulently. They buy goods and services, and many purveyors of these goods and services are not beyond providing inferior products or otherwise inflating their invoices. Governments raise taxes, and many taxpayers evade payment. Government employees may divert public assets for private use. When governments are defrauded, all honest citizens pay the price. To the extent that funds defrauded would otherwise be spent on worthwhile government programs, the public suffers twice.

Fraud against employers

Organisations, whether in the public or private sector, may be at risk from their employees. Embezzlement or theft of money, goods or services by employees can mean the difference between economic survival and bankruptcy. When an employer's business fails because of employee theft, law-abiding employees are among those who pay the price.

Fraud against consumers

Purveyors of goods and services can cheat their customers in many ways. They may provide defective or inferior products or fail to deliver goods and services altogether. They may advertise their products in a deceptive manner. In the extreme, this can lead to death or injury in the case of dangerous products purported to be safe. At the very least, the consumer or will pay more for a product than he or she should.

Telemarketing fraud

The media of commerce are also changing. The days of face-to-face exchange are giving way to an increased volume of sales by mail-order and telemarketing. Telemarketing may involve the use of the telephone or increasingly the internet, which may well become the dominant medium of commerce this century. While these new forms of media offer greater opportunity and choice for consumers, they also pose greater risk. *Ceteris paribus*, the greater the uptake of new technologies for commercial application, the greater the risk that they will be exploited for criminal purposes.

Fraud against shareholders and investors

The directors of large companies may divert company assets for personal use. When this occurs on a scale sufficient to affect the company's financial performance, shareholders and investors suffer. At the extreme, companies may collapse, leaving investors and creditors at a loss. Endemic fraud can taint an entire economy, leading to capital flight and discouraging foreign investment.

Superannuation fraud

The world's industrialised nations are at present experiencing certain economic changes at a dramatic pace. One of the most dramatic examples is the growth of the superannuation industry, which establishes and manages private pension funds. Over 100,000 superannuation funds currently exist in Australia alone. Around the world, vast sums have accumulated, and the superannuation savings pool contains trillions of dollars.

This is not to suggest that persons charged with the stewardship of such funds have unusual criminal propensities, but the sheer volume of money constitutes what may be an irresistible temptation to the unscrupulous. Abuses of superannuation funds in the United States and the United Kingdom illustrate the attractiveness of such enormous amounts of money to those who would commit fraud. Short of the risk of outright fraud, the risk of imprudent management cannot be ignored.

Bribery and corruption

Public officials may demand or accept a financial or other consideration as a price of doing business. This can erode the legitimacy of an entire government. Companies in the private sector may require side payments from suppliers. In the long run, the cost is borne by consumers. Widespread, entrenched corruption can detract from a nation's economic competitiveness and may discourage foreign investment.

Money laundering

The term is used to describe the process by which the proceeds of crime ('dirty money') undergo a series of transactions which disguise their illicit origins and make them appear to have come from a legitimate source ('clean money'). This makes criminal activity more difficult to detect, can lead to the criminal infiltration of legitimate business, and can distort the economies of small nations.

Telecommunications fraud

As telecommunications services become more widely accessible, the theft of such services becomes more common. From the 'cloning' of cellular telephones, to the unauthorised access and use of telephone switchboards, and the fabrication of stored-value telephone cards, millions of dollars of telecommunications services are misappropriated.

Credit card fraud

There are four basic vulnerabilities of plastic card payment systems.
- Vulnerability of cards to alteration and counterfeiting.
- Vulnerabilities arising from the issue of cards.
- Vulnerabilities arising from card holder identification systems (PINs).
- Vulnerabilities arising from the misuse of cards.

As plastic cards eclipse currency as a method of payment, opportunities for their misuse will increase. The costs will be borne by merchants and by card issuers.

Industrial espionage

The world of international business is in some respects a jungle. Competitors at home and abroad, and nations which might be hosts to a company's investment, may have a strong interest in a company's trade secrets and other economic intelligence. The lengths to which some will go in order to acquire such information are substantial, and at times illegal. Industrial espionage by governments and private sector institutions is a fact of contemporary commercial life. Companies', indeed, nations' competitive advantage may be at stake.

Theft of intellectual property

Copyright infringement can occur quickly and easily, greatly facilitated by the advent of digital technology. Text, video, sound, designer labels and computer software can be copied and reproduced as never before. Unrestrained, such modern forms of piracy can discourage invention and innovation and deprive artists and creators of the royalties to which they are entitled.

Forgery

Currency, negotiable instruments and a variety of other valuable documents may be forged or counterfeited. The advent of digital technology, including scanning and copying, enables almost perfect reproduction. Not only may the recipient be left holding a worthless piece of paper, but forged documents can be used to facilitate a variety of other economic crimes.

Business opportunity fraud

In the industrialised world, the downsizing of organisations in both the public and the private sectors has generated growing numbers of individuals in mid-career with significant disposable income. With increasing sums of money to invest, the temptations of fiduciary fraud are bound to increase.

In addition to entrusting their funds to financial managers, those with money to invest may wish to start a small business. Unfortunately, they are also within reach of others who can exploit them. Business opportunity fraud or other 'get rich quick' scams may be an unfortunate by-product of nation's transition to a more competitive economy.

One of the easiest avenues into small business is through purchase of a franchise. It has been estimated that, in the United States, over half of all retail sales were through franchised establishments in 2000. Short of the most blatant form of franchise-related fraud—simply taking the new franchisee's up-front money and disappearing with it—there remains the potential for a variety of lesser misrepresentations, such as overstatement of earnings potential and understatement of risks or other hidden costs of a franchise agreement.

Electronic funds transfer fraud

The move to a cashless society has significant implications for both law enforcement and society. Although reducing the use of cash in the community may help minimise traditional forms of bank robbery and theft, new cashless payment systems will create new problems. The proliferation of electronic funds transfer systems will enhance the risk that such transactions may be intercepted and diverted. Existing systems such as automatic teller machines (ATMs), and electronic funds transfer at point of sale (EFTPOS) technologies have already been the targets of fraudulent activity. Most of the large-scale electronic funds transfer frauds that have been committed have involved the interception or alteration of electronic data messages transmitted from bank computers, sometimes with the complicity of bank employees. The development of electronic commerce will be impeded to the extent that the security of electronic transactions is threatened.

Commonalities

One common thread running through most if not all of the types of economic crime listed above is that they are greatly facilitated by recent developments in information technology. This does not mean that we should 'pull the plug' on our computers. Indeed, if mankind were to reject all technologies because of their potential for abuse, we would have rejected the wheel. Rather, we must learn to exploit the benefits of new technologies and manage the risks which accompany them. But we should not underestimate the challenges the digital age poses to those involved in the prevention and control of economic crime.

Where computers are used in the commission of fraud, difficulties of investigation are exacerbated as offenders are able to disguise their identities and activities through the use of complex electronic technologies. Those who seek to mask their identity through the use of computer networks are often able to do so by means of looping or weaving through multiple sites in a variety of nations. Electronic impersonation—colloquially termed 'spoofing'—can be used in furtherance of a variety of criminal activities, including fraud. Anonymous re-mailers and encryption devices can shield one from the scrutiny of all but the most determined and technologically sophisticated regulatory and enforcement agencies. As a result, some crimes may not result in detection or loss until some time after the event, thus making the process of investigation even more challenging.

Other issues which may complicate the investigation of computer-based fraud entail the logistics of search and seizure during real time, the sheer volume of material within which incriminating evidence may be contained, and the encryption of information, which may render it entirely inaccessible or accessible only after a massive application of decryption technology.

Economic crime in a shrinking world

It is worth noting that not only can many fraudulent initiatives originate on the other side of the globe, but few remedies are available to the unfortunate individual who might fall victim to transnational economic crime. Even if one is able to mobilise the law, the chances of locating the offender, obtaining extradition, mounting a prosecution, or recovering compensation may be minute.

Particular problems arise when financial crimes are committed against a local company or government agency by a person situated in a foreign country. Enlisting law enforcement assistance in the foreign country may be difficult, as their resources are limited and their priorities may well lie elsewhere.

Even where a perpetrator has been identified, two problems arise in relation to the prosecution of offences which have an international aspect. First, the determination of where the offence occurred in order to decide which law to apply; and second, obtaining evidence and ensuring that the offender can be located and tried before a court. Both these questions raise complex legal problems of jurisdiction and extradition.

Additional problems are reflected in the difficulty of exercising national sovereignty over capital and information flows. Jurisdictional issues may arise from transborder online transmission. If an online financial newsletter originating in Albania contains fraudulent speculation about the prospects of a company whose shares are traded on the Tokyo Stock Exchange, where has the offence occurred?

Even if the host law enforcement agencies are willing and able to assist, collection of evidence in the foreign country may be problematic. Distance will be more of an impediment to the thief-taker than to the thief. The cost of sending law enforcement officers abroad to assist in an investigation, or the cost of bringing witnesses from abroad to testify in proceedings, may be prohibitive. Even then, there are often legal impediments which must be overcome. The laws of evidence of one's own country are not likely to be instantly hospitable to all evidence obtained from abroad. In nations where a degree of thought has been given to these issues, mutual assistance arrangements may be reached with selected nations for the collection of evidence on their soil, and special legislation may be enacted to provide for the admissibility in one's own courts of evidence taken abroad.

It must be emphasised that none of these impediments to the investigation and prosecution of transnational economic crime are unique to high technology offences. They exist for more conventional forms of criminality as well. However, their significance is heightened, given the increased opportunities for transnational offences which new technology provides.

Extraterritorial law enforcement costs are also often prohibitive. Moreover, the cooperation across international boundaries in furtherance of such enforcement usually requires a congruence of values and priorities across nations which, despite prevailing trends towards globalisation, exists only infrequently. This may be less of a problem with fraud than with matters relating to political or artistic expression.

Countermeasures

The extreme diversity of economic crime means that no single institution of prevention or control will suffice. The police alone are unable to cope with economic crime; there can be no 'magic bullet' or panacea. Rather, each separate type of economic crime is best addressed by a combination of countermeasures. Some of these will be governmental, some will lie in the hands of the prospective victim, and some will be at the disposal of third parties.

- The first line of defence against economic crime is awareness of one's vulnerability.

The popular term for this is 'risk assessment'. This applies to the individual consumer or investor, who should become familiar with the basic pitfalls of the marketplace; to companies, who should be aware of the procedures and processes which are likely targets; and to governments, whose various functions (such as payment of benefits and the purchase of goods and services) may be targeted for criminal exploitation.

- The next step is to take necessary precautions.

The key to fraud prevention on the part of organisations, whether public or private, is the development and refinement of a fraud control system. Having identified points of vulnerability, individual systems and processes should be put in place to protect these vulnerabilities from 'attack'. These principles apply to the control of 'electronic' economic crime, those offences committed with or against telecommunications and information systems, as well as the more conventional forms of crime. The foundation for such a system is a management philosophy which is sensitive to fraud risk. The basic elements of such a system are careful recruitment of staff, a culture of integrity and loss prevention within the organisation, and formal procedures for the protection of assets.

The design of systems can be an important means of fraud prevention. The introduction of a requirement that the recipients of public funds have an account with a financial institution in which the funds can be deposited automatically, has dramatically reduced the risk of lost or stolen cheques and fraudulent claims. Fraud control systems may include technologies as diverse as the requirement that company cheques be signed by two people, to sophisticated systems of biometric authentication (based on physical characteristics such as fingerprints or retinal images) required for access to a computer system.

There are some basic principles for the prevention and control of economic crime.

Audit

The scrutiny of a company's accounts by an independent auditor is an important safeguard against economic crime. It is by no means fail-safe, as accountants often fail to detect irregularities, but the very necessity of having to prepare accounts in a form suitable for independent scrutiny and then subjecting them to a degree of examination is an important first step.

Transparency

It was once said that 'sunlight is the best disinfectant'. Procedures for the public disclosure of basic aspects of a government's or a company's operations can help safeguard against a variety of crimes. Freedom of information legislation can facilitate citizen access to government information. This is not to suggest that trade secrets—or military secrets for that matter—be made available to anyone who wants them. Rather, it means that fundamental information is available to keep markets and citizens informed.

The requirement that organisations in both the public and private sectors publish regular accounts which disclose details of income and expenditures, including the salaries of executives and liabilities relating to environmental pollution, has become an international standard of best practice. Markets are beginning to expect nothing less.

Procedures for independent review of administrative decisions

The possibility of bias or other irregularities in the administrative decisions of governments can be addressed through the system of administrative law (Allars 1997). Procedures for the independent review of administrative decisions by a specially constituted court (Aronson and Dyer 2000), the institution of an Ombudsman with investigative powers who can hear complaints by individual citizens (Caiden 1983), and freedom of information legislation which provides public access to government documents (Birkinshaw 1997) are three elements of an administrative law system which can contribute to the integrity of governments.

Specialised bodies for the investigation and prosecution of serious economic crime

In many nations, the investigation of complex and sophisticated economic crime lies beyond the capacity of conventional law enforcement agencies. Some have thus created new agencies with special powers and expertise to address specific issues. The Independent Commission Against Corruption in Hong Kong, the Serious Fraud Office in the United Kingdom, and their variations elsewhere, are all examples of such agencies. This is not to suggest that specialised bodies are essential to resolving all problems in all jurisdictions. Where more general law enforcement bodies are adequate, there may be no need to create new ones. Indeed, a proliferation of agencies may lead to overlap and duplication, to bureaucratic rivalries, and to important cases 'falling between the cracks'. The effective exchange of intelligence and operational information can be made difficult. Such lack of cooperation may often be to the advantage of offenders, who may be able to delay or avoid detection and prosecution through a lack of coordination on the part of law enforcement agencies. However, the increasing specialisation of economic life suggests that designated organisations may be appropriate in some circumstances.

Cash transactions reporting

The challenge of money laundering and tax evasion is made much easier when the offender is able to shift funds around undetected. To this end, a growing movement among nations around the world has seen the development of cash transaction reporting systems. Banks and other financial institutions are now required to report all transactions over a specified amount to a central authority, or any transaction of any amount which appears in some manner to be suspect. In those jurisdictions where cash transaction reporting systems are in place, it becomes that much easier to 'follow the money trail'.

A free press

The famous adage that sunlight is the best disinfectant has already been noted. To the extent that an open and free press exists within a nation, questionable practices will be subject to questioning. This is important across a range of offences, from bribery and corruption to consumer fraud and fraud against shareholders and directors. This is not to suggest that the media are always virtuous and responsible in their coverage.It could be said, however, that the best antidote for irresponsible speech is more speech.

An adequate regulatory system

Freedom of expression does not extend to the freedom to publish false or misleading advertising or spurious commercial claims. A regulatory system which can identify such misconduct and respond to it effectively will help ensure the integrity of markets is maintained. This need not be the exclusive province of government. Private remedies such as civil litigation, and self-regulatory regimes by individual companies and industry associations, are no less important than government agencies. A regulatory system which combines private and public remedies is likely to be more effective than one based solely on government or on self-regulation.

Mechanisms for building public awareness

By no means should knowledge about fraud and fraud risks remain a monopoly of law enforcement agencies. Because the first line of defence against fraud can and should be self-help, appropriate knowledge should be shared with private citizens, businesses and public sector agencies. All prospective victims of fraud—and this includes almost everyone—should be aware of the types of fraudulent activity to which they are most vulnerable, the 'red flags' or *indicia* of fraud, the most appropriate means of prevention, and best avenues of response when they detect an offence. New developments in communications permit not only the dissemination of basic fraud control information, but also the reporting of suspicious activity to appropriate authorities. The internet abounds in materials on fraud control; some industry-specific, others focusing on certain vulnerable groups such as senior citizens. Other sources of information are medium-specific—sites are dedicated to warning of fraud on the internet. Moreover, many law enforcement and regulatory agencies have established hotlines which are available to fraud victims or civic-minded third parties to report illegal or questionable conduct.

Freedom for individuals to form non-government organisations

Some of the most effective actions to combat economic crime are implemented by citizen groups. Before the rise of the modern state, citizens performed a number of functions (including policing, prosecution and imprisonment), which later became functions of government. Even in modern times, citizens' groups undertake activities that complement the work of government agencies. Two examples are victim assistance and prison aftercare associations. The control of corruption is facilitated by organisations such as Transparency International. Consumer groups and Better Business Bureaus remain vigilant against unfair trading. Citizens' crime commissions are vigilant against activities as diverse as abuse of power by law enforcement agencies, bribery and electoral fraud.

Responsible banking

In addition to their role in the prevention of money laundering, banks and other financial institutions have an important role to play in the prevention and control of economic crime. Prudent lending practices will deny opportunities to the unscrupulous. The challenge facing governments today is to allow sufficient flexibility in the financial services industry to permit the economy to flourish, but to provide sufficient safeguards to protect against irresponsible or predatory conduct.

Commercial third parties

A variety of other third parties can complement the work of governments in the prevention and control of economic crime. A burgeoning industry in information security can assist clients in the public and private sectors to ensure the integrity of their systems. All of the large multinational accounting firms offer fraud control services to clients anywhere in the world. Many have established departments or subsidiaries specialising in fraud prevention. Their products range from a total review of risk management practices to more narrowly focused issues such as security of information technology systems.

Private fraud control services are by no means limited to prevention. Private organisations which find themselves the victims of fraud may retain their own in-house investigators or may engage specialised private sector fraud investigators. These private investigators may conduct an entire investigation, handing the matter over to the police for prosecution. This is common in the Australian insurance industry in response to insurance fraud.

Market forces themselves may exert positive effects from time to time on the behaviour of some public and private organisations. There are opportunities for the second-order operation of market forces through the guidance provided by financial and insurance institutions, and by institutional investors.

Open political system

An open political system permits individual citizens, interest groups or an organised opposition the freedom to question policies and programs. A viable political opposition can be alert to financial irregularities in the public and private sectors and can make them more difficult to conceal.

International cooperation

Because many fraud offences do not involve face-to-face interactions in their commission, it is possible for offenders and victims to be located in more than one jurisdiction. More sophisticated conspiracies may involve individuals in three or more jurisdictions within Australia or overseas. Few remedies are available to the unfortunate individual who might fall victim to such activities. The transnational dimension of many economic crimes requires unprecedented multilateral international cooperation, from formal treaties and mutual assistance arrangements to informal liaison between and exchange of law enforcement personnel. Transnational electronic crime will require very timely cooperation, involving the capability of contacting overseas authorities at a moment's notice.

Sanctioning of offenders

While some would argue that severe penalties do not always deter crime, or that increasing penalties is unlikely to achieve a commensurate decrease in crime, one should not ignore the potential usefulness of punishment for economic crime. Economic crime is often based, to an extent greater than in other areas of crime, on rational decision making. Embezzlement does not occur in a moment of passion; corrupt payments are not made in an alcoholic rage. Penalties proportionate to the seriousness of the crime can send a message to would-be offenders, and educate the public that economic crime is serious and will not be tolerated.

Economic crime prevention

None of the solutions presented here is guaranteed to prevent economic crime, but each helps reduce the risk of such crime. The greater the number of preventative measures in place, the more difficult it is to perpetrate fraud and other forms of economic crime. It may be useful to use the analogy of a web. Any one strand of a web may be insufficient to support a load. But many strands, interwoven, may be very strong indeed.

The prevention and control of economic crime should not impose unrealistic burdens on commerce or on agencies of the state. Absolute integrity may be unattainable, and its pursuit may have counterproductive consequences. One might speak of 'burning the house to roast the pig'. It is ultimately the overall health of the economy and the integrity of its markets which are of greatest importance. Initiatives for the prevention and control of economic crime should be undertaken according to a risk-benefit calculus. This would see the most stringent controls operating where there is significant vulnerability to catastrophic loss, with fewer controls in place when risk is correspondingly less. The challenge for the future lies in implementing systems which will reduce opportunities for fraud, while at the same time allowing commerce to flourish.

10

Use of information technology to address institutional failure

Asim Barman

This chapter describes the experience of deploying information technology (IT) in Calcutta Municipal Corporation to arrest corruption in the municipal administration of Calcutta, a bustling metropolis in India. In the face of apparently insurmountable problems, IT was used as a means of institutional strengthening in the public sector organisation. Introduction of IT in Calcutta Municipal Corporation has had many benefits, including fast and accurate flow of information, increased revenue generation, decentralised planning, effective operational control, a paperless environment, and strengthening of both intra-organisational and inter-organisational communication systems.

The chapter specifically focuses on how the introduction of IT checked corruption, and helped improve efficiency and effectiveness in dealing with

- property tax assessment and collection
- expenditure management
- solid waste management.

The Calcutta Metropolitan Area is 1,380 square kilometres in area, and has a population of about 12 million (about 59 per cent of the urban population of West Bengal). It has three municipal corporations (Calcutta, Howrah and Chandannagar), 35 municipalities, three notified areas, and 540 rural units. The city of Calcutta itself is 187 square kilometres in area, with a population of 4.38 million (at night), which increases by 2 million floating population during the day. With an average population density of 23,381 persons per square kilometre, there is tremendous pressure on land as well as civic services and amenities available for residents in the city. Calcutta Municipal Corporation's area of jurisdiction and population offer many challenges in providing efficient and effective municipal services across the city limits.

The Calcutta Municipal Act 1951 came into effect on 1 May 1952. It was revised in 1980, and the subsequent Act came into force on 4 January 1984. Under the Municipal Act, the Calcutta Municipal Corporation is the principal agency responsible for water supply, sewerage and drainage/water disposal facilities in the urban metropolis of Greater Calcutta. The Corporation's major service sectors include

- solid waste management
- health
- water
- sewerage
- roads
- trade licences
- property records maintenance.

The context

A new global information economy based on knowledge and intellectual capital is fast replacing the industrial economy of today. The global marketplace and its technological infrastructure reflect shifts from manufacturing and distributing physical products to the development of products that are differentiated only by the information that is contained within them. Indeed, the information is often itself the product. Further, these information products are delivered through a combination of advanced digital networks that cannot be contained within geographic borders.

Like industries, many governments are engaged in internal reengineering of their activities so as to improve efficiency through use of technology and to deliver government services electronically to citizens. Economic benefits accruing to governments from technological integration have historically been viewed in terms of cost savings and returns on investments from specific projects. However, in a rapidly expanding information-based economy, governments must deal with a complex set of issues including regulation, deregulation, unbundling, licensing, incentives, and risk management among service providers. The successful governance of cities and urban areas requires both sophisticated IT strategies and institutional reforms in government organisations, based on fundamental rethinking of associated public policy.

In India, it was only during the Eighth Five-year Plan (1992–97) that some state governments initiated a program of institutional reforms in the urban planning, water supply and sewerage sectors. These were through

- imparting a commercial orientation to the sector
- exposing the sector to market forces through encouragement of private participation

- financing projects in the sector through a well-developed secondary debt market
- consolidation of gains already achieved in creating the best possible regulatory framework
- introduction of information technology to aid governance.

This chapter examines the introduction of IT in Calcutta Municipal Corporation beginning in 1994–95, and the effects it has had in streamlining the Corporation's dealings with the citizens. Information technology became the crucial lever for dramatic change. 'Lead us from captivity to freedom, from darkness to light and from despair to hope' was how the role of IT was envisaged when the change began. Calcutta Municipal Corporation was captive because it could not share its information with citizens of the metropolis. Its staff was captive because they had no access to information about the outside world. Citizens were in the dark about the Corporation's functions, as they had no access to information about the Corporation. Taxpayers and others directly or indirectly associated with the Corporation did not know what was in store for them, due to the Corporation's poor data and knowledge bank. In the pre-IT scenario the effectiveness and efficiency of any organisation depended, among many other factors, on the quality of personnel it possessed. In other words, human resources used to be the biggest asset to a vast organisation like Calcutta Municipal Corporation where the establishment cost, inclusive of wage bill, was more than the development cost.

Unfortunately, for various reasons, Calcutta Municipal Corporation had been deprived over the years of the services of the best talents available in the market. As a result, the Corporation was overstaffed and generally underskilled. In the absence of new recruitment at middle management level or lateral transfers in the Corporation's services, supervision, monitoring and evaluation of programs were poor. This was primarily because creativity and innovation could not be expected from the people who had risen from the ranks and also because they were not respected by their juniors. Consequently, municipal services suffered from poor supervision and management skills.

Calcutta Municipal Corporation's databank was very weak. The citizens at times fell prey to the unscrupulous elements of the organization. Manipulation of data, and distortion of information, exploitation and extortion of the citizens in general, were common. Consequently, the negative image of the city was firmly anchored in the minds of both the citizens and the outside world. This negative image emboldened the Corporation's staff to engage in corrupt practices. Institutional failure thus propagated varying degrees of corruption.

The primary task for top management in the mid 1990s was to address this institutional failure. It was not possible to replace existing staff, within the existing framework of the staff policy, with quality personnel. Nor was it desirable to create many new posts and recruit quality staff in addition to the existing employees. Therefore, the only remaining option was to introduce information technology into the Corporation in a phased manner.

In introducing information technology in Calcutta Municipal Corporation, political factors had to be kept in mind. Calcutta was a centre of opposition and protest during the age of automation of the early 1970s. The state government lead by Leftist parties was initially not favourably inclined towards automation. The employees of the state government, including the staff of Calcutta Municipal Corporation, feared job losses with the advent of automation.

Information technology implementation—three case studies

Information technology was progressively introduced in 1994–95 in Calcutta Municipal Corporation's three key areas of operations—property tax assessment and collection, expenditure management, and solid waste management.

Case 1   Property tax assessment and collection

The main areas of revenue generation within Calcutta Municipal Corporation are its Property Tax Assessment and Collection and Property Mutation Services. Under these, major activities undertaken include

Annual tax billing

From 1993–94 to 1999–2000, the Corporation's assessee base for property taxation grew from 350,000 to 400,000 households. Consolidated annual tax bills for assessees owning property in their name are payable in four instalments (one bill for each quarter) for each financial year. These bills are based on an annual valuation made by the Corporation for each assessee through a standard legal assessment procedure.

The need for automation

There were many reasons for automating this service.
- The volume of bills is huge—ensuring they are correct using manual methods is nearly impossible. Currently, consolidated tax bills are computerised and mailed under certified post from

the data processing department. If an assessee claims that they have not received the tax bill, an information database can be accessed to verify the complaint and a duplicate tax bill can be generated at the counter.

- Corruption inherent in the system had led to tampering of data in case of high valued property. Previously, discrepancies could be noted only at the time of general revaluation after every six years. By automating the business process of the hearing system, the immunity of the annual valuation is ensured.
- If the tax bill cannot be served, the assessee cannot be declared in default even if the due date of payment lapses. Therefore, the mailing address is vital to ensure that the collection is proper and the Corporation's revenue claims are valid.
- To ensure functionality, the areas under the Corporation are marked as wards. A ward has a number of streets under its jurisdiction; a street has a number of premises; and a premise can have a number of assessees (for example, multi-storied buildings). Identification of assessment backlogs are impossible manually but are successfully handled using IT.
- Once the bill is generated successfully, the problem shifts to collection and reconciliation of payments. Manual procedures produce huge gaps, which result in improper updating of assessee's records. Also, Calcutta Municipal Corporation can never ascertain the defaulter list. The Corporation has around 18 consolidated tax collection centres where the counterfoils of the bills are retained, on the basis of which manual summary information and computerised information summaries are tallied. The Corporation's counter clerks often receive a tax with rebate even after the rebate date has lapsed, leading to loss of revenue. This bottleneck has been removed by using collection software at the counters. It has also assisted in reconciliation of the non-realisation of payment made by cheques by providing receipts only after the cheque has been cleared.

Introducing automation

A system of progressive automation was incorporated in the following areas.

- Present demand bills. Previously, present demand bills were printed quarterly and mailed separately. In cases where the bill did not reach a person on time, was lost, or not paid on time, the person had to come to the Corporation's head office to get the bill details or to have the penalty interest calculated manually. The computerisation of present demand bills has resulted in one-time printing and mailing of the bills for all quarters, thereby reducing expenses. Reprinting of bill and interest calculation has also been automated and has reduced corrupt practices. Taxpayers' addresses are kept on file, hence reducing the chances of the bill being lost. Accurate reconciliation of the payment due and the amounts received is also possible.

- Supplementary bills. Previously, re-evaluation of property was manual and subsequent applications from the taxpayer and the hearings were supervised by local councilors. This generated a lot of corrupt practices. The system has now been automated and the assessee numbers are being generated by the system, which means that re-evaluation can be done accurately and on time.
- Fresh bills. New assessees register with Calcutta Municipal Corporation after mutation and the fresh bill is raised to calculate the amount due between date of registration and the next financial year.

Streamlining the hearing system

The hearing system was also streamlined in the following ways.

- A proposed annual valuation is intimated to each assessee for general or intermediate revaluation through hearing notice. In the manual system, the assessee was often never informed and the backlog cases therefore used to rise. The annual variation proposed in the intimation was not known to the assessee, and he was thus trapped in a situation where a higher annual variation could be intimated to him, which he was required to pay unless he went in for a deal that also involved a corrupt practice.
- On completion of the hearing, the assessee received a rate card in which the confirmed annual valuation was written along with the surcharge (if any). There were no controls on the number of adjournments provided to an assessee or the gap in the hearing dates, which resulted in a lengthy hearing cycle. There was also no control on the number of cases heard, number of adjournments, or the number of hearings done.
- If the annual valuation for any completed general or intermediate revaluation quarter is fixed on a subsequent quarter, then the difference of taxes between the previously

fixed annual valuation and the newly fixed annual valuation is collected through a supplementary bill. This bill is handed over to the assessee along with the new annual valuation (rate card) after completion of the hearing. The supplementary bill was never updated in the manual system and the assessee had great difficulty in getting his records cleared.

* By automating the full cycle of the hearing system through the use of an online integrated information system, the process is reduced to a few hours, incorporating the following activities
  i) generation of hearing notice on the proposed annual valuation
  ii) generation of a computerised rate card after the rate is confirmed
  iii) handing over the rate card to the assessee
  iv) generation of fresh/supplementary bill
  v) immediate payment by the assessee at the receiving counter
  vi) online reconciliation of the fresh/supplementary bill demand
  vii) simultaneous updating of the tax register and all related records.

The automation of the hearing system has greatly increased the assessee's confidence. It has also saved time and money. Calcutta Municipal Corporation is now able to complete the backlog of bill payments and also maintain the general revaluation cycle.

Property records

Under the Calcutta Municipal Corporation Act, maintaining property records is one of the statutory functions of the organisation. Mutation is the process by which the name of the property owner is changed when ownership of a property is transferred. The Calcutta Municipal Corporation keeps a record of these changes and ensures that the change is reflected on the assessee's consolidated tax bill. Under the old manual system, effecting this change in records was a cumbersome procedure that was inconvenient for the assessee.

Developing integrated software, where the mutation is classified under various heads, and business rules are provided in a logical information database, has resulted in the registration process being a short single-window process (simple mutation).

A variant of mutation is Suo-Moto, a mutation process initiated by the Corporation to bring a new building into the tax net quickly. This process has resulted in a significant increase in revenue for Calcutta Municipal

Corporation, and there are plans to attach the Building Department's 'Issue of completion certificate' process, which is the new building sanction authority.

The taxpayer has benefited from computerisation of property records in several ways. Payments can be made across the counter at any of the 14 counters located in the city. Even if the assessee does not receive prior payment notice, he/she can approach a payment counter with his/her assessee number or residential address and the computer will provide the information on the exact amount due. Calcutta Municipal Corporation staff have also gained. The replacement of the obsolete cash register system with the computerised system has relieved staff of the drudgery of work, freeing up time to devote to their other activities. It has also led to a reduction in overtime and better utilisation of staff.

Table 10.1 shows the increase in revenues over the period 1993–2001. During this period, as a result of automation, the realisation figures increased substantially—from around 45 per cent in 1993–94 to about 65 per cent in 1999–2000, thus lowering the gap between dues and recoveries.

Challenges faced

Due to lack of automation in this function, Calcutta Municipal Corporation had not been able to monitor tax collection or mutation proceedings. Manual procedures propagated currupt practices, resulting in large monetary losses for the Corporation and harassment of taxpayers at the hands of the Corporation's clerks.

In carrying out its activities under this function, Calcutta Municipal Corporation faced several challenges.

- The manual system was highly personnel-dependent. Knowledge was concentrated among a small group of employees who had a lot of power. In addition, due to the

Table 10.1   Annual demand (Rs. Crores)

	Calcutta	Tollygunge	Jadavpur	S.S. Unit	G.R. Unit	Total
1993–94	57.93	5.27	0.72	0.84	0.64	65.4
1994–95	62.68	5.26	0.94	1.08	0.76	70.72
1995–96	68.16	6.08	1.24	1.24	0.8	77.52
1996–97	80.08	6.64	1.44	1.58	0.8	90.54
1997–98	88.4	7.2	1.68	1.84	0.84	99.96
1998–99	99.99	7.6	1.91	2.29	0.88	112.67
1999–00	107.71	8.29	2.22	3.22	0.81	122.25
2000–01	125.00	9.28	2.70	4.22	0.85	142.05

system of lateral transfers, it was difficult to retain this knowledge across departments. Further, in the absence of a centralised repository, there were no standards, and business rules varied widely across the wards. In effect, the small group of employees took advantage of this state of affairs and indulged in corrupt practices. There was the case of an employee whose services had to be extended for 12 years simply because he could not be replaced.

- Calcutta Municipal Corporation must obtain the correct valuation that is to be billed for a financial year. Generally, this figure is revised once every six years (general revaluation) or in any instance when the value of the property changes dramatically, for example through Mutation, addition of a new area, alteration or amalgamation of property (intermediate revaluation).
- Maintaining the correct name of the owner. The name printed on the tax bill is of paramount importance as the bill is considered an authentic document for proof of ownership.
- Maintaining the mailing address to ensure that the bill is served correctly and remains authentic evidence of the property premises.

When the new municipal commissioner took charge at Calcutta Municipal Corporation, this was the first area to become computerised. This activity is now fully computerised and maintained in an online database.

Cost and time implication of automation

It took roughly two years to automate the system. Investment expenditure was about Rs 1.50 crores for hardware and software (for the headquarters, treasury and suburban centres) and another Rs 1.00 crore for associated infrastructure (buildings, electrical cabling, air conditioning, and so on).

Case 2   Expenditure management

The need for automation

When the new municipal commissioner took charge, Calcutta Municipal Corporation's accounting records were hopelessly behind schedule—some accounts were in seven years arrears. The manual system was not efficient in tracking the enormous volume of data and transactions generated daily. Accordingly, the budgeting was based on the system of estimated values of allocations and expenditures, and there was no method of collecting information on actual expenditures incurred under different accounting heads during the year. Further, while the accounting period was supposed to close at the end of March, payments to external parties continued to be made as late as September or October of the next financial year. One of the major concerns was that it was impossible to track expenses *vis-à-vis* the budgetary allocations of various departments. Hence, many expenses were booked more than once against the same order. This was not only due to oversight on the part of the Corporation's staff, but also due to devious methods adopted by contractors in collusion with some officials in the Corporation.

Introducing automation

One of the foremost goals of the municipal commissioners was to fix the accounting system, and establish a system of financial discipline. This involved introducing budgetary control, introducing a system of checks and balances, as well as making the accounting system accurate and up-to-date. Now the processing of bills ceases around 10 March each year in order to ensure accounts are finalised by the end of the month.

Expenditure management has been improved by creating budget heads, which are maintained on the system. All expenses are booked against work order numbers generated by the system and the total expense against any head of account in a financial year is fixed. The cash book and the journal have been automated. The list of vendors is also maintained in the system, preventing favouritism towards select vendors. An inventory of the Corporation's assets has been published for the first time in many years.

Challenges faced

To overcome resistance to the introduction of IT, the system was introduced progressively and focused initially on the critical applications. Enormous effort was required to bring about this financial discipline among employees. In effect, close monitoring of expenditures became possible and, for the first time, actual expenditure statements for the previous year began to be recorded in budget statements.

Cost and time implication of automation

It took about two years to automate the system and involved an investment of about Rs 70 Lakhs in hardware and software.

Case 3   Solid waste management

The need for automation

Previously, the city's garbage collection system was not only inefficient but also corrupt. Garbage was irregularly picked up from several areas of the city. In addition, since garbage collectors were paid bonuses based on the number of trips made and the amount of garbage collected, they would make false trips and state incorrect tonnage. It was common practice to make false trips, make trips with half-full trucks, or even use the same load of garbage and show multiple trips in the records. While garbage used to pile up in the city, records showed remakable diligence amongst the city's garbage collectors, with some trucks making as many as many as 1200 garbage disposal trips per day. This resulted in excess expenditure on petrol bills and wages. Further, the garbage dump was controlled by a mafia group who encouraged this malpractice.

Introducing automation

The municipal commissioner sought to improve this state of affairs. During a tour to Chicago in 1995, he learned how IT had been deployed in Chicago to correct these types of failures in garbage management. He decided to adopt a variation of the Chicago practice in Calcutta.

As the first stage of IT implementation, a Foxpro-based rudimentary system was introduced in the garbage dump at Dhapa. This system would note the garbage trucks' time of entry to, and exit from, the dump. This simple measure streamlined the system significantly. False trips by particular trucks were reduced and the average number of trips fell to roughly 700 per day.

Three other initiatives were also introduced. Despite stiff opposition, private garbage collection was introduced to complement the CMC's system. This was based on the fact that, even if the CMC's own system of garbage collection and disposal was fully operational, it could only ensure disposal of 60 per cent of the total garbage generated daily in the city. Second, the incentive system was rationalised. The tonnage of garbage dumped was used as the measure of productivity rather than the number of trips made. This rapidly reduced the number of trips made. Finally, a weighbridge mechanism was introduced so that the weight of each truck's contents could be easily determined, and payments made on that basis. Thus, measurement of the weight and number of trips made by each vehicle has been automated, reducing the scope for falsification of data. This has also resulted in more efficient garbage removal, a cleaner environment, and greater resident satisfaction. Currently, CMC and private contractors' vehicles make an average number of 500 trips per day, and the trucks always carry a full load of garbage.

Challenges faced

It initially appeared that the workers at the garbage dump—who were controlled by the mafia—would not allow the new system to be implemented. Garbage was dumped next to the computer centre, and the road leading to the dumping site was deliberately lined with lorries to prevent smooth movement of the garbage trucks operated by private contractors. In addition, the electric power lines did not extend all the way to the rather remote garbage dump, which meant there was no way of powering the new system. Initially, the system was implemented using generators. Senior officials of Calcutta Municipal Corporation had to keep a vigil to ensure that the system began without any hitches.

Cost and time implication of automation

The system took about one year to automate, and involved an investment of about Rs 30 Lakhs (computers and weighbridge), Rs 50 Lakhs (building, electrical cabling and air conditioning) and roughly Rs 2 crores on road development within the dumping yard.

Incorporating Information Technology—how did it happen?

Introduction of IT was based on a three-pronged strategy adopted by the new municipal commissioner. The aims were to
- improve employee morale
- raise revenue
- control expenditures.

Gaining employee confidence

A series of free and frank dialogues with various employees' unions was initiated to win the employees over to the computer program. The dialogues centred around the following points.

- The process of computerisation would not pose any immediate threat to the staff as far as their tenure in Calcutta Municipal Corporation was concerned.
- Automation did not necessarily imply diminished job opportunities.
- Computerisation was being introduced to aid their efficiency and effectiveness.
- Manual compilation and tabulation processing of these data was fraught with risk. Disciplinary proceedings were initiated against some staff for mishandling of data.
- The entitlement of staff in terms of disbursements of Provident Fund could not be properly ascertained due to the volume of transactions. As a result, many staff suffered.
- It was impossible to meet the growing establishment costs, particularly the ever-increasing wage bills due to the huge

number of Calcutta Municipal Corporation staff, if the resource base was not augmented. It was not possible to bring more citizens into the tax-net through traditional manual methods. Moreover, raising huge numbers of bills manually was not possible. The necessary decentralisation and mechanisation was only possible through computerisation.

- If Calcutta Municipal Corporation staff did not become acquainted with modern technology they would become redundant as the massive changes in IT occurred all over the world.
- Institutional pride amongst staff is the essence of any organisation. Only through such pride could the negative image of Calcutta Municipal Corporation be countered, and that was only possible if computerisation—devoid of any discretion or favouritism—could be introduced, particularly in the public service oriented departments.
- Calcutta Municipal Corporation has a big role to play in making Calcutta environmentally-friendly, citizen-friendly and investor-friendly. Only through that process can more job opportunities be created in the city. Therefore, the staff of the Corporation have a big responsibility in ensuring a better future for Calcutta.

Dialogue with employees' unions can only yield results when it is accompanied by concrete action. Several steps were taken to restore employee confidence in the organisation by making it clear that the authority meant business and had no intention of replacing manpower with machines.

A special training institute was set up to train all Corporation staff in the new system. Training programs ranged from orientation courses to three-month and one-year courses, and were successful in making the staff extremely computer-literate. A new environment, favourable to computerisation, was gradually established.

Calcutta Municipal Corporation has 18 treasury counters. They used to handle cash and calculate the transactions using cash register machines. At the end of the financial year, and on many other occasions, staff were required to work until late evening counting cash and processing transactions. It was felt that computers should be introduced at the treasury counters to make the work more accurate, smooth and effective. Where before there were heated arguments between Corporation staff and ratepayers regarding delays in the collection of money, and incorrect compilations and tabulations, the introduction of computers in Treasury improved customer–staff relations. A sense of institutional pride was also established among CMC staff.

There were other benefits from computerisation.

- Staff were concerned that the compilation of their contributions to Provident Fund was incorrect. The accounts of Provident Fund had been in arrears for a long time. As a result, staff were unsure about their entitlements. The introduction of computers in Provident Fund dispelled staff fears.
- It was very difficult to prepare cash journals involving large amounts of bill and cheque transactions in the Finance and Accounts Deptartment. Even with their best efforts, they could not prepare proper accounts on time. At one point, CMC accounts were more than seven years in arrears. Hence, Corporation staff in the Finance and Accounts Department welcomed computerisation.
- Previously, the process of promotion and transfer of staff was inefficient. Manual preparation of gradation lists and issuance of promotion orders through traditional methods took a long time. Corporation staff in the Personnel Department welcomed the introduction of computerisation to ease this problem.
- With the gradual introduction of production incentives to Corporation staff, staff confidence grew. But preparation of correct incentive bills for the huge number of staff was a major problem. Moreover, the clerical staff who were to prepare the incentive bills were reluctant to do so because they were not the beneficiaries of the incentive program. Therefore, the field staff welcomed the computer program for making the preparation and disbursement of incentive bills smoother and more accurate.
- Printing and electronic media was effectively utilised in gaining public confidence in the Corporation's computerisation program. The benefits that accrued to citizens through the computerisation process were highly publicised. The response from the citizens was so encouraging that both the management and the employees' unions proceeded to implement further computerisation in other departments.

Gaining political support

Calcutta Municipal Corporation is run by a democratically elected Mayor-in-Council system. Judging the public mood and assessing the benefits of computerisation both for revenue collection and expenditure management, the members of the Mayor-in-Council became ardent suporters of computerisation. Some of the members of the Mayor-in-Council thought that computerisation was a panacea for all the evils of administration.

Being elected representatives, the members of the Mayor-in-Council have many responsibilities to the citizens. Therefore, they were very concerned about the image of the organisation. They wanted to introduce transparency and accountability and thought that computerisation would achieve this.

Because Calcutta Municipal Corporation is a vast organisation, the directives of the management were not always strictly adhered to by its staff. This could be attributed primarily to the lack of proper supervision by middle management, and also to the lack of knowledge in interpreting various circulars issued by the management. Close scrutiny of the transactions in various departments revealed that actual field operations differed within various sections of the same department, not to mention other departments, and contravened both the objectives and the spirit of the Calcutta Municipal Corporation Act. Essentially, a huge gap existed between the statute and rules and what was actually practiced. The Mayor-in-Council believed that the only way to bridge the gap was to analyse the business rules through development of proper computer packages, and enforce them with uniform implementation. They thought that introduction of proper business logic and uniform application of various packages would enable Calcutta Municipal Corporation to create greater transparency. For example, raising supplementary bills on account of property tax and providing facilities in terms of rebates and instalments in a uniform manner was welcomed by taxpayers and also helped the CMC raise more revenue.

Streamlining operations

The municipal commissioner felt that for any new institutional strengthening initiative to succeed it was vital that the endemic problems of generating resources for the cash-starved Corporation, controlling avoidable expenditure, and gaining public confidence needed to proceed in parallel. Accordingly, the specific areas in which IT was to be introduced were chosen with care. Targets and objectives of the IT Implementation Program were defined in a phased manner. The main hindrances were ambiguities associated with the business rules definition, information on data availability, and assigning responsibilities to ensure the process worked smoothly.

Developing a vision

Keeping these constraints in mind, the following objectives were set
- incorporate transparency into the system
- reduce process completion time
- eliminate manual procedures

- add control and audit trails to the system
- simplify the business process for faster decisions
- increase revenue
- reduce multiple data capture points (reduce data redundancy)
- ensure better management control
- enforce standards (like usage of pre-printed stationery).

To achieve these objectives, a high-level task force was set up under the direct supervision of the municipal commissioner. Use of the latest reliable hardware and software was encouraged and high quality networking solutions were adopted. Within three years, a huge computing resource was established.

Implementing the action plan

As expected, the implementation of the IT system encountered strong resistance from many quarters. One of the main sources of resistance was employees. This was manifested in the form of non-cooperation or slow response, but commitment of the management team and the strong support of the municipal commissioner have gone a long way to solving this problem.

Initially, the new system was implemented through contract staff. This was slowly changed, and the system is currently run by the CMC's own employees. In order to train its own staff to use computers, the CMC has started a computer-training institute. Education and computer awareness among employees has had a positive effect on the management's pro-IT stand. Fresh recruitment of IT-oriented staff and IT training of staff in key managerial positions has also helped.

Lessons learned and recommendations

Computerisation of CMC processes is not simply a matter transferring of the data in paper documents to electronic media. The process has sought to introduce logic into the system. This logic is based on fixed parameters. At the Corporation, much work used to be done without any logic or well-defined parameters. Therefore, under computerisation, establishing the parameters with uniform logic was the greatest challenge. Computerisation thus necessitated the initiation of a series of administrative and financial reforms.

The management felt that the reforms could be undertaken alongside computerisation. The informal practices originally followed by CMC staff for their personal aggrandisement gave way to stratified uniform business rules. Transparency has been the key parameter in the administrative reforms, and there has been a major transformation in the work attitude of the staff and the attitude of citizens and other external entities, such as suppliers and contractors, towards the Corporation as a result.

The implementation of IT has eliminated many unscrupulous aspects of the system. The uniform policy prescription, coupled with the attitudinal change of the top and the middle management, gave a new dimension to the dealings between the Corporation and its clients. It enabled the Corporation to augment its resources and establish a new image.

Upon its deployment, IT became an important tool for better governance and institutional strengthening in the hands of the Corporation's decisionmakers. An analysis of how the IT intervention brought about institutional change delivers certain interesting insights. Reforms and improvements can be initiated in a system irrespective of the extent of its existing malaise. It is necessary to draw up a strategic plan and implementation program, secure top management commitment and build stakeholder buy-in. In addition, IT can be an effective mechanism to arrest institutional failure and provide good governance in public sector/government organisations interfacing with citizens. Finally, implementation of IT to arrest institutional failure is most successful when adopted in a progressive manner, with sufficient prior work on planning, pilot implementation, organisational development and discipline enforcement. At the Corporation, the process was implemented under a five-stage model.

Stage 1—set strategic agenda. The success of deploying IT in government organisations such as municipal corporations is dependent on a sponsor setting a strategic agenda for implementing IT and showing commitment to a program of institutional change. In the case of the CMC, it was the organisation's municipal commissioner who, upon assuming responsibility, ensured that he understood the benefits of IT in establishing better governance in critical municipal services and took an active interest in the project, reviewing its progress at regular intervals.

Stage 2—launch pilot project. Rather than deploying IT all at once across the entire organisation, it is preferable to launch the IT project on a pilot basis. At the Corporation, IT was initially introduced in one critical area—property taxation and assessment.

Stage 3—reconfirm strategic agenda. At this stage, based on the successful results from the initial pilot implementation, the sponsor reconfirms the priorities and benefits of IT implementation and pledges support for it. The scope of the pilot project is then widened. In CMC, this stage included reaffirmation of the Commissioner's commitment to the IT initiative and inclusion of a number of other critical functions in the implementation program. These functions were—budgets and expenditure and solid waste management.

Stage 4—project roll-out. By this stage the results of computerisation are evident. At the Corporation, this stage involved parallel implementation of the IT program in the three chosen areas and increased coverage of the organisation's employees. Thus, from its beginnings at the headquarters, the program was extended to the Corporation's eighteen nodal receipt centres and the waste dump-yard at Dhapa.

Stage 5—drive benefits and change. Finally, it is imperative for the organisation to distribute the benefits throughout the organisation and reaffirm support for an organisation-wide process of IT-enabled change. The Corporation is currently undergoing such change and has ambitious plans to expand its IT base in its core business operations.

11

Depoliticising key institutions for combatting corruption
the new Thai constitution

Borwornsak Uwanno

Corruption has been rampant in Thailand for many decades. It has been one of the pretexts used by the Thai military to legitimise coups against civilian governments. Thailand's most recent coup, enacted by the National Peacekeeping Council (NPKC) in 1991, was justified by coup leaders on the grounds that members of Chatichai's government were greatly corrupted. A committee for asset inspection was formed to investigate the assets of 'unusually wealthy' ministers. The case ended with the Supreme Court annulling the NPKC's Order No. 26 on account of its unconstitutionality.

Following that, the movement for political reform became widespread among opinion leaders and the media. This led to the amendment of the 1991 constitution by the NPKC's nominated National Assembly, creating the 99-member Constitutional Drafting Assembly (CDA) to prepare a new constitution for reform. The drafting committee of the CDA was chaired by Anand Punyarachun, a former liberal Prime Minister. The drafting committee proposed three main directions for reform

- increased people-participation in government at all levels, and stronger guarantees of human rights
- the creation of 'watchdog' agencies and emphasis on more transparent and accountable decisionmaking processes
- the creation of mechanisms to ensure government stability and efficiency.

After nationwide hearings and consultations, the CDA prepared a draft constitution which was sent to the joint sitting of both houses of Parliament for consideration. Parliament voted to adopt the draft without amendment. The new constitution received royal assent and, with its publication in the Royal Gazette, came into effect on 11 October 1997.

This chapter highlights key constitutional institutions that have a direct or indirect mandate to fight corruption. It then assesses practical difficulties surrounding the creation and operation of these organisations.

Depoliticisation of key constitutional institutions and procedural reforms

It has been generally accepted that a holistic approach is needed to fight corruption. It has been pointed out that '[a]lthough anti-corruption strategies should focus on priorities, they should also be comprehensive. All the agencies designed to fight corruption—prevention, investigation, research, education and enforcement bodies—have to work in concert, harmonise their efforts and complement each other to develop one strategy' (Stapenhurst and Kpundeh 1999).

This holistic strategy highlights the institutional aspect of anti-corruption efforts. No single agency can effectively combat corruption alone. Various organisations need to be created and/or mandated to perform corruption-fighting tasks. The drafters of the present Thai constitution decided to adopt comprehensive institutional reform by creating new 'watchdog' agencies and modifying existing institutions' methods of operation. This 'national integrity system' has, for the first time in Thai constitutional history, been installed to create a 'clean' government.

The national integrity system in the Constitution

The 1997 Constitution has been labelled the 'anti-corruption constitution' because it has created a comprehensive national integrity system. Within the constitutional innovations, there are eight 'pillars' of integrity, as presented in the national integrity system model developed by Langseth, Pope and Stapenhurst (1997) (Figure 11.1).

Political will. Political will, or the determination to fight corruption, is one of the pillars that creates good governance. Countries such as Hong Kong (Speville 1998) and Singapore (Quah 1988) that have been successful in fighting corruption are proof that political will is one of the most important factors.

Quah proposed a matrix to demonstrate four characterisations of government anti-corruption strategies, depending on commitment of political leaders and adequacy of anti-corruption measures. With strong commitment and adequate measures, the strategy is considered to be most effective. In contrast, weak commitment and inadequate measures will result

Figure 11.1   The pillars of integrity

National integrity system

Political will	Administrative reforms
'Watchdog' agencies*	Parliament
Public awareness	The judiciary
The media	Private sector

Note: ¹Anti-corruption agencies: Ombudsman; Auditor-General.
Source: Langseth, P., Pope, J. and Stapenhurst, R., 1997. 'The role of a national integrity system in fighting corruption', *National Integrity System Country Studies*, The World Bank, Washington, DC.

in a 'hopeless' strategy. Strong commitment with inadequate measures, and weak commitment with adequate measures will both yield ineffective strategies (Figure 11.2).

Quah (1988) concluded that Singapore had succeeded in minimising the problem of corruption because its anti-corruption strategy was characterised by several key features. These included

- commitment by the political leaders, especially Prime Minister Lee Kuan Yew, to eliminating corruption both within and outside the public bureaucracy
- adoption of comprehensive anti-corruption measures designed to reduce both the opportunities and need for corruption
- creation and maintenance of an anti-corruption agency with honest and competent personnel to investigate corruption cases and enforce the anti-corruption laws.

The Thai Constitution tends to follow these same principles. In respect of political will, the charter in Chapter V on Directive Principles of Fundamental State Policies sets forth various provisions to forge political will and to assess annual performance of political leaders in all governments in relation to the battle against misconduct in the administration of the country. These mandates are

- the duty of all governments to ensure rule of law, efficient and expedient administration of justice, and equal opportunity to justice (Section 75 § 1)
- the requirement for all governments to adopt and enforce moral and ethical standards for politicians and public officials in order to prevent corruption and misconduct and create efficiency (Section 77)

Figure 11.2   Matrix of anti-corruption measures

Commitment of political leadership	Anti-corruption measures	
	Adequate	Inadequate
Strong	Effective strategy	Ineffective strategy II
Weak	Ineffective strategy I	'Hopeless' strategy

Source: Quah, J.S.T., 1982. 'Bureaucratic corruption in the ASEAN countries: a comparative analysis of their anti-corruption strategies', *Journal of Southeast Asian Studies*, 13(1):175.

- the mandate to promote and encourage public participation in checking the exercise of state powers at all levels and in all decisionmaking processes (Section 76), including public participation in natural resource management and the protection of the environment (Section 79)
- the obligation to allocate sufficient funds to independent watchdog agencies (the Election Commission, the Ombudsman, the Constitutional Court, the National Human Rights Commission, the Courts of Justice, the Administrative Courts, the National Counter-Corruption Commission and the State Audit Commission) (Section 75 § 2)
- the requirement to adhere to the market economy and the mandate to deregulate, with prohibitions on the expansion of the public sector in the market (Section 87).

These requirements are to be guiding principles in legislating and forming policies and platforms for all Thai governments. They are not intended to be enforceable through courts of law. As the Constitution requires the government to state clearly in its declaration to the joint sitting of both houses at the beginning of its term the strategies and activities to enact these requirements, each newly elected government has to take these constitutional mandates seriously. Failure to do so will induce severe criticism from members of parliament (MPs) and the media for lack of commitment and clarity of purpose. This political sanction is important in forging political will.

Moreover, the Constitution imposes a duty on the government to submit an annual report to the joint sitting of both houses of Parliament indicating the results of its policy implementation, including a description of problems and obstacles encountered during the year. This accountability mechanism created by the charter seems to be very effective in promoting debate on the floor of the houses. The annual report also serves to draw the attention of the media and the general public to the operation of government and provides a good incentive for the government and state agencies to review their plans and put more effort into achieving their mandates. Opposition criticism of the current government in the past two annual report joint sittings has been described by the press as the equivalent of a no-confidence debate.

In any case, improvements are possible in two areas. Before taking office, coalition parties should seriously prepare an action plan to address each mandate. Plans should identify attainable, manageable and measurable targets. The practice of allowing bureaucrats to draw up the plan (as is the case with the present government) should be strictly avoided, as such a practice allows bureaucrats' agendas to prevail, as in the past. Both houses of Parliament should ask their relevant committees to monitor the initial declaration and the annual report. A monitoring system would enable the houses to effectively oversee agencies throughout the year.

Administrative reforms. The new constitution has brought about many reforms in the Thai public sector. There is now an emphasis on the duty to act impartially in compliance with the law in order to protect public interests and provide convenience and services to the public; in other words, the necessity of separating personal matters from the duty of office (Section 70). Conflict of interest provisions in the Organic Law on Counter Corruption, 1999 have been imposed on public office holders and their spouses (see Appendix 1). These include restrictions on concurrent and post-employment, prohibitions on contractual and monopolistic concession with the state and local governments, and restrictions on holding shares in corporations and on accepting gifts (Sections 100–103 and 122 of the Organic Law on Counter Corruption, 1999 and Sections 110, 118, 126, 128, 208 and 209 of the 1997 Constitution applying to MPs, senators and ministers). Prohibitions have been imposed on MPs and senators from interfering or intervening in the recruitment, appointment, reshuffle, transfer, promotion or elevation of salary scale of government officials. Members of parliament and senators who violate these provisions will be removed from office (Sections 111 and 128). The Constitution requires adherence to ethical codes by political figures and permanent staff of the state (Sections 77 and 191). Improvements have been made to the pension scheme for MPs, senators and ministers (Section 229 § 2). Finally, the requirement for an efficient system of administration to meet people's needs has been recognised (Section 75).

Parliament. The third pillar of the national integrity system is the reformed Parliament. The changes are dramatic, to ensure more effective, efficient and accountable chambers.

The first feature that needs to be addressed is the Senate (the upper chamber). For many decades, appointment was the manner of selection for members of the Senate. The Prime Minister proposed a list of military officers, important public officials, and leading businessmen for royal approval. For this reason the Senate was considered a group of government 'supporters'. The Prime Minister's power to nominate was severely criticised for creating a 'winner-takes-all' situation. In addition to forming government, parties that won a majority in the lower house were entitled to distribute all senatorial posts among supporters. This encouraged particularly fierce competition in general elections, often manifested as vote-buying.

The drafters of the constitution decided that the upper chamber should be directly elected. However, the electoral mechanisms used to select members for the two chambers differ greatly. First, each candidate to the House of Representatives (the lower house) must be a member of a political party so that they can promote party discipline for the sake of efficiency and government stability. Lack of efficiency and stability have been serious impediments to the continuity of national management under the civilian regime. However, candidates for senatorial seats must not have any party affiliation. Those with past affiliation must have resigned from their parties at least one year before registering candidacy in a Senate election. This measure of depoliticisation was introduced to render senators non-partisan so that they could exercise their control over political figures and high-ranking officials more impartially (in this context, depoliticisation means a de-linkage of candidates from political parties).

Furthermore, while political campaigning is permitted during House of Representative elections, it is not allowed during Senate elections. Senate candidates are only permitted to 'introduce' themselves to the public using posters and pamphlets, the contents of which are prescribed by the Election Commission. The Election Commission also provides radio and television fora for candidates' introduction. Although this method has been criticised as being unnatural, it resulted in less electoral spending than in previous elections, and an absence of the usual 'mud slinging' among candidates.

Constituencies for the Senate election are provincial and are typically multi-member, though some low-population provinces select only one senator. This contrasts with the single-member constituencies of MP elections. Despite the fact that many Senate election constituencies are multi-member, each elector has only one vote. For example, Bangkok has 18 senators but each voter can only cast one vote for the candidate of his or her choice. Though strongly criticised, this method offers advantages because it basically gives all citizens' votes equal weight and allows the realisation of a pluralist Senate. Such pluralism is in sharp contrast to the majoritarian politics of the House of Representatives (see Figure 11.3). The true representation of various groups within Thai society can help provide civil society groups—historically dominated by élites drawn from the bureaucracy, the military and big business—with a more equitable share of legislative and administrative power.

The constitution bars senators from running for two consecutive terms. This rule was instituted out of concern that senators' political ambition would induce them to affiliate discreetly with political parties. As compensation, the term of office for senators is six years, two years longer than for MPs. In addition, while the House of Representatives can be dissolved, the Senate cannot (Sections 126(3) and 130).

Senators are not eligible for appointment to ministerial posts or other political positions. A former senator may be nominated for such a position only after one year has elapsed since he or she vacated office. This prohibition aims to prevent the possibility of senators being bribed with offers of government positions (Section 127).

Efforts to de-link the Senate from party politics were undertaken to make the institution central in the fight against corruption. The Senate is armed with two important powers which the House of Representatives lacks.

- the power to vote for nomination of Constitutional Court judges, Supreme Administrative Court judges, Ombudsmen, members of the National Counter Corruption Commission, the State Audit Commission, and the National Human Rights Commission
- the power to impeach political figures, including the Prime Minister, ministers, MPs, senators, presidents of the constitutional control bodies mentioned above and other high-ranking officials. The impeachment power can only be exercised after an investigation is conducted by the National Counter-Corruption Commission which must recommend that the case for impeachment is a *prima facie* one. The vote for impeachment should receive the support of not less than 60 per cent of the Senate's 200 members.

Depoliticisation in this case theoretically guarantees impartiality and neutrality of the Senate in its quasi-judicial function.

Some political observers are not confident about this institutional neutrality, arguing that in reality many candidates would have links with the parties. Some candidates would be former MPs, many would seek support from parties' canvassers, and so on. Figure 11.4 shows an estimate of the possible affiliations between the senators elected on 4 March 2000 and political parties.

In fact, personal connections between some senators and MPs are natural. This, however, does not imply a direct link to the parties of those MPs. Even in cases where party connections exist, they will not be formal. No party line can be legally imposed on the theoretically free members of the Senate. In matters of little importance, lobbying by MPs and parties can occur. When the Senate is considering high profile issues, however, the public will be able to observe closely, and such pressure should prevail over secret affiliations. The proceedings of the CDA are an illustration of this safeguard. On important policies opposed by political parties, such as the incompatibility of ministerial function and parliamentary representative function, the majority of Assembly members who had personal ties with parties voted against the parties' preferred policies.

The House of Representatives—chamber of partisan politics. Unlike the Senate, the House of Representatives is designed to be a politically partisan institution. No candidate or MP is allowed to be independent from a political party. Strict party discipline stands as the ultimate sanction, through expulsion from the party and loss of the office of MP (Section 118(8)). This is intended to entrench the stability of Thai civilian governments which historically have an average term of office of 1.2 years.

Figure 11.3   Senators' backgrounds by occupation

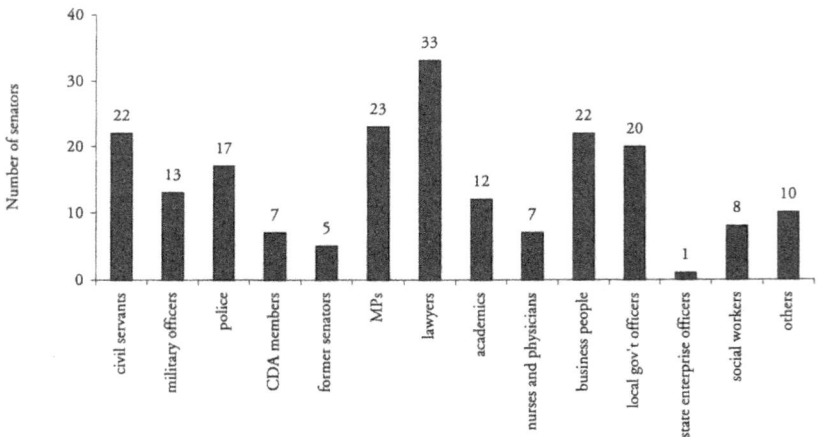

Note: The figures may change following the election on 29 April 2000 election in which 78 seats will be contested again because the Election Commission disqualified the winners.
Source: *Matichon,* 6 March 2000.

Figure 11.4   Senators' possible relationships with political parties

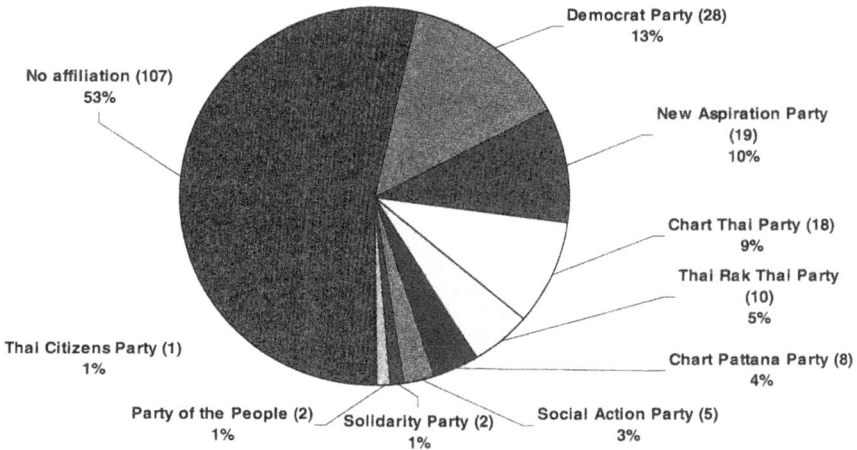

Democrat Party (28)
13%

New Aspiration Party
(19)
10%

No affiliation (107)
53%

Chart Thai Party (18)
9%

Thai Rak Thai Party
(10)
5%

Chart Pattana Party (8)
4%

Thai Citizens Party (1)
1%

Party of the People (2)
1%

Solidarity Party (2)
1%

Social Action Party (5)
3%

Source: *Matichon*, 6 March 2000.

The interesting feature of the election system is the combination of proportional representation and a simple majority system. One-hundred seats are allocated by proportional representation to candidates drawn from national party lists, and 400 seats are allocated on the basis of first-past-the-post single-member constituency contests. The aim of this innovation is to avoid vote-buying and electoral fraud. The party list system should be especially effective because the national constituency is too large to allow efficient voter bribery to take place.

Furthermore, compulsory voting is prescribed in order to render vote-buying more difficult—it makes it very difficult to buy all or even a majority of votes. Furthermore, in the past, ballot counting took place at the polling stations and was thus easily controlled by party canvassers. Now, ballot counting takes place at a central counting venue in each constituency, as specified by the Election Commission (Section 104 §4).

Two aspects of the 'rationalised parliamentary system' prescribed by the new constitution are particularly striking. The first is the incompatibility of ministerial and parliamentary function. Members of parliament who become ministers must resign from their offices as MPs within one month after the royal command of appointment is issued (Sections 118(7) and 204). MPs resigning from single-member constituencies are replaced through by-election. Resigning party-list MPs are automatically replaced by the next candidate on the list. In opting for this choice, the drafters of the constitution seemed to favour party-list MPs as ministerial appointees. This strict separation of powers adopted in the French Fifth Republic Constitution is, for Thais, a means of enhancing the monitoring function of the lower house over the government. The logic is simple: the controlled (ministers) cannot concurrently be the controllers (MPs). Moreover, this measure should contribute to government stability because rebelling ministers (not uncommon in Thailand's coalition governments) will not have parliamentary seats to retreat to if they are sacked by the Prime Minister.

The second constitutional measure is the requirement that when accusing any minister of corruption, unusual wealth, malfeasance or intentional violation of the law or constitution, the opposition must first launch an impeachment accusation before submitting a motion of no-confidence to the House of Representatives (Sections 185, 186). This condition is laid down in order to avoid a frustrating situation where the opposition may present convincing evidence of ministerial corruption during a no-confidence debate, but the House still votes in support of the government and there are no lasting repercussions for seemingly corrupt ministers. Under the new mechanism the National Counter-Corruption Commission must become involved in the impeachment investigation, so, regardless of the outcome of the no-confidence vote, impeachment proceedings will take place and corrupt ministers will be subject to punishment.

'Watchdog' agencies. Before the new constitution came into force, all control institutions were quite politicised in the sense that political interference could be real and effective. For example, the Constitutional Tribunal was chaired by the speaker of the House of Representatives. The speaker of the Senate, the president of the Supreme Court, and the prosecutor general were *ex officio* members. Other members were elected by the sitting parliament and remained in office only during the life of that parliament. The Tribunal was, in this respect, more of a political institution with political biases than an impartial judicial body. The Counter Corruption and Malfeasance Commission (CCMC) and the Office of the Auditor General were under the Prime Minister's responsibility. The Council of State, which decided on administrative disputes between individuals and state officers, was also under the Prime Minister's direct control. In order to remedy this problem, the new constitution adopted four principles for the creation of watchdog agencies: comprehensiveness, depoliticisation and independence, reinforcement of powers, and checks and balances.

Comprehensive control institutions. Thailand has a huge bureaucracy which includes 15 ministries, 207 departments including public enterprises, and 2,668,000 public servants, as well as 585 acts of Parliament that enable these entities and officials to act. The risk of abuses of power resulting in violation of people's rights and freedoms is therefore high. Previous control agencies were limited to courts of law and the non-independent bodies mentioned above. It was therefore the task of the constitution to create a comprehensive system of control bodies that could oversee all aspects of state administration so as to uphold the principle of rule of law. Nine such bodies were established.

- The Election Commission (Sections 136–48)—empowered to organise and control elections at different levels, tasks which were formerly executed by the Ministry of the Interior which had long been accused of having a bias towards the party in power
- The National Counter Corruption Commission (Sections 297–302)—entitled to verify the asset and liability declarations made by political figures and high-ranking officials, and to conduct investigations into cases of unusual wealth, corruption, malfeasance in office and intentional violation of laws and the Constitution
- The Supreme Court of Justice's Criminal Division for Persons Holding Political Positions (Sections 308–11)—instituted to adjudicate cases in which political figures are declared *prima facie* corrupt or unusually wealthy by the National Counter-corruption Commission (NCCC). This first and last-instance criminal court is composed of nine Supreme Court judges elected by the plenary session of the Court; criminal procedure is inquisitional but bears due process to ensure the accused's right to self defense
- Three Ombudsmen (Sections 196–98) entrusted with the power to investigate cases where public officials are suspected of failing to perform their duties, or to have exercised powers beyond their official prerogative
- The State Audit Commission (Section 312) oversees and audits public spending of all public organisations including constitutional independent control institutions
- The National Human Rights Commission (Sections 199–200) investigates human rights violations by both public and private entities and reports to the Cabinet and Parliament

- The Constitutional Court (Sections 255–70) controls the constitutionality of bills and acts of Parliament and is the supreme arbitrator in cases of constitutional disputes among constitutional bodies
- The Administrative Courts (Sections 276–80) judge cases of illegalities committed by the administration or its agents
- The Courts of Justice (Sections 271–75) judge civil, commercial and criminal cases.

These independent bodies have different mandates and powers so as to avoid redundancy and duplication of jurisdiction. They have to work in concert to fight aberrant behaviours.

Depoliticisation and independence of watchdog agencies. Independence is a fundamental aspect of effective control institutions. To achieve independence, eradication of political interference is essential. Past failure proved that the work of the CCMC was quite deceptive. One of the reasons for the CCMC's lack of achievement was that the institution was under the pressure and control of the government.

The new constitution tries to cope with this problem by depoliticising the process of nominating members of the watchdog agencies to make them independent *vis-à-vis* their clients. The selection process is basically the same for all these agencies.

A depoliticised method of nomination. Members are chosen by a selection committee comprising, on one hand, representatives of political parties and, on the other, non-partisan judges or academics.

In the case of the NCCC, the selection panel consists of 15 persons: the president of the Supreme Court of Justice, the president of the Constitutional Court, the president of the Supreme Administrative Court, seven rectors self-selected from among all state higher-education institutions and five self-selected members from among all political parties that have at least one MP in the House (Section 297). The selection committee prepares a list of 18 qualified persons for submission to the Senate (Section 257 applied *mutatis mutandis*). After receiving the list, the Senate, through its investigation committee under Section 135, scrutinises past records and behaviours of the 18 candidates and then votes to select the nine most qualified persons to be appointed by the King as members of the NCCC. The vote is by absolute majority in the first round and by simple majority in the second round, which is necessary only if an absolute majority is not obtained in the first round.

This complicated method has two merits. It ensures the legitimacy of the selected members because they are chosen by the elected representatives of the Thai people in the upper house. In addition, it minimises political interference and partisanship. This method proves to be effective and efficient because NCCC members selected in this way can perform their function freely without allegiance to parties.

Guarantee of independence. The constitution has various other mechanisms to ensure the independence of watchdog agencies. These include

- single-term, non-renewable offices of long duration: nine years for NCCC, seven years for Election Commission, six years for Ombudsmen, the National Human Rights Commission (NHRC) and the State Audit Commission
- incompatibility of these offices with other public and private offices (examples in Sections 139, 141, 256 and 258)
- an independent secretariat attached to each agency, entitled by organic laws to freely conduct personnel management, administration and financial operations without being bound by laws and regulations applied to the government (Section 270 for the Constitutional Court, Section 275 for Courts of Justice, Section 280 for Administrative Courts, Section 302 for NCCC, Section 327(8) for Election Commission, Section 330(4) for Ombudsmen, and Section 333(3) for State Audit Commission)
- the fact that sufficient funding for the operation of these agencies is prescribed by the Constitution for fear that the government and parliament may try to jeopardise the agencies' operations through budgetary constraint (Section 75 § 2)
- the chairmen of these bodies are in charge of the control and execution of the organic laws creating the bodies, to avoid political pressure.

Reinforcement of powers and capacity. The charter reinforces powers of the controllers. The Senate is empowered to impeach high-ranking politicians and officials. The Election Commission can annul elections which are not free and fair. The NCCC can freely conduct investigations in cases of unusual wealth or corruption, including verification of public figures' asset and liability declarations. The State Audit Commission can audit agencies under the government, the Parliament and all independent bodies.

Apart from powers specific to the functions of each agency, the watchdog agencies all have the power to order government agencies, officials, the police, prosecutors and courts to supply assistance and evidence as required in the course of agency activity. The penalty for non-compliance varies from disciplinary to criminal action.

Checks and balances. Bearing in mind the adage 'power corrupts, and absolute power corrupts absolutely', the drafters of the constitution did not allow any agency to have supremacy without controls. Every watchdog agency is controlled under a comprehensive system of checks and balances.

All holders of office, including senators, ombudsmen, members of the NHRC and State Audit Commission, and judges of the Constitutional Court, the Supreme Administrative Court and the Supreme Court of Justice, must declare their assets and liabilities to the NCCC. Members of the NCCC must make asset and liability declarations to the president of the Senate. This method allows verification of declarations and the investigation of unusual wealth cases if declarers cannot justify unusual increases in their assets. Questionable assets are subject to confiscation by the Supreme Court of Justice's Criminal Division.

All holders of offices are impeachable after investigation by the NCCC and a vote of impeachment by 60 per cent of the Senate. All holders of office may be charged with the criminal offence of malfeasance. Penalties for members or officials of the NCCC who are found to be corrupt are double those normally provided for by the law concerning such offences. All agencies and their officials are under the jurisdiction of other watchdog agencies—that is, the NCCC will be audited by the Supreme Administrative Court, and be controlled by the Ombudsmen and the Administrative Courts in matters of maladministration and illegal acts.

The classical notion of separation of powers into the three branches of the executive, the legislature and the judiciary is necessary but not sufficient. The Thai Constitution goes further in instituting a fourth branch—various constitutional controllers have been established in such a way as to give them legitimacy to control, and have been vested with substantial control powers with which to perform their duties. These bodies are the fourth power to be added to the Montesquieu Doctrine because they exercise substantial and effective checks and balances over the other three classical branches.

The judiciary. The Thai Constitution accounts for the importance of the judiciary as the central pillar of rule of law. The Constitution attempts to reform the judicial process in three respects: the destruction of monopoly control of judicial function by a single institution, reinforcement of the independence of the judiciary, and provision of an efficient and fair judicial process.

De-monopolisation of judicial powers. Formerly, the Courts of Justice monopolised judicial power over public and private law cases. This situation was unsatisfactory due to lack of expertise and delay in the judicial process. For example, cases disputing lower house election results took years to reach a conclusion. The majority of cases ended with the dissolution of the House and the dismissal of the cases on the grounds that there was no need to annul election results because dissolution had produced the same outcome!

To de-monopolise judicial power, the Constitution separates judicial functions to be vested in different jurisdictions. The Constitutional Court will be in charge of constitutional disputes, while the Administrative Court will adjudicate administrative cases opposing individual and state agencies, except for election cases, which are under the Election Commission's jurisdiction, and taxation cases, which are heard in the Courts of Justice. The Courts of Justice will have adjudicative powers different from those of the other two courts and will decide mainly private law and criminal cases.

This separation of judicial function ensures greater relevance and should improve the quality of decisions rendered, as well as creating a speedier process. The separation of functions also allows the possibility of comparative evaluation of the judicial processes and outputs from the three main court systems.

Reinforcement of independence. The independence of judges is the central feature of justice. The Thai Constitution reinforces this feature through various means, including

- depoliticisation of judicial nomination. In this respect, the Courts of Justice have been recognised as being independent from political interference since their establishment. The Judicial Commission, which is vested with the power to appoint and promote judges to judicial offices, is composed solely of judges (Sections 274 and 279). Furthermore, there is no external appointment; all judges are career judges and their promotion is determined by seniority
- sufficient remuneration for judges—in accordance with Section 253—and preventing application of the salary scale or emolument for civil servants. This is to ensure not only adequacy of salaries and emoluments, but also to prohibit the use of promotion criteria and schemes practiced in the civil service, which may jeopardise judges' security in office
- installation of independent secretariats for the various courts (Sections 270, 275 and 280) and guarantee of adequate funding (Section 75 § 2) are required by the charter.

Efficient and fair judicial process. Good justice needs not only qualified and independent judges but also efficient and fair trial. The Constitution sets forth many principles for this purpose. Discriminatory process (Section 75) is prevented by not allowing special courts or special procedures for particular cases (Sections 234 § 2 and 235). A full quorum of judges is required in all types of cases; judges may not serve as judges in their own cases; only judges who sit and hear the full case are entitled to decide that case (Section 236). In performing their functions, judges are independent and must decide each case according only to the Constitution, the law and their consciences. Judges are not subject to any hierarchical or supervisory pressure. They cannot be transferred, removed or promoted without their prior consent (Section 249).

In criminal cases, suspects and accused are presumed innocent until proven otherwise. They are entitled to a speedy, continuous and fair trial (Section 241). They are also entitled to legal assistance from the state (Section 242) and to the opportunity for bail during the process, except in certain cases provided for by law. Even after final decision, the accused can have recourse to retrial if substantial new evidence emerges that can prove his or her innocence. In this case, the state must pay compensation to the wrongfully convicted party (Section 247). A detainee has the right to *habeas corpus* and, if he or she is proven innocent by the final decision of the court, he or she will be compensated by the state (Sections 240 and 246).

Injured persons and witnesses must be properly protected by the state (Sections 244 and 245). To ensure transparency in all cases where the public prosecutor decides to drop the prosecution, the injured person has the right to examine facts and opinions employed by the prosecutor and the police. This right is also granted to suspects and accused (Section 241 § 3, 4).

The three remaining pillars for integrity—public awareness, the media and the private sector—will be discussed in the next section.

Procedural reforms to enhance participation, transparency and accountability

Institutional reforms to create a comprehensive system of checks and balances may be ineffective if the work processes of the institutions lack people's participation, transparency and accountability. Introversion and internal collusion could make the institutions prone to failure. The Constitution tries to create an environment to help them survive and grow by opening up the process. There are three main directions in this endeavour.

Public awareness and public participation. In the new era, public affairs are the domain of all citizens, not only the government or state as the public provider of services. If the aim of public affairs is to improve the wellbeing of all citizens, then all citizens should be in a position to participate in those affairs.

Understanding this changing climate, the drafters of the constitution decided to place emphasis on public participation in public affairs at all stages of decisionmaking processes and at all levels of government from national to local.

Section 76 requires that the state shall promote and encourage public participation in policymaking, decisionmaking and planning processes, together with public involvement in controlling the exercise of state power.

Various types of public involvement are described in the Constitution. Access to public information is guaranteed in order to keep people informed of the progress of the ongoing process. This right has been exercised in many cases—disclosure of notes for the entrance examinations of various public schools and universities; disclosure of an NCCC investigation concerning a drug scandal; disclosure of contracts concluded by the Debt Restructuring Agency and foreign consultants; disclosure of letters of intent to the International Monetary Fund; and revelation of a toxic substances scandal in Hua-Hin, among others. Corruption, normally imbedded in a 'closed and secret' environment, should decrease with increased public access to information.

Freedom of expression is guaranteed so that censorship cannot be imposed. Closure of printing houses and radio and television stations is unconstitutional. Independence of reporters and columnists *vis-á-vis* employers in both the public and private sectors is guaranteed (Section 41). This should be the central part of free expression of facts and opinions through media. If the media is theoretically and practically free from state intervention, but falls into the hands of corrupt private owners or shareholders with only pecuniary interest, who will ensure 'freedom of expression'—reporters or owners? If it is the latter, freedom of expression would only be freedom for them to propagate commercial and selfish interests! This situation is as undesirable as advocating government control of information.

In order to achieve impartial radio and television and eliminate government monopoly over these two media, Section 40 requires that transmission frequencies were to have been be redistributed by 11 October 2000. Redistribution is to be done with consideration for public benefit in education, culture, state security and other public interests. Television and radio broadcasting business should be conducted on a free, fair and competitive basis under the supervision of an independent regulatory body. The right to public hearing and consultation in decisionmaking processes that affect the interests of the people is assured (Sections 56, 59 and 60).

Autonomous civil service entities are created under the Constitution to provide public authorities with opinions on environmental impact assessment (Section 56 § 2) and law, regulations and measures to protect consumers (Section 57 § 2). Moreover, the National Economic and Social Advisory Council will be established to consult with the government on economic and social development plans (Section 88). Laws are now being drafted to establish advisory institutions to represent the relevant factions in civil society. Hopefully, the advisory institutions will contribute to more balanced decisions in important areas.

The Constitution guarantees that citizens have the right to propose bills to Parliament by producing a petition with the signatures of 50,000 voters. Local bylaws can also be initiated in this way(Sections 170 and 287). Civil society groups are now preparing at least two bills—one on public welfare and one on community forestry. This action bodes well as an indicator of this mechanism's effectiveness as an instrument for participatory democracy.

Co-management of the environment and natural resources is a central aspect of participation. The Charter enables at least five groups to be involved—individuals (Section 56 § 1), traditional local communities (Section 46), autonomous environmental organisations (Section 56 § 2), local administrations (Section 290) and the state itself. Section 79 stipulates clearly that the state shall promote and encourage public participation in the preservation, maintenance and balanced exploitation of natural resources and biological diversity, together with protection of the quality of the environment. It is now clear that these affairs are no longer the domain of the government, but are public affairs that call for the involvement of all parties. The issue is now one of how to orchestrate these participatory efforts to achieve the goal of genuine co-management.

Lastly, the Constitution empowers voters to launch impeachment accusations against politicians and officials suspected of corruption, again through the 50,000-signature petition mechanism (Section 304). Similarly, this power can be exercised at the local level (Section 298). This power has already been exercised at the national level during a drug scandal. The result was the resignation from office of two accused ministers. In addition, all individuals who feel they are victims of maladministration, corruption or illegality are allowed to bring cases before the Ombudsman, the Administrative Court, the Court of Justice and the NHRC.

If the way is paved for public engagement, strong civil society organisations should lead the journey. In fact, Thailand is lucky enough to have a tradition of involving civil society in various important changes. The tradition is exemplified in the student uprising of October 1973 led by the Thailand Student Center, the Black May incident involving pro-democracy groups that led to the overthrow of General Suchinda's government in 1992, the political reform movement led by Dr Prawase Wasi and networks of the Central Organisation of Poll Watch, and very recently the network of Rural Doctors and People's Counter Corruption group that successfully revealed drug-procurement corruption. Moreover, a group of important opinion leaders has been formed as a national chapter of Transparency International. Led by former Prime Minister Anand, its task is to monitor and report corruption, and to protect good public officials who do not yield to corrupt practices of their superiors or colleagues. It is hoped that joint citizen–state action will bring about changes in society.

Transparency, accountability and the media. The new Thai charter focuses on transparency and accountability at all levels. It prescribes freedom of information and freedom of expression. Furthermore, it imposes an obligation for disclosure of important information useful to fighting corruption, such as the assets and liabilities of the Prime Minister and other ministers, their spouses and children (Section 293 § 2). Already, six cases of false documentation in such declarations have been sent to the Constitutional Court by the NCCC. The Constitutional Court has judged three cases and the remaining three are pending, including that of Sanan Kachornprasart who has resigned from his posts of interior minister and deputy Prime Minister over the issue. False declaration is grounds for dismissal from office and imposition of a five-year ban from politics, in addition to any criminal penalties. Other information subject to disclosure includes voting records in Parliament, political parties' expenditures and sources of income, including names of donors, and electoral spending by candidates and parties.

The media have an important role to play in monitoring information that can be disclosed and drawing public attention to questionable matters. A free press is therefore crucial because it can expose and make accountable those suspected of corruption. Figures suspected of corruption are obliged to defend their conduct before the public and the press. In many cases, public declarations and press interviews have been used as evidence in NCCC corruption investigations and as grounds for political debate during no-confidence motions in the lower house.

In practice, the press reveals most corruption cases in Thailand. Examples include mega-project kickbacks such as in the HDS project, and corrupt practices surrounding MPs' fund for provincial development. Examination of daily newspapers indicates how strong and free the Thai press is in fighting corruption.

Three issues, however, should be addressed. First, a free press needs to exhibit responsibility and accuracy in reporting. Some newspapers do not distinguish between 'news' and 'views' and, by failing to do so, distort issues. Even worse, this failure can bring disgrace to innocent and honest persons. If reporters and columnists do not verify their information, innocent people's reputations could be injured. It seems that two remedies can be effective—strong commitment by the press to a code of ethics sanctioned by an autonomous professional press association, and libel action in the courts. The Thai press has united to create the Press Council to address grievances of individuals who believe they have been wronged. The Press Council has in many cases pointed out malpractices of their colleagues. Hopefully this institution can render members of the press more responsible for their statements.

Second, the commercial interests of the media should be monitored closely. Even if the media is free from state intervention, it may not be free from interference by owners or businesses with personal or institutional interests that may not coincide with the public interest. As an example, advertisers can exert influence on owners and reporters. For this reason, the new charter guarantees employees of the media freedom in their reporting of news and opinion in the hope that this can protect them from the private interests of their employers.

Third, corrupt practices by journalists should be carefully explored. Journalists, like all human beings, may be tempted by greed. Politicians and public figures try to befriend journalists by offering benefits such as travel, luxurious meals and gifts. This may bias reporting. Therefore, it is necessary that the Press Council enforce a code of conduct to discourage and punish corruption in the press.

Private sector and good corporate governance. Corruption often involves two principal actors—the government and the private sector. When cases involve the provision of goods and services, consumers are typically the victims. Private monopolies established through corrupt practices will take advantage of consumers. Business leaders who have access to high-ranking politicians and officials are able to offer 'discreet support' to parties in return for business advantages. Measures to discourage the corrupt practices of individual officials have already been discussed. To discourage corruption at the party level, the Constitution calls for a scheme for the state financing of political parties (Section 328 (5)). The Organic Law on Political Parties established the Fund for Political Party Development under the control and supervision of the Election Commission. Hopefully this mechanism, in conjunction with controls on party spending, can help free parties from dependence on private funding.

Even so, corruption in business cannot be eradicated without major reform of corporate governance. One reason for Thailand's economic crisis was poor governance in the private sector. Corrupt directors and private auditors contributed to corporate weakness. Corporate governance reform should be a priority, especially for companies listed on the Stock Exchange of Thailand. Private auditors must overhaul their practices because only audit institutions with integrity can guarantee corporate transparency and accountability and protect shareholders.

Suggestions for improvement to the integrity system

While the pillars of integrity exist in Thailand, some improvements should be considered in order to ensure efficiency and effectiveness of the institutions. Qualitative changes in three areas will improve the integrity system engendered by the Constitution considerably. These areas are—institutional improvement, commitment to public and private sector reform, and enhancement of public awareness and involvement.

Institutional improvements

In order to make the eight pillars of integrity more effective, various strategies should be adopted.

Measures to ensure the integrity of watchdog agencies. The nine watchdog institutions should be improved to ensure they operate successfully. Though members of the watchdog agencies are chosen by the Senate, the selection process is still imperfect. Criteria by which the Senate assesses candidates proposed by the selection panels should be clear, open and impartial. Over the past two years, the Senate Investigation Committee has had no clear review criteria. Some candidates have been rejected merely because they were former constitution drafters. This was the case in the selection of Constitutional Court judges, where at least three prominent and well-respected scholars were rejected on these grounds (perhaps an act of revenge against those who abolished the nominated senate). Anonymous letters accusing candidates have been taken into consideration, and calumnies have also played an important role in undermining candidates.

Moreover, investigations were conducted—contrary to practice in the western world—*in camera*. Even the debate on the floor was secret for the purpose of protecting the dignity and reputation of the candidates! Questionable practices described above are known only because some senators have chosen to speak out. It is true that secrecy may protect candidates from public criticism, but it can also engender bias and abuse of power. We can hope that the newly elected Senate will amend rules and procedures to establish clear criteria for the scrutiny process as well as open that process up to ensure impartiality. This would further ensure that members of the watchdog agencies are truly honest and able to perform their important functions.

Remuneration and other emoluments are equally important for guaranteeing the integrity of control institutions. In Thailand, only senior watchdog organisation members elected by the Senate and nominated by the King are well paid. Most staff are paid according to the government pay scheme, which is inadequate. This creates the risk of anti-corruption officials becoming corrupted themselves. The problem of inadequate pay should be addressed quickly before systematic corruption permeates the new system.

A continuous training program should be implemented to ensure high quality work skills. Technologies should be introduced to increase ease of work; millions of pages of asset and liability declarations can only be managed successfully with the help of information technology.

Internal organisation of agencies. Each agency should be designed to fulfil its multi-dimensional role. To this end, a number of specialist divisions should be present in each agency, such as

- a public relations division. Public relations and promotion campaigns are important in the prevention of malpractice and illegality. A public relations and campaign division (for example, the ICAC of Hong Kong) is needed to inform communities, the private sector and public officers about correct and clean behaviour.

- a coordination unit. This body should be created to network and work in concert with other bodies whose operations are related to the agency's function. Coordination units can help eliminate duplication of work and avoid potential conflict.

- a monitoring unit. The monitoring unit would oversee potential sources of corruption and conduct secret checks to gather information to suggest *sui generis* action by the agency.

- a research unit, which would supply facts, figures and policy options to support the policymaking process. Comparative studies of tools, practices and experiences of similar institutions in foreign countries would be valuable for improving agency performance. The research unit could also make suggestions for improving government processes to avoid corruption.

Adequate staff and funding. Staff and funding are critical factors in agency performance because control agencies cannot operate effectively without qualified personnel and adequate resources. Even though the Constitution requires sufficient funding for the watchdog agencies, the budgetary process is under the direct control of the government. The Budget Bureau under the Prime Minister's Office prepares all public expenditures for Cabinet approval. After approval, the budget is tabled in the lower house and government whips try to pressure coalition MPs to vote in support of the Budget Bill. Even at the committee stage, the Minister of Finance traditionally chairs the scrutiny committee. Traditionally, the government uses its majority in the House to control budget allocations to all state institutions, including Parliament and the overseeing institutions. Budgetary independence for the latter is more theoretical than real.

As long as this situation prevails, true independence and effectiveness of watchdog institutions is jeopardised. Serious correction measures must be taken immediately, beginning with revolving fund and standard unit cost together with block grant and direct access to Parliament as first priorities.

Adequate numbers of qualified personnel are also a success factor. Inadequacy results in delays in the work process. Unqualified personnel can damage cases under investigation. This problem is linked to inadequate funding and remuneration.

As an example of the staffing situation, the NCCC, with its wide mandate for combating corruption, has only 346 officials. This compares poorly with the ICAC of Hong Kong, which has approximately 1,200 staff. Furthermore, the number of personnel is not in proportion to the number of cases the NCCC has to investigate

- 5,741 asset and liability declarations of politicians and high-ranking officials
- 530 accusations launched against holders of public office
- 1,967 cases of corruption transferred from the now defunct CCMC
- 19 criminal cases transferred from investigation and prosecution police in the Supreme Court's Criminal Division for Persons Holding Political Positions
- 73 cases of unusual wealth
- 48 urgent cases.

Furthermore, a law has been passed to criminalise cartel practices in government procurement of military supplies. The NCCC is charged with the cumbersome task of pursuing these cases even though this work may be more suited to public prosecutors.

Without adequate funding for new staff and an appropriate pay scale, it is difficult to imagine how the NCCC is to operate effectively. If the situation is not improved the NCCC risks being labeled a 'paper tiger'—an appellation often assigned to the CCMC. In such a case the blame rests squarely on the shoulders of the government.

Priorities. Good strategies must be adopted in advance to cope with corruption. Prevention is likely to be more effective than suppression. Petty corruption is less problematic than large-scale corruption in huge government projects. Hence, piecemeal graft should draw the attention of overseeing institutions less than systematic corruption. Each agency should focus on meaningful and significant corrupt practices. The most severe forms of corruption should be attacked first.

Privatisation and decentralisation are two important areas for attention because they have great potential for harbouring corruption. Control institutions should coordinate and subscribe to the principle of division of labour in order to cope adequately with the potential corruption.

Transparency required. Overseeing bodies must be prepared to open up the investigation process at appropriate times. The media and the general public must have the opportunity to observe important sessions so as to stay informed about what is going on. This practice, which has proven effective in Australia and Hong Kong, has two merits. It fosters public awareness through public debate, and it pre-empts undue pressure from powerful individuals or groups under investigation. Furthermore, public proceedings help protect the watchdog agency's staff from the temptation of corruption.

Public sector reform accelerated

The success of the political reform movement, which resulted in the adoption of the Constitution against the will and interests of parliamentarians who nevertheless voted for it was the result of three factors—strong research back-up, public campaigning and public involvement, and political will.

Reform must be based on good strategies and produce mechanisms, tools and techniques to be adopted. Successes and failures from other countries serve as good examples. Research is fundamental for producing good policy options in any reform endeavour.

Public campaigns and involvement create awareness that, in turn, puts pressure on policymakers and prevents vested interests from resisting reform. The constitution drafting process involved wide public participation to raise public awareness and to put pressure on the government and Parliament to approve the draft despite their opposing interests. Political will comes at the end because it can be forged by public pressure.

In public sector reform, weakness stems from the fact that reform has been conducted only *within* the government circle. This is not conducive to good results because the reformed agencies and officials can stage active or passive resistance. Moreover, the reform package was not comprehensive. It would have been rejected if it had been too great an assault on the *status quo* and the vested interests of those involved. Thailand has been preaching administrative reform for a long time, but with limited results. In order to accelerate the process, continuous campaigning and public participation should be of the highest priority in order to overcome internal resistance and produce the political will to push for rapid reform.

Public awareness

Since corruption often involves two actors—the individual and the public official—both should be informed of the costs of corruption from legal and economic perspectives. In many cases, actors involved do not even realise that what they are doing is an act of corruption. For example, gifts offered without anything asked in return are considered customary and thus acceptable practice, regardless of worth and occasion. Personal relations between individuals and law enforcement officers are commonplace in Thailand's patron–client oriented system. Worryingly, the study *Corruption and the Thai Democracy* (Pongpaijit and Pirijarongsan 1994) indicated that 70 per cent of those questioned thought that giving a minor tip after receiving a service is not a form of corruption.

The situation would improve if the public and officials were informed that these behaviours are illegal. Campaigns not only help prevent unintentional corruption but also to create new values. Subsequently, emphasis should be placed on continuous public relations campaigns at all levels. This has not yet been done to promote government anti-graft strategies and the overseeing agencies.

At the domestic level, indicators for integrity, participation, transparency and efficiency in various public agencies are one of the most powerful tools for drawing media and public attention. Indicators also enhance the image of agencies with good records and encourage all agencies to improve their services. Corrupt agencies are vulnerable because they are forced to reveal their service records. Unfortunately, most existing indicators are international ones. They measure on a comparative basis and, in the majority of cases, are predicated on subjective perception rather than objective evaluation. It is of the utmost importance that relatively objective tools be used in order to arm the media and the public against corrupt agencies.

Conclusion

Thailand has already gone a long way down the path of fighting corruption. Much, however, remains much to be done. This chapter does not suggest that the tasks are too difficult or too trivial to perform. Instead, it insists that there is interdependence between all eight pillars of integrity and that those pillars should function in concert. The Constitution is only the beginning of a new era. It is not, and cannot be, a perfect instrument unless it engenders a continuous process for improving efforts to end corruption.

Appendix 1

Excerpt from Organic Law on the National Counter Corruption Commission (Chapter 9)

Conflict between personal interest and public interest

Section 100 No state Official shall be allowed to do the following acts:
  (i) to be a party or have an interest in the agreement entered into with a government agency in which the State Official acts as the official who has the powers to direct, supervise, control, audit or take legal action;
  (ii) to be a partner or shareholder in a partnership or a company which has entered into the agreement with the government agency in which the State Official acts as the official who has the powers to direct, supervise, control, audit or take legal action;
  (iii) to obtain concession or hold the concession from the State, a government agency, a state enterprise or local administration or entered into the contract with the State, a government agency, a state enterprise, or local administration which has a characteristic of monopoly, whether direct or indirect, or be a partner or a shareholder in a partnership or a company which obtains the concession or be a party to the above;
  (iv) to have an interest as a director, consultant, agent, worker or employee of a private enterprise which is under the direction, supervision, controlling or auditing of the government agency in which the State Official acts as the official by the nature of the interest of private sector conflicts with the interest of public or government interest or affect the independent of the State Official.

State Officials who are prohibited from carrying out pursuant to the first paragraph shall be as prescribed by The National Counter Corruption Commission in Government Gazette.

The provision of the first paragraph shall apply to the spouse of the State Official pursuant to the second paragraph and the business of the spouse shall be considered as the business of that State Official.

Section 101. Section 100 shall apply to business activities of former State Officials who have vacated their offices within the last two years, *mutatis mutandis* with the exception of shareholdings not exceeding 5 per cent of total shares sold by a limited-liability public company, not a party in the agreement entered into with a government agency under Section 100(2) licensed permitted by stock and stock market regulation.

Section 102. Section 102 shall not apply to a State Official carrying out the business in which they have the powers to direct, supervise, control, or audit limited companies or public companies limited assigned to perform duties in the limited company or public co., Ltd. where government agency has its shareholder or joint venture.

Section 103. State Officials shall not be allowed to receive assets or benefits from any person, apart from those given and receive within the law or rules, regulation by virtue of statutory provision law with the exception of assets or benefits justly received by according to rules and amounts issued by The National Counter Corruption Commission.

Provision in first paragraph shall apply to former officials for two years after the date of vacating office, *mutatis mutandis.*

Section 119. Any State Officials who intentionally fail to submit the declaration of assets and liabilities and its supporting documents to The National Counter Corruption Commission within issuing date of the organic law designated, or intentionally submit the same with false statements or conceal facts which should be revealed, shall be sentenced to imprisonment or fine not exceeding 10,000 Baht or imprison and fine.

Section 122 Any state official who violates the provisions in Section 100, Section 101 or Section 103 shall be sentenced to imprisonment not exceeding 3 years, or fine not exceeding 60,000 Baht, or imprisonment and fine.

In cases of wrongdoing in accordance with Section 100, third paragraph, if the State Official can prove him or herself innocent of, or unconnected with, the spouse's wrongdoing, that official shall be deemed not guilty.

12

Combatting corruption in the Philippine Customs Service

Guillermo Parayno, Jr.

In the 1970s and 1980s, the Philippine Customs Service undertook anti-corruption campaigns to combat the perceived defects in the inherent character of the Customs personnel. They used a combination of negative reinforcement, value formation, and attitudinal change which have all been found to be ineffective. The programs entailed the establishment of specialised government watchdog, investigative and prosecution agencies against corruption. Generally, however, all ended up being the same tools of the corrupt practitioners against the government officials whose mission it was to combat this social malady.

On the other hand, recent programs, implemented from 1992–98, had as their focus the reengineering of the environment within which customs officers operate. By reducing the opportunities for corruption, heightening the risk for committing corrupt acts, and reducing the rewards thereof, they achieved better results in curbing, if not totally eliminating, negative bureaucratic behaviour. In the reengineering process, information technology was employed as the essential tool for lifting customs administration into the realm of electronic governance.

There are, however, limits to the effectiveness of these environmental approaches to combating corruption in customs. The most significant and real limitation was that the measures were perceived by Customs itself as external temporary stopgap impositions to be supported only when their main patron was still occupying the seat of power. The leadership recognised this and designed contingencies to ensure sustainability of the reform. The business sector was extensively involved in the reform process and was repeatedly made aware that the responsibility of ensuring continuity rested upon them. To date, this 'friendly force' is still responding to the challenge and is helping to ensure that the reform program does not become a brief shining moment in the history of the Philippine Customs Service.

Public perceptions of the Customs Service

The general impression that the Philippine Customs Service is one of the most corrupt government agencies dates back to the time of Spanish colonial rule.

More recently, in August 1990, the Social Weather Station—the most reliable survey agency—conducted a survey on the perceived extent of corruption in a number of government agencies. The Bureau of Customs was viewed as the most corrupt agency, with 74 per cent of respondents considering the extent of corruption to be large (24 per cent perceived the level to be small and 1 per cent had no opinion). In the same survey report, Customs ranked alongside the police force in registering the lowest margin of satisfaction—negative 49 per cent (dissatisfied 56 per cent; satisfied 7 per cent; undecided 36 per cent)—on the issue of actions in place to reduce corruption (Dayag and Laylo 1994:2).

Many published reports show huge customs revenue losses due to corruption. The extent of smuggling in the Philippines is widely believed to be between 12.2 per cent and 53 per cent of recorded imports. Figures from the IMF's *Direction of Trade Statistics* (1990) show that, at 11.59 per cent, the Philippine has the second highest level, after Thailand, of import undervaluation as a percentage of total imports.

In a privilege speech before the House of Representatives, a Congressman reported that for a six month period alone (first half of 1992), an estimated one billion pesos ($37 million) in duties and taxes were lost by government from goods either diverted or illegally withdrawn from Customs Bonded Warehouses. Over 100 such warehouses were involved and were closed accordingly.

The nature and causes of corruption in Customs

Many factors predispose the Customs Service to a high incidence of corruption. Almost all of these are environmental in nature rather than inherent defects or flaws in the character of the Customs officers. It is only fitting, therefore, that the anticorruption programs be focused on addressing these environmental factors, but without neglecting the psychological underpinnings of corrupt acts. The more important contributors to the incidence of corruption in the Customs Service are as follows.

Abundant opportunities

This is the single most important cause of widespread corruption in Customs. About 1.5 million import entries, the same number of export entries, 200,000 requests for goods transfers, 500,000 liquidations of raw material imports, 500,000 bond applications and tens of thousands of other transactions (duty drawback, accreditation, accountability clearances, licenses renewals, and so on) are filed each year. Face to face interaction in these transactions is essential owing to complex and bureaucratic procedures exacerbated by the still restrictive and complex foreign trade regime. This provides fertile ground for corruption. Opportunities for corruption are as numerous as the total number of transactions, which is easily 4 million. Multiplying this by the number of processing stations—which, conservatively, is 10—yields a potential 40 million opportunities for corruption each year. Special mention must be given to the many exemption laws and the absence of clear guidelines and procedures for the grant of such exemptions. Billions of pesos have been lost to syndicates and their conspirators through the granting of undeserved or questionable exemptions and refunds.

Irresistible rewards

The legitimate salary of Customs officers pales in comparison to the rewards they receive from their corrupt practices. Smugglers share their profits with their conspirators and, since the profits are magnified by the high tax and tariff walls and the inflationary valuation method, the attraction is almost irresistible. Even legitimate business is disposed to giving attractive rewards because the cost of the delay in the clearance of goods can be more than the financial cost of illegally accelerating the process. Although the majority of businessmen would want to deal with the government above board, many are forced to pursue illegal channels and methods in order to stay in business.

Low-risk endeavour

In addition, insurance is often provided by smuggling syndicates to their conspirators in government. Conniving officials are provided the best legal counsel money can buy and, in the rare case that one is found guilty, he or she is well provided for during his incarceration.

Damaged values system and culture

'Everyone is doing it!' There is pressure to do what everybody else is doing. Even before a Customs officer joins the organisation, he or she already has the preconception that corruption is a ticket to riches. This is confirmed on entering the organisation. There is practically no indignation against corruption in Customs, probably because it is perceived as an open crime without a victim, and hence not considered much of an offence. Professionalism is utterly lacking in the Customs Service. The organisation offers its staff very little in terms of status and pride in being part of the organisation.

There is also the 'live and let live' culture and the code of *omerta* or silence. Officials and businessmen who are unwilling to live by these rules are subjected to discrimination, and are even ostracised.

Weak controls and justice system

There is a dire need for effective systems that make it difficult for officials to engage in corrupt practices and make detection of corrupt acts more likely. The chance of being found guilty after being caught is also low due to ineptness and corruption in the justice system. All these factors encourage officials to behave in a corrupt manner. Syndicates even offer insurance to their conspirators in government by footing the cost of their defence and taking care of their families while they are undergoing investigation, trial, or serving punishment.

Lack of means and support

Many men and women who join the organisation do so with the right ideals, but they quickly realise that sincerity and dedication alone are not enough. For example, they may strongly suspect that a shipment is undervalued or that it is wrongly classified but since they are not technically trained or equipped to prove this, they may ignore it. The easiest thing is to go along with everybody else.

Insincere and opportunistic media

Many in the media are using their facilities to share in the fruits of corruption instead of performing their role as neutral observers in a democratic society. Their *modus operandi* ranges from threats, coercion and intimidation through media exposure to blatant participation in illegal activities. Unfortunately, corrupt officials have no difficulty keeping these media practices alive. It is just considered an additional expense.

Typical acts of corruption

Being or threatening to be difficult

These are actions not involving the commission of a criminal act. They may involve threatening to take actions, under the guise of performing official duty, that would create difficulties to the subject of the action, such as the issuance of Alerts, Hold Orders and Mission Orders; Submission of Derogatory Information; Recommendation to Stop the Operations; Uplifting of Values, or sending the shipment for laboratory examination; requiring additional supporting documents, such as a CRF, price list or product brochure.

They may involve the threat of submitting derogatory reports (valid or otherwise) that could create difficulties for the subject of the report, or of submitting exaggerated assessments/audit findings coupled with recommendations for punitive measures as a means to extort certain sums.

Further, they could involve delaying initiation or completion of official action until a favour is given or promised. For example, attending to those who have given favour first; being absent when the requested action is much needed; prolonging hearings in seizure cases; conducting detailed examinations; asking for documents that are difficult to produce.

Sins of omission

This includes not performing one's duty in order to give favour. Examples would be not acting on violations that come to one's attention; dereliction of duty, such as when an examiner does not conduct examination of a smuggled shipment or releases the same notwithstanding the violations observed; officers who allow goods to be illegally withdrawn; customs guards who allow shipments to be removed without the duties and taxes having been paid; hearing officers deciding a case in favour of the offender.

Direct participation in criminal activities

These acts are the most risky but also the most rewarding. Examples include assisting the introduction of spurious documents leading to fraudulent release of a shipment; grant of a license to operate a CBW (radio) which is clearly to be used as a conduit for smuggling; non-remittance of collections or delayed remittance coupled with the illegal placement of the fund; pilferage of goods from security warehouses, shipments or public bonded warehouses.

Previous initiatives to curb corruption

Previous initiatives were mainly focused on the customs personnel—their shortcomings, weaknesses and vulnerabilities. Underpinning these initiatives was the belief that acts of corruption spring from a character defect or lack of moral fibre. Thus, anticorruption activities were centred on establishing specialised offices and agencies which were charged with altering the character of a customs official through punishment or threat, as well as through value formation and attitudinal change programs.

Large-scale investigations, prosecutions and purges had limited effect, and many of those who were removed from the service managed to rejoin the organisation through their connections to officers with power. The legal proceedings that attended the dismissal procedures only served to drain top management's strength and time. Some effort was taken to reduce the opportunities for corruption by streamlining the cargo clearance process and by limiting the number of signatories to the clearance documents, but the initiatives failed.

Martial law and the dictatorship years

Common knowledge that the Customs Bureau was one of the most corrupt government agencies was probably the reason that it was one of the first to undergo large-scale purges during the early days of the Martial Law Years (1972–86). On 29 September 1972, seven days after the declaration of martial law, some 200 senior customs officers were dismissed by the President (244 if those performing customs-related functions in other offices in the Department of Finance are included). This was followed on 1 November 1972 by a second wave of dismissals involving some 111 senior personnel. These two purges cleared out more than 8 per cent of the Bureau's workforce.

The 1972 purges also took place in several other government offices and formed part of the nationally-implemented emergency measures, such as the midnight to dawn curfew, the warrantless arrests and seizure orders, the operation of military tribunals, the assignment of military supervisors in sensitive government offices and the campaign against loose firearms. For a short while they had a positive impact in reducing the level of corruption in government, including the Customs Bureau.

By 1976, it became clear that the impact of the emergency measures had waned—particularly in Customs—prompting a third wave of purges. The impact of this was even more short-lived.

In 1977, faced with a return to the old ways—so-called 'backsliding'— the President appointed for the first time a military man as head of Customs. The new Commissioner brought with him a small number of young, highly educated military officers who later assumed sensitive positions in the Intelligence, Investigation and Police departments of Customs. They also assumed leadership in the two most sensitive ports, the Port of Manila and the Manila International Airport.

The tenure of the military officers saw the introduction of a number of initiatives against bureaucratic corruption, albeit on a limited scale. Cargo clearance procedures were simplified not only to remove the system's vulnerability to fraud and also reduce the number of steps and signatories required to complete the process. The system remained fully manual, however, and all transactions went through the same 'one size fits all' clearance procedure. The result was that new steps crept in almost as quickly as other steps were removed by management. Consequently, the opportunities for corruption remained widespread.

The nine-year military administration did produce significant results in restricting fraud against government revenue. This was partly because there was much opportunity at the time for engaging in illegal trade and the rewards were substantial. Tariffs were high and were placed on many essential consumer and producer commodities. Coupled with very tight foreign exchange controls, these 'incentives' pushed a significant segment of trade underground.

While the success of the military leadership in the fight against corruption was noteworthy, it was the economic restructuring undertaken by the national government in the 1980s that laid the foundation for the gradual reduction of the rewards and opportunities for fraud against Customs revenue. The two major reforms instituted—the Tariff Reform Program and the Import Liberalisation Program—were not actually even intended as anticorruption measures.

The revolutionary government years

The change of government following the February 1986 People's Power Revolution, which toppled the 14-year old dictatorship, sparked a renewed effort to rid society of graft and corruption. Initially, the campaign was limited to information drives such as poster displays in government offices calling for an end to graft and corruption in government. Subsequently, a program based on the theory that corruption thrives most in an environment where the rewards are high and the risks low was launched. Responsibility for this national anticorruption program rested upon a national committee called the Public Ethics and Accountability Committee (PEAC). Spearheaded by the Development Academy of the Philippines, PEAC Task Forces were established for each Department and measures were implemented to reduce the rewards and opportunities for corruption as well as heightening the risk of detection. In the Customs Service, several orders were issued limiting the level of control officials had over the clearance of goods, as a means of reducing corruption in the Bureau.

Actual government behaviour deviated from this progressive view of fighting corruption, particularly at the Customs Bureau. As with the Martial Law Years, over 300 customs personnel—many of them senior officers—were purged under the guise of reorganising the Bureau. Concerned officials challenged the legality of the purges in court. The ensuing legal battles, which went all the way to the Supreme Court, effectively prevented the customs leadership from making significant headway in its anticorruption campaign.

While measures were initiated to streamline the cargo clearance process, to limit the number and participation of law enforcement agencies, and to curtail the discretion of customs personnel in assessment, these measures were too little and too late to make any significant dent on corruption. The overall result was disappointing, particularly since reputable surveys showed that the Customs Bureau and the national police were the two most corrupt government agencies by mid 1992.

National government agenda to curb corruption, 1992–98

The three national anticorruption programs of the Ramos Administration were the Moral Recovery Program (MRP), the Resident Ombudsman Program, and the Presidential Commission Against Graft Commission.

The Moral Recovery Program (MRP)

The MRP became established on 18 September 1987 when the Senate passed Resolution No. 10 on the urgent need for an MRP and decided to inquire into the strengths and weaknesses of the Filipino character with a view towards solving social ills and strengthening the nation's moral fibre. It became a national program on 30 September 1992, when Presidential Proclamation No. 62 was issued declaring an MRP and enjoining active participation of all sectors in Filipino society.

The aim of MRP was to strengthen those values and attitudes in society that would make it difficult for corruption to persist. One particular prescription in the program was to establish a more efficient bureaucracy, with a minimum of red tape. The focus of the drive, however, remained the individual and the means was value formation.

The Presidential Commission Against Graft and Corruption

The Presidential Commission Against Graft and Corruption, a three-man special commission, was to investigate administrative complaints against presidential appointees in the executive department, including those in government-owned and controlled corporations. It was a failure, and was actually utilised by syndicates to file harassment charges against government officials who were forcefully doing their work and hurting the syndicates in the process.

The Resident Ombudsman Program

Resident ombudsmen were assigned to several sensitive government agencies. A significant drop took place in the number of cases filed against officials of the agencies where there was a resident ombudsman. It is not clear, however, whether the presence of resident ombudsmen contributed to a reduction in corruption cases filed or if the program actually contributed to a reduction in the level of corruption.

Customs Anticorruption Program, 1992–98

The common focus of all three national government programs was the individual. The array of measures were likewise similar—investigations and prosecutions supplemented by behaviour modification through value formation. As Professor Jon Quah of the National University of Singapore pointed out during the 1999 Manila ADB/OECD Workshop on Combating Corruption, however, the Philippines has had the greatest number of these anticorruption agencies. Because of what he termed a 'lack of political will', these and similar initiatives in the past have not been effective in curbing corruption. Experience shows, however, that negative bureaucratic behaviour will continue, irrespective of strong political will for change, as long as the customs officer continues to work in the same poor environment.

General principles and strategies

The Customs leadership under the Ramos Administration had a running start in its anticorruption program. A Blueprint for Customs Development for the Year 2000 was immediately drafted in consultation with many interested parties (organisations and individuals), both in the business sector and in government. The document analysed the changing environment within which the organisation will operate in the coming years. It defined the demands on Customs from the government, the business community, and the rest of society. It anticipated the realities or constraints that the Customs Service faced. Finally, the environment of the Customs Service was examined for opportunities that could be harnessed to support the developmental thrust. Only after that were the objectives clearly determined and the general strategies for the attainment of such objectives laid down.

Particular care was taken to make the document look more like a development plan than an anticorruption program. This was done to gain the organisation's support for the plan. The only reference to corruption in the plan was a general statement that a 'climate that promotes involvement, commitment, integrity and professionalism shall be cultivated'.

Reengineering of the Customs environment

The main philosophy underlying the Customs Service anticorruption program from 1992–98 was the same as during President Aquino's tenure—reducing the rewards to corruption, emphasis on reducing the opportunities for, and increasing the risks of, engaging in corrupt acts. During this period, however, there was a massive reengineering of the environment in the Customs Service.

With information and other technologies as essential enablers, customs systems and procedures and the work environment were re-engineered with the goal of attaining

- full automation of the processes (no officer intervention) for 80 per cent of transactions, with the percentage to be gradually increased to 95 per cent
- repositioning of controls to where they are most effective without obstructing business and trade (before goods arrival and after their release), as well as the removal of queues and choke points
- provision of remote lodgment facilities to enable the public to interact with the organisation without the need for face-to-face interactions
- complete paperless and cashless processes
- privatisation of certain operations
- electronic linkage of all the participating agencies in the system
- the development of clear and simple rules.

Measures addressing systemic weaknesses and vulnerability to fraud

To ensure that revenue generation is not sacrificed while bureaucratic corruption is being addressed, short and long-term revenue enhancement programs were set in place to remove system weaknesses and vulnerabilities as follows.

- Concerned private sector associations were empowered, enabling early detection of violations as they police violations within their own ranks.
- Friendly and constructive competition was encouraged among the various law enforcement units.
- Extensive information and encryption technology was introduced into the electronic transmission and utilisation of payments, release instructions, exemptions and other sensitive data.
- Advanced technology, such as a global positioning system, was introduced to allow tracking and accounting of transit cargo.
- Customs warehouses, container yards, freight stations and other customs facilities used as conduits for smuggling were closed, and the regulations for the licensing of new facilities were tightened.

- The auditing process was strengthened.
- Investigation, prosecution and hearing offices were strengthened.

Electronic governance

Electronic governance is the creative application of information technology in government operations to allow more effective delivery of services to the citizenry. Information technology was applied extensively in a range of Customs operations.

Collection system

Project Abstract Secure. Project Abstract Secure ended the losses in Customs revenues arising from the introduction of spurious payment documents in payment abstracts and official receipts delivered to Customs by the bank's couriers.

The project was conceived after the discovery in 1992 of shipments released with the use of spurious bank documents by a syndicate in collusion with bank and Customs personnel. Estimated losses of duties and taxes ran into hundreds of millions of dollars.

The main feature of Project Abstract Secure is the use of security software in the encryption of payment data by the agent banks, their transmission to the Bureau in an electronic form, and their decryption at the Bureau offices. The software provides a highly sophisticated data security system and cryptographic algorithms to protect data and prevent unauthorised access to sensitive information. Data cannot be decrypted without a smart card and the cryptographic keys. The transmission process was overhauled and only electronic card-bearing personnel from the Bureau can gain access to the system. The Bureau also developed a feedback process designed to catch break-ins in case the security system is breached.

Automated collection from special accounts. Raw material imports for Customs manufacturing warehouses are released without duties and taxes but are charged fees. Prior to the reform, five separate fees were collected by five different collecting officers. These were the cost-of-entry forms, documentary stamps, processing fees, boatnote and overtime charges. The face-to-face interaction at each of these payment stations presented opportunities for extracting grease money and creating delays in the clearance process. Further, problems were discovered in the handling of these collections, with cashiers running away with their collections to 'kiting' operations (collections are placed in high yield financial instruments in the name of the collecting officer instead of being immediately remitted to the Treasury).

Under this reform, manufacturing companies open up special accounts in an in-house Customs bank from which the above fees are electronically debited. The greatest benefit is the speed of the electronic processing. In addition, the various illegal practices of collecting officers were curtailed as these officers no longer handle cash. A further benefit to the Customs Service is that some companies make payments up to three months in advance to ensure they have sufficient credit from which their payments can be debited. **Mandatory payment to the authorised agent banks and in-house banks.** Prior to this reform, only shipments covered by letters of credit were required to pay duty and tax through the banks. Taxes for the majority of shipments were paid directly to Customs collecting offices. As with the payment of the various fees for warehousing entries described above, a number of anomalies were discovered in the direct payments to Customs. Spurious checks took place, and cheques were often diverted to other accounts.

Under the reform, mandatory payments of duties and taxes had to be made to the banks for all shipments as the first step in the clearance process. As a convenience for those living far from Customs House, in-house banks were established in each district port with computer workstations directly connected to the Customs port servers. With this reform, Customs collection operations became paperless and cashless, thus eliminating many of the anomalies arising from a collection system which was based on cash and cheque payments and where payments documents were handled by numerous staff. **Projects Reconcile 1 and 2.** Electronic filing of payments under the computerised collection system made possible the replacement of the old manual system of reconciling payments collected by the banks and bank remittances to the National Treasury with an electronic reconciliation process. The manual process typically had a four-month backlog, whereas the electronic reconciliation process can be completed within a day. Thus, agent banks that fail to remit any collection are immediately detected and penalised. Under Project Reconcile 1, the amounts collected by the banks and electronically transmitted to the Bureau under Project Abstract Secure are matched with the amounts actually remitted to the National Treasury through the Bangko Sentral.

Under Reconcile 2, the electronic files of payments, with which the assessments are compared prior to the release of the goods, are regularly compared with the Central Headquarters filex that received directly from the banks. This can show whether tampering of electronic records occurred at the ports.

Declaration processing

Automated Customs Operating System. The implementation of this main Customs operating software drastically changed the processing of clearance documents and declarations. Under the system, Customs works with the electronic record of a clearance document, thus rendering the process virtually paperless. With electronic declarations, the entire process has been fully automated for most of the transactions from entry reception to assessment, collection, and release of the goods. Record-keeping and the generation of both operational and management reports have likewise been automated.

Remote lodgement of declarations. The electronic record can be created and lodged by the importer himself through computer workstations linked to the Customs network. Following the Direct Trader Input (DTI) procedure or the alternative Electronic Data Interchange (EDI) procedure, importers can file declarations from their own office. Under the DTI system, importers make use of the declaration module of the main Customs software to compose the declaration and then lodge it electronically by establishing a direct connection with the Bureau's computer system. Under EDI, declarations composed in the EDIFACT message format are likewise electronically lodged, but via a commercial communication network. From there, the message is forwarded to a gateway which converts the message into a data declaration stream that the Customs system can process.

Private sector operated service centres. Importers who are not capable of using either DTI nor EDI must go through service centres operated by the Philippine Chamber of Commerce and Industry. Through these facilities, the declarations are digitised and then electronically transmitted to the port computer system for automated processing. As with DTI and EDI, there is no face-to-face interaction between an importer and a customs officer in the service centres, thus removing opportunities for corruption at this stage of the Customs clearance process.

Risk assessment, selectivity and green lanes. At the heart of the Automated Customs System is a computer program called Selectivity. It analyses the risk profiles of shipments and categorises them as high, medium or low risk by comparing their particulars with some 18 reference tables and files. Low-risk shipments are diverted by the computer system to a Green Channel where the only activity undertaken is the automated calculation of tax payable and matching of the calculated amount with the amount paid. Only when the declaration is considered to be of high risk is it necessary to conduct a physical examination and a verification of submitted documents.

These interrelated measures represent a shift in strategy for reducing corruption—from reducing the number of steps and signatures required in the process to reducing the number of transactions. These measures allow customs authorities to focus limited enforcement resources on a manageable number of shipments and thus allow greater depth of Customs intervention. Just as important is the application to the majority of trade, to reduce the cost and extent of corruption.

Customs–cargo handler computer systems interface in the release of goods (Online Release System). One of the weakest links in the cargo clearance chain is the handover of the cargo release authority from Customs to the cargo handler. This stage of the cargo clearance process is where spurious release documents usually appear. In most cases, investigations to pinpoint responsibility for the introduction of such documents and the fraudulent release of goods are unsuccessful.

The first version of the initiative to address this weak link was the Online Release System (OLRS). This system facilitates and makes secure the final release of shipments from Customs control. For the in-dock OLRS, Customs is connected online to the cargo handler for the simple matter of removing a stop flag and for red channel shipments, the lowering of the examination flag. The off-dock OLRS utilises the public telephone system to download the encrypted release instructions to the computers of the container yard–container freight station, located away from the ports. The off-dock OLRS removes the need for messengers to physically carry the release authorisations. In the past, traffic congestion in the metropolis meant that authorisations took at least a day to deliver. Fraud and corruption frequently took place in the physical handling of the release authorisations by messengers.

Unfortunately, the first version of the OLRS had weaknesses. OLRS clerks were commonly given spurious matching documents and fraudulently lifting the duty stop. The release procedure has subsequently been strengthened further. The results of the computer matching of payables and payments are automatically downloaded into a communications gateway from which the cargo handler computer can draw release authorities. With this interface, the entire process from reception to assessment and collection and thence to cargo release has become seamless.

Tax exemption system

The manual system for issuing and transmitting tax exemptions has been breached many times, resulting in the introduction of fictitious or tampered exemption papers and fraudulent release of shipments. The solution adopted was to computerise the receipt and processing of exemption applications at the Department of Finance and to provide a secure electronic communication channel for transmitting the approved exemptions to Customs. The work flow system, on top of a lease lines network, removed many if not all of the weaknesses and vulnerabilities of the operation. Now that the notes can be encrypted, the process is secure and has been dramatically shortened—much to the delight of the business community.

Use of VTS to secure the transfer of cargo

A highly political issue in Customs corruption involves the control of goods in transit from the various ports of entry to the special economic zones (SEZs), most notably to the former American military bases of Subic and Clark. Domestic producers and manufacturers have drawn attention to the diversion of goods destined for these SEZs as a source of competing smuggled goods. Since the use of guards has not worked, vehicle tracking using global positioning system technology has been put in place. The movement of goods is tracked via computers and reported on a real time basis in order that emergency response teams can take immediate action in case of diversions.

Customs Service–Federation of Philippine Industry Data Link-up

The Federation of Philippine Industry Data Link is a partnership between the government and the private sector to enforce Customs laws. It is also a showcase for the provision of easy access to Customs data for businesses. Through this data link, business is able to access records of sensitive imports as they enter the system so that an analysis can be immediately undertaken as to possible violations committed. Cases of undervaluation, and even mis-classification, can be detected through this link-up. The objective is to establish a level playing field and bring about transparency in the conduct of business.

Results and lessons learned

The overall results of the ACI were positive for the Bureau and for the country. The achievements were also recognised internationally by such prestigious organisations as the World Customs Organisation, UNCTAD and by numerous customs administrations and customs regional groupings.

Probably the best testimony to the success of the 1992–98 anticorruption program is the passion and commitment with which the business sector and other concerned groups—including many in the executive and legislative areas of government—are now fighting to preserve the gains captured during the period. There is also strong support from such international organisations as UNCTAD, the International Monetary Fund and the World Bank. The Asian Development Bank in Manila also showed its appreciation for the gains produced, by organising symposium workshops on the reforms.

Following the 1998 national elections, the new administration not only slowed the reform process but caused setbacks for some components of the program. The Direct Trader Input system at the Ninoy Aquino International Airport was discontinued for almost a year and was resumed only after the business sector—particularly the Semiconductor and Electronics Industry

Federation Inc.—and other private sector groups strongly pushed for its resumption. The business sector, led by the Philippine Chamber of Commerce and Industry and the Federation of Customs Brokerage Companies of the Philippines, is strongly advocating the removal of manual procedures that have been added to the once fully-automated and paperless system.

The experience of the Philippine Customs Service shows that anticorruption initiatives that promote good governance and provide a working environment with limited opportunity for corrupt practices are most effective in bringing about a significant reduction in the incidence of this social malady. Experience also indicates that the successes and difficulties encountered in implementation of these initiatives were strongly influenced by a number of factors, some of which were within the ambit of management influence and control.

Leader's role

The most important determinants of the success of an anti-corruption program are related to the extent to which the leader 'owns' the program and displays 'hands-on' management. He or she can demonstrate these qualities by participating in the design, development, implementation, and monitoring of the project, and by dealing with the problems encountered. Also important are the rewards and recognition given to those contributing to the success of the program and the sanctions meted out to those who refuse to cooperate. Perhaps most important, however, is leadership by example—the extent to which he or she actualises the program and conducts himself, officially and unofficially, throughout the program.

Private sector role

The business sector can be the Customs Service's strongest ally in the development and execution of the initiatives. While material and technological support are important, the private sector can be of most help in change management and sustainability. Efforts must be made to involve the CEOs of businesses affected by the program. They must ensure that their own organisations work with the Bureau on the various components of the program, instead of simply relying on 'representatives' and 'agents'. They are the ones in contact with the top government officials and are hence in the best position to impress upon them the necessity and value of the reforms and the need for continuity and sustainability. The private sector must be vigilant and courageous in demanding improved services and higher ethical standards from government civil servants. Customs management must protect them, and it must be made known to the internal staff that it is policy to encourage the private sector to speak its mind on the reforms.

Role of the IMF, World Bank and other international organisations

At times, donor and international organisations are more forceful than the private sector in calling for vigilance, sustainability and continuity in the reform program. In undertaking an assessment of their respective projects that directly or indirectly relate to the anticorruption initiatives, these organisations must objectively report any deviations from the program. Managers of the reform process must be able to work with these institutions to ensure continuity.

Negative reinforcement

While it is highly desirable to obtain support and commitment for the anticorruption program from the formal and informal leadership in the organisation, it is not realistic to expect real commitment and support when the organisation's interest is not properly aligned with the program objectives.

Audit

Related to the readiness to apply negative reinforcers is the need for strong monitoring and auditing of the reform progress. The leadership must make use of external assistance in this activity, given the propensity of internal staff to fail to present an objective picture of the level of corruption and to cover up for one another. It is desirable to have an independent auditing unit reporting directly to the top leadership. The business sector should also endeavour to conduct their own surveys to provide independent feedback.

Resource availability

In bringing about reforms, availability or adequacy of resources is not the issue. The issue is availability of sectors concerned or interested in the need for the reform. If there are enough concerned groups, there will be enough resources.

Some factors are beyond the control of the reform managers and are better addressed at the national policy level. Complex tax and tariff systems which create many rate bands and exemptions and entail numerous non-tariff barriers, such as licenses, approvals, quotas and permits, make for complicated administration and create opportunities for corruption. The Philippine government is aware of the ill-effects of such a policy framework and has done much to improve the situation, particularly on tariff and tax reforms. But stronger political will is required to ensure that vested interest groups do not jeopardise the positive things that have been accomplished in previous years.

13

Corruption as a social process

from dyads to networks

John Warburton

The problem of corruption can be stated in relatively simple terms. What is it? How does it function? If we could answer these questions we should be able to discover ways of combating what is now perceived as the scourge of the modern world. However, every complex problem has a simple plausible answer, which is invariably wrong. The problem of corruption may be able to be framed in uncomplicated terms but this is where the simplicity ends.

In general terms, corruption is an artefact of social and political organisation and, as such, is a phenomenon of infinite complexity. I have never seen a definition or paradigm that comprehensively describes corruption in all its guises and manifestations, nor do I propose one here. In this chapter I will argue that understanding corruption as a social process has implications and advantages that provide insights into the way corruption functions. I will be suggesting that such insights can also inform corruption prevention programs.

The orthodox way to approach corruption these days is to examine the institutions and systems that allow corruption to occur. To some extent I am turning this on its head by suggesting that if we are to understand corruption as a social process then we need to understand the individual actors who are the participants in this social system. I'm not suggesting that the institutional approach is wrong but we are attacking the same problem from somewhat different directions. Larmour and Wolanin are right to point out, in the introduction to this volume, that the managerialist approach to corruption invariably fails because of a failure to address the atmosphere of integrity surrounding the institution. I would add that this approach fails to incorporate the cognition, motivations and actions of individuals. Addressing the individual seems to be out of fashion because it reminds some of the unsophisticated 'rotten apple theory' that was usually trotted out to explain corruption in simpler times.

We have now moved full circle with several contributors in this volume citing Zipparo's (1998) argument that deviance stems largely from the nature of the organisation rather than the nature of the individual. Instead, I would suggest that to come to some fundamental understanding of the way corruption functions it is essential to understand it firstly from the individual's perspective and to then build the individual into a complex social world. This has not been done to date, probably because it is such a difficult and complex task, requiring an interdisciplinary approach. In any case I will attempting to propose a different paradigm describing the way corrupt transactions occur and the way corrupt networks develop.

Corruption as a social process

Corrupt transactions occur between actors as the result of social interaction. For corrupt transactions to occur there must be communication between two or more individuals. Individuals intend to participate in corrupt transactions. They may not call them corrupt or they may have some rationalisation to hand to justify their behaviour, but they intend to promote their interests over the interests of others. The precise nature of those interests and how actors come to have them is not my concern here. Actors have interests/goals/desires/needs/preferences[1] and they act to achieve them.[2] The most important factor is not the nature of the interests but the strength of the actor's desire to achieve them. Petri refers to the 'energy' inherent in motivation that drives actors to act (1981:18).

Promoting your own interest is essentially identifying and attempting to realise personal goals. In order for an actor to achieve her goals she must have 'power' (Lamberth 1980:295). It is my contention that both parties to corrupt transactions are resource holders and power seekers. They possess differing resources of power that cannot easily be converted to promote their own interests. The purpose of corrupt transactions is to conduct a swap, which converts resources into usable power. The participants in the transaction can then use the power they have obtained from the transaction to promote their own interest.

In any such transaction each individual actor has to make a personal decision as to whether they will instigate or accede to an attempted corrupt transaction. If the actor participates in such a transaction then it can be assumed they have crossed a decisional threshold. I contend there are two competing forces acting on them as they reach the decisional threshold. Firstly, there are motivational, or excitatory forces, energising them toward participation in the corrupt transaction. Principally, they are fuelled by the strength of the actor's desire to promote the interest that the corrupt transaction will satisfy. This strength of desire will be a function of the actor's dependence on the resource that the other actor in the transaction controls and is offering as part of the transaction.[3] Secondly, there are inhibitory forces lowering the tendency of the actor to cross the decisional threshold. These would include such factors as moral inhibition, perception of the risk of sanction and perception of the consequences of sanction.

It becomes obvious from this discussion that the systemic effects of organisational culture are only one of the factors that affect the individual at the decisional threshold. It is true that organisational culture and systems change can affect the scale or opportunity for corrupt transactions. Such factors address the inhibitory forces acting on an individual actor's decision to behave corruptly. They do not however address the motivational forces impelling an actor to behave corruptly. I would like to address these forces and examine how they can lead to the corrupt transactions and the development of corrupt networks of exchange.

Corruption and power

The connection between corruption and power has been poorly understood to date, with few theorists explicitly drawing a connection. Rogow and Lasswell's *Power, Corruption and Rectitude* is one of the few works to link corruption and power but sheds little real light on the connection (1963). It concentrates on power in its broadest political sense and failed to place it in the context of individual transactions.

It is my contention that corrupt transactions are a special form of power relations that involve a mutual swapping of the resources of power. The precise nature of power is contentious and I will only say here that I will draw on the Weberian causal concept of power,[4] combined with Emerson's theory of resources dependency.[5] My view is that power is a generic term used to describe the state of being of an actor,[6] possessing, controlling, or having access to resources which allow them to potentially promote their interests over the interests of others. Resources refers to money, influence, personal charisma, sporting prowess, family ties, control of the media or any other personal or external assistance capable of being used to promote the actor's interests (Clark 1968:57). Power vested in public officials is more correctly described as authority, the defining characteristic of which is its political legitimacy. Authority refers to being given administrative control of decision making processes and scarce resources on behalf of 'the public' to be administered on their behalf. I now turn to the links between power and corruption.

It is not the intention of this chapter to haggle over definitions of corruption. Most authors tend resignedly to accept the Transparency

International definition: 'the misuse of public power for private profit'.[7] I propose to expand it slightly.

Corruption refers to the actions of government officials, whether elected or appointed, who use power, in the form of the authority vested in them on behalf of 'the public', to promote their own interests over that of the public.[8] Corruption also refers to the actions of private actors who conduct transactions of power with public officials, characterised by supplying the official with a convertible resource of power for the purpose of gaining access to government controlled resources that allow the private actor to promote their interests over that of the public. It will be noted that corruption has been the mechanism by which the authority possessed by public officials has been transformed into power that can be used to serve the private interests of both parties to the transaction.[9]

The key point of this definition is that it focuses on the dichotomy between public versus private interests and the link between power and goal achievement (Etzioni 1970:19). It becomes clear when you overlay the definitions of corruption and power that corruption is a technique of goal achievement, not an end in itself. Given that power is essentially a social process these definitions place corruption centrally within the ambit of all social and therefore power relations.[10] We are talking about the most fundamental human characteristics: cognition; goal achievement and the use of power; and, human relations in social networks. Which brings me to the basic building block of social relations, the dyadic interaction between two actors.

Social relations and corrupt social networks

The precise nature and conditions under which social interactions take place are the subject of much debate (Parsons 1951). I will focus on only two aspects of social interaction crucial to corrupt transactions—secret communication and trust.

Secret communication

Corrupt transactions are by definition sanctionable. If they are sanctionable, whether legally or otherwise, those that participate in them know they must keep such participation secret from others. This raises the first and perhaps most difficult hurdle to overcome for actors wishing to instigate a corrupt transaction. They must open a channel of communication with the intended target of their corrupt approach.

A channel of communication must have a medium by which communications are maintained. In normal social interactions this is simple to conceptualise. One person meets another in a restaurant and has a conversation. They talk on the phone, send a letter or communicate by any recognised means. The opening of the channel of communication is a difficult dance for the instigator and the target. The approach can't be too obvious, lest the target denounce the instigator and expose them to sanction even before any benefit is possible. Nor can the approach be too abstruse lest the target misunderstands the true nature of the overtures being made and the opportunity is lost. The instigator doesn't want to be in situation where they have to spell out the nature of the approach to clear up misunderstandings. I would suggest, and experience bears this out, that corrupt approaches are usually made in face to face meetings where as much non verbal information can be conveyed and received in what is a highly complex social interaction. In my ten year's experience as a corruption investigator, I have never seen a first corrupt approach made by telephone or by letter.[11]

This is why interest groups are willing to pay huge amounts to have 'the ear' of political decisionmakers. They know that without a channel of communication there is absolutely nil prospect of influencing a decision maker's decision. Most modern political systems, which have safeguards against corruption, are still struggling to deal with the payment of large sums for 'access' to politicians. Indeed, in Australia, it is standard practice for political parties to hold policy 'forums' where interested business groups pay tens of thousands of dollars for guaranteed access to the Minister.

Once a channel of communication has been established and one corrupt transaction executed, the nature of the communication changes between the two actors. There is no longer an instigator and a target, only two willing participants. The corrupt transaction is sanctionable and secret ensuring the channel of communication *cannot be closed* even if one actor decides they no longer want to participate.

Trust

The two actors are now locked in to a relationship that has its own demands. At any time they could be revealed and exposed to sanction. This requires that the corrupt relationship be conducted in total secrecy and with a great degree of trust between the participants. Luhmann (1979) describes trust as a generalised expectation that the 'other' will continue to behave in accordance with the way they have portrayed themselves. In essence, trust is the rational response of actors to increasing social complexity. It is impossible to have all the information we need to make decisions about the behaviour of others and where it will lead so we make an assumption of trust. Such assumptions vastly reduce the computational complexity of decision making in a social world. As Luhmann notes, one can reduce complexity and therefore the need for trust in modern society by relying on structure. Trust in most commercial relationships has been to some degree displaced by complex legal and normative frameworks, which govern the way business is conducted (Luhmann 1979:34).

In corrupt transactions there is no such structure to rely on. The secret and sanctionable nature of the transaction ensures that the actors must 'trust' each other.[12] Once trust is established, the actors are locked into a complex social interaction in which trust must be nurtured and maintained. Therefore, the channel of communication between the actors must be of a nature that nurtures and maintains such trust. I would argue that this is why personalised relations are so important to ongoing corrupt transactions. It is often the case that corrupt actors must meet face to face, socialise and generally enjoy some sort of empathy that engenders trust between them. Face to face personalised relations actually affect the nature of the corrupt relationship. Trust, empathy and desire to fulfil the actors' personal interests interact in complex ways.

The need to build and maintain trust through face to face relations may explain the fact that in many corrupt transactions the target will accept a resource as the bribe which is vastly lower than the 'rational market value' of the publicly owned resource they are swapping. Public officials simply sell out for a lower than expected price. This is particularly evident in police culture where police will risk their reputation, career and superannuation for a few cartons of alcohol, a free night at a brothel or a very small amount of money. The annals of the New South Wales Independent Commission Against Corruption (ICAC) are full of examples.[13]

Corrupt networks of exchange

Most of the theorising about corruption is based on the corrupt dyadic exchange. With a few notable exceptions very little work has been done on corrupt networks.[14] Corrupt networks of exchange highlight the essentially social nature of corrupt transactions. I will now attempt to outline a model of how corrupt dyadic transactions can develop into corrupt networks of exchange. It should be noted this is a theoretical model in its infancy and much further work is needed. To assist in the understanding of corruption as a social process I draw on insights from a mode of inquiry which uses networks to understand social interactions. This approach goes under many guises but is commonly known as Social Network Theory (SNT).[15] SNT focuses on actors as nodes in a network and the importance of connections between actors (Emirbayer and Goodwin 1994). SNT sets out to understand the patterning of actor's interactions. It is based on the intuitive idea that the patterns of interactions between actors in a social network have a strong affect on the way that actors live their lives (French 1956). This approach combined with increased computing power has led to the development of a way of visually representing social networks that allows comprehension of their complexity in terms of space and over time.

Imagine that every person in the world is a node in one gigantic network.[16] Every actor has links with other actors in the network, which form complex sub networks. Some have a few links and some have many. Some actors have high quality connections through which high quality communications flow. Some have low quality connections and their communication with others will be degraded and unsatisfactory for their lifetimes. A feature of this social network is the interconnectedness of the actors who form the its nodes. Social researchers have been continually surprised by the interconnectedness between actors, even in a huge and complex society like the United States.[17]

This system is not static but dynamic. Connections are constantly growing, connecting, and dying. These social connections are modified by the experiences of each individual actor. Social connections require energy investment to be maintained. If individual actors do not invest in each connection then eventually they will atrophy.[18] Unlike biological neural networks, social networks do not have a central organising principle, in response to stimuli external to the network. Actors in social networks grow connections according to their own needs, desires, environmental and social influences. They respond to the connections grown toward them in a similar manner.

Typically, for each actor, they have strong, smooth, wide and well-serviced connections with their immediate family, mother, father, partner, siblings and children.[19] They will have connections of a different character with friends and acquaintances. Connections with family will generally stay constant throughout life. Connections with friends and acquaintances will grow and die in accordance with the particulars of each relationship. Each actor will have connections with their employer and other employees in the workplace. They may have a formal hierarchical relationship with the boss, but formal and informal connections with fellow employees (Argyle 1988:174). Actors may have connections with other actors who share their interests.[20] They may belong to a political party or a gardening club or be the local scoutmaster. They may go to a dance group on Thursdays and Church on Sundays. Everywhere they connect with other actors thus increasing the complexity of their relationships and their place within networks (Brown 1965:160).

Generally the connections actors make are the result of circumstance and intention.[21] Actors join or become part of definable groups or less definable networks.[22] Initially their main connection with others in such groups is the common interest of the group. As connections grow and mature within the group, this changes over time, although the group interest will always be in the background providing an underlying structure for the group connections.

Actors are intentional and can form connections in directions that suit their needs and desires. Actors do this to varying degrees and fall on a continuum between being passive and shaped by the forces acting on them, to actively forging connections strongly in the direction they want to go (Fischer 1977b). The question then becomes what are their needs and desires and how much capacity does each actor have to achieve them?

The precise mechanism of needs/desires/goal formation need not concern us here. Humans often act irrationally out of fear, greed, envy, jealousy or just plain stupidity. They do not act the same way all the time, in all situations. The complexity of human action falls within the realm of psychology the most that can be said is that humans act in accordance with their *perceived* interest at that particular time and place.[23] Once needs/goals/interests have been established in the mind of the actor they must then be sufficiently motivated to act.

I have described a social network where every actor inhabits a location within the network connected to others. The connections are growing and changing and the actor can intentionally create connections to assist in achieving their goals. Actors can only achieve their goals if they have possession, control or access to resources that allow them to do so (Burt 1977:269; see also Etzioni 1970:19). In the context of a social network, the possession, control or access to such resources gives the actor 'power'. In modern economies the most commonly possessed and used resource of power is money, however anything at all can be a resource of power if it assists an actor to promote their interest over the interests of others. Charisma, public speaking ability, media resources, advertising, and information that others don't have can all be resources of power (Olsen 1970:5).

Gathering resources is the way an actor gathers power. After all, power is a potential state, not an actual one. When an actor uses power and actually achieves their interest over the interest of someone else then power has been used. If the actor has the ability to promote their interest over another but they haven't actually done so then they have power but they haven't used it.[24] Emerson goes one step further and suggests that power is not an attribute of a particular actor *per se*, but of the social relations between actors. If an actor controls resources that another actor is dependent on, then to that extent the first actor has 'power'.

Every actor controls resources that they can call upon to promote their interest. They also possess or control resources that can't be used to promote their interest. Money is such a useful resource of power because of its convertibility. It can be handed from one actor to another and be immediately converted to the use of the new owner. This analysis appears to lead to corrupt transactions being a straightforward market in resources. Rose-Ackerman is right to point to the allocation of scarce government controlled resources leading to the creation of a market, as being central to understanding corrupt conduct (Rose-Ackerman 1978:2). What Rose-Ackerman and most economists fail to comprehend is that the market is merely a simplified representation of complex networks of social exchange and social action. The general population is so used to participating in the buying and selling of material goods that the layers of social exchange that underpin such transactions are invisible and instinctive (Jackson, Fischer and Jones 1977:43). Social exchange theorists propose that social exchange occurs between connected actors in relation to all transacted resources, whether material or non material. Such transactions are based on dependency relations, which lead to the operation of power (Cook 1987).

The above discussion brings us to the dyadic corruption transaction which always includes an instigator and a target. Once the instigator has made the decision to make a corrupt approach they will attempt to contact the target and persuade them to comply. It will be obvious from the above discussion that this attempt at convincing another individual to be part of a corrupt transaction involves power from both the instigator's and target's point of view. This attempt at a corrupt transaction will either succeed or fail—there is no in between state. It can only have a chance of succeeding if the following conditions are met

- The instigator has a channel of connection with the target (Dahl 1994:292).
- The instigator has a resource the target wants or needs.
- The target is dependent on this resource.
- The target cannot easily obtain this resource another way.
- The target has a resource the instigator wants or needs.
- The instigator cannot easily obtain this resource another way.
- The connection between the instigator and the target is of sufficient quality that allows 'trust' between the actors to support the transaction (Della Porta and Pissorno 1996:76).
- The transaction can be conducted in secret (Alatas 1968).
- The target will have no moral objection.[25]
- The target perceives that the risk of sanction and the

consequences of sanction are low enough to allow the
transaction.
• The instigator perceives that the risk of sanction and the
consequences of sanction are low enough to allow the
transaction.

Whether the instigator makes the attempt at a corrupt transaction at all
will be contingent on a combination of the above factors accumulating a
sufficient 'weight'. The acceptance of the corruption attempt by the target
will also be contingent on the above factors accumulating a sufficient weight
to allow receipt of the attempt. It is clear from the above discussion that
any corruption/power attempt (CPA) involves excitatory factors that motivate
the attempt and inhibitory factors that prevent it.

If the CPA is successful then two consequences ensue. First, the connection
between the actors is strengthened. Second the channel along which such
CPAs occur will remain open. All the above conditions having been met,
the instigator merely has to provide a resource that the target desires to
continue such transactions. In addition the instigator has the power resource
of information regarding the target's previous corrupt transaction.[26] Gaining
evidence of the original or subsequent transactions strengthens this. If the
target is dependent on preservation of her good name, as all public officials
are, then this resource further adds to the instigator's power in the
relationship. This connection is now ready to be used in continuing corrupt
transactions.

For actors in the corrupt network the connection itself will have to be
maintained and both actors in any transaction (either a power attempt or a
corrupt power attempt) will have to expend resources to preserve the secrecy
of their transactions. The two actors are now tied together in such a way
that continuing trust is required.[27] Although the transaction began with
an instigator and a target, future transactions will be characterised by their
mutuality. Further improvement of the connection by personalising relations
via social means may take place.[28]

The instigator in a corrupt transaction can be either a government actor
or a private actor. I would suggest that if a government actor has high
motivational forces and low inhibitory forces then they will probably be
the instigator. This is not usually the case in modern democracies where
the rule of law is established and enforced. The rule of law and widespread
education about the unacceptable nature of bribery ensures that moral
inhibition, perceived risk and consequences of sanction are generally higher
than in jurisdictions where the rule of law is not well established or
enforced, such as in developing countries. In addition, public officials in
developing countries, due to their poverty, are highly resource dependent

on material goods to just survive therefore ensuring they have high levels of motivation.[29]

If the instigator's desire for resources to increase his power has been satisfied then their relationship may remain static. A non-government instigator may attempt further corruption attempts against other government actors, through the target, if the instigator has a desire for power that exceeds the ability of the target to satisfy. Corruption will tend to flow upwards through the authority hierarchy to the next level of management, in order to gain access to greater discretional authority. This is particularly significant in democracies and modern bureaucracies where authority is usually scattered among a number of actors. It is not usual for one actor to possess monopoly decision making authority over significant government controlled resources.[30] An instigator may attempt to corrupt other public officials if other actors in the instigator's own network wish to access the instigator's connection to further their desires for resources of power.

The key point is that the instigator (who we will assume is a non-government actor) is unlikely to have a readymade connection with potentially corrupt government actors who can provide government resources that she desires. Having gained access to one corrupt government actor the instigator now has the ability to connect with all the government actors linked to the original corrupt actor. Through one connection there is potential for corruption to pervade the entire network. The process of opening up the network to corruption can repeat itself for as long as: there are targets in the government agency amenable to such an approach; the agency has resources of power desired by the instigator(s); and the instigator(s) have resources that can be converted to the use of the targets. In addition, any attempt has to satisfy the conditions specified above. This however is complicated by the fact that as the network grows, corrupt network actors are in the unique position of being able to use organisational power to negate some of the inhibiting conditions.

It should be noted that prior to the establishment of a corrupt network there is no overriding organising principle patterning the actor's relations with the other potentially corrupt actors, with the exception of the pre-existing organisational structure and informal social influences. Once the corrupt network has been established then it is subject to dual influences. Firstly the corrupt network is subject to the personal agendas of the actors, fuelled by the relative power of each actor in the network. Secondly the corrupt network is subject to the overriding influence of the whole corrupt network. The consequences of this is that actors in the network will fire power attempts and corrupt/power attempts in directions that promote the network as well as specific acts of corruption.

The result will be a continual firing of power attempts between actors in the corrupt network, and between actors in the corrupt network and other organisational actors. Organisational power, power attempts and corrupt/power attempts, will be used by corrupt network members to grow the network toward places in the organisation where discretionary power resides and can be utilised to the network's advantage. This will include the promotion of network members and the isolation and ejection of non-network members. Individual actors will interact with this process in a complex manner, patterning the way the network grows.

Internal motivating forces will drive or inhibit the corrupt actor's corrupt behaviour combined with external organisational factors such as low morale, poor leadership, lack of moral leadership, poor training, ambiguous organisational ethics and impractical policies and procedures which act to corrode moral inhibition.[31] Other factors such as poor accountability, internal audit review, performance management and supervision can lead to a perception of low risk of sanction and reduced consequences of sanction.

Once a corrupt network of actors is established in an organisation then the use of power is expanded through resource transferral. The corrupt actors maintain and protect themselves and the network through the use power in all its forms.[32] Participating in a corrupt network places the actors within a group that possesses a collective interest—that of furthering corrupt transactions and protecting the network.

Members of the corrupt network do not have to go outside the network to gain power in the organisational context. They all have access to organisational power to varying degrees, however the collective nature of this power means that as the network grows the organisational power available to its members grows exponentially. At a certain point the accumulation of organisational power reaches a critical mass and at this point the corrupt network has captured the organisation. It should be noted that the power of the corrupt network does not relate necessarily to the number of actors involved but the scale of organisational power available to the corrupt actors in the network.[33] A few corrupt actors with a high degree of organisational power can capture an organisation as can a large number of corrupt actors with a smaller amount of organisational power.[34]

Corruption networks and corruption prevention

How does understanding corruption in terms of social interactions and social networks assist in preventing it? Firstly it provides a theoretical basis for the value of the organisational integrity approach. As Boardman and Klum note in this volume, 'unethical behaviour' is causally linked to a number of risk factors. Through experience and some descriptive research it has become apparent that corruption can flourish where certain risk factors are present. An examination of the literature suggests that at present there is no theoretical understanding of the functioning of corruption which explains how these risk factors lead to corruption.

The organisational approach can be successful because the culture of public sector agencies is to some extent controllable. Through education, corruption prevention and the promotion of corruption 'resistance' a powerful atmosphere of organisational integrity can be created. Such an atmosphere can contribute significantly to an actor's inhibitory motivational forces. The approach does however have its limitations as it fails to appreciate the other side of the equation—the excitatory factors that impel the individual to action. If such factors outweigh the inhibitory forces created by the organisational integrity measures, then corruption will still occur.

Two examples will illustrate my point.

1   A public official in a developing country could be still be strongly impelled to act corruptly, even if her agency has implemented successful organisational integrity measures, if her family is starving and corrupt transactions will feed them.

2   In the United States of America narcotics interdiction officials are highly trained, well paid, and subject to strict codes of conduct, oversight, auditing and other measures. Corruption is still a problem partially because of the massive sums available to narcotics traffickers to bribe officials. Those that can't be bribed can be intimidated through threats to their families.

It is not true to say that everyone has their price. It is however true to say that there will always be some individuals for whom the impulsion to act corruptly under certain circumstances will be stronger than the inhibitory forces resident in the institution to which they belong. The above examples highlight the importance of the effect of resource dependency on human action. Corruption prevention programs should strategically target resources available to corrupt private actors as well potential resource dependencies for government actors. Understanding resource dependency could inform programs of risk assessment targeted at vulnerable officials.

The social networks approach alerts us to the importance of channels of communication. Without a channel of communication a corrupt transaction is impossible. Corruption prevention programs should include the monitoring of channels of communication with potential corrupters. Payment for access to public officials should be seen for what it is—an attempt to open a channel of communication that allows influence.

Once a channel of communication is opened between two actors in the network which have conducted one corrupt transaction, it remains open, even if the actor in the public sector agency moves to another position. Public sector officials suspected of corruption cannot be just moved or 'promoted out' as so often happens with problem employees. Those suspected of corruption must be dealt with by the agency through the disciplinary process. If sufficient evidence is available strong steps should be taken to remove them. If this is not possible then they should be the subject of overt or covert surveillance to affect and monitor the suspect officer's behaviour.

The social networks approach to corruption focuses on the way power is an integral part of the functioning of corrupt networks, both in terms of the gathering of resources for goal achievement, and as a medium of exchange in the network itself. Corruption is a technique used by power holders and power seekers to gain or maintain power. Corruption is not an end in itself, merely a technique of goal achievement and corruption is but one technique of gathering the power needed to achieve such goals. Actors willing to use corruption to achieve their goals are also willing to use more subtle techniques to achieve their ends. In particular, this approach suggests that the misuse of organisational power, even though it might not appear to be for private gain, is a clear indicator of the potential for corruption in an organisation. In corrupt networks, operationalising the network can, at certain stages, be a lot more important than the exchange of resources. The use of organisational power to facilitate nepotism may be of much more significance than traditional examples of corruption. Once a corrupt network has been operationalised in key areas of the organisation, the chance for discovery and change have been vastly reduced.

Focussing on the interests of actors in corrupt networks suggests that the shared interests of actors in corrupt networks is a key issue. Any corruption prevention program should target the potential for strongly shared interests of public sector employees where such shared interests are not identical to that of the organisation. As we have seen, trust is a key component of relations between actors when the first corruption attempt is made and in ongoing corrupt relationships. Shared interests between actors facilitate trust and provide a common motivational stimulus that can override the inhibitory forces that may be active.

Shared interests can provide a readymade network that contains its own culture, norms and goals, which can displace or negate organisational cultural norms. The most obvious example in Australian political life is the strong culture of political parties. This can lead to, and has in many cases, the corrupt elevation of party political shared interests over the democratic institutions of parliament, which the members of the party are supposed to serve. Any corruption prevention program would do well to identify shared interests of power holders in public sector employment and to focus on these as potential nodes of corrupt influence.

Finally, and perhaps most importantly, the social networks approach to corruption allows the corruption investigator to conceptualise the operation of corrupt networks in terms of power flows and relationships rather than the attributes of actors. The question to be asked by the corruption investigator is not whether actor A is corrupt. The question should be, what is the relationship between actor A and other potentially corrupt actors in the network. Understanding corrupt networks in this way allows us to comprehend that corrupt transactions can occur across the network between individuals who are not directly linked. Such transactions, on their face may not appear to be reciprocal and may be removed in space and time. It is only by understanding the relationships between the actors in the network that the true nature of such transactions can be revealed.

Conclusion

The problem for corruption prevention programs is that corrupt networks and social networks look similar to each other and function in the same way. We all operate in a world of differentiated social networks based on communication, personalised relations and shared interests. To act socially is a human need. It is simply not realistic to believe that rational managerialism can prevent the creation of social networks involving public sector agency officials. To radically restrict personalised human interaction would reduce efficiency in public sector agencies to such a low level as to make them non viable. Weber's totally rational bureaucracy is an idealised fiction that is not possible and not desirable. The challenge for anti corruption agencies is to attempt to formulate a model of bureaucracy and policy formulation that can integrate the reality of personalised relations and social networks whilst ensuring decisions are always made in the interests of the 'the public' alone.

Notes

[1] For the sake of brevity I will condense these concepts into the word 'interests'.
[2] This is a relatively uncontroversial view in modern psychology. See for example Lamberth (1980:295) and Atkinson, Atkinson and Hilgard (1983:317).
[3] I am utilising concepts of power dependence relations derived originally from social exchange theorist Richard Emerson. See for example Emerson (1962).
[4] Weber defined power as the ability to achieve one's goals despite opposition from others in a social relationship (quoted in Giddens (1971:156)).
[5] Emerson wrote, 'The dependence of actor A upon actor B is (1) directly proportional to A's motivational investment in goals mediated by B and (2) inversely

proportional to the availability to those to A outside of the A–B relation' (1970:45). In essence, he is saying that A has power over B to the extent that B is dependent on resources controlled by A.

6 Which can be an individual or an organisation

7 Originally proposed by Joseph Senturia, 'Political Corruption', Encyclopaedia of the Social Sciences, Vol iv: p448.

8 One problem with this definition is that the public official may rationalise that they have used their power in a way that benefits both themselves and the public interest. In this case they have promoted their interest in equal proportion to the public interest rather than over it. My view is that they intend to promote their interest regardless of the public therefore the fact that these interests may coincide is irrelevant. In addition, by promoting their interest they have distorted the process of achieving the 'best' policy, which in itself is against the public interest.

9 It will also be noted that this definition faces the difficult problems of how you identify the private interests of the public official/private actor and how you identify the 'public' or 'common' interests of the populace? These are issues I don't intend to address here.

10 It is almost self-evident that power can only be exercised in relation to others. See for example Bierstadt (1994).

11 An extraordinary example of this has recently occurred in Peru where it is estimated that 2400 video tapes were made of corrupt approaches between the head of Peru's secret police, Vladmiros Montesinos and politicians. All of the corrupt approaches occurred at videotaped meetings in a hotel room. See Associated Press (2001).

12 It should be noted that one off corrupt transactions which have no prospect of being repeated, such as the license providing official who extorts a 'fee' from the hapless applicant, have a somewhat different nature and are not included in the current discussion.

13 Perhaps the best example is an investigation conducted into the unauthorised release of government information. Police were risking their careers for $10–20 per item of information even knowing their computer use could be audited. Independent Commission Against Corruption (1992).

14 See Cartier-Bresson (1997) for one of the most thoughtful and interesting discussion on corrupt networks.

15 'Social network analysis is not a formal or unitary 'theory' but rather a broad strategy for investigating social structure' (White and Brudner 1996). See also Leinhardt (1977). SNT also goes under the name of network analysis (Fischer 1977a).

16 The concept of each individual as an actor enmeshed in a social network links to early work by sociologist George Simmel in 1922 (Fischer 1977b).

17 See for example Travers and Milgram (1969). They conducted an experiment to see how many people through personal acquaintances could transmit a letter from the West Coast of the USA to the East Coast. Approximately 30 per cent of the sample letters made it to the East Coast, travelling through a mean number of acquaintances of 5.2. This was the basis for the so-called 6 degrees of separation where every person on the planet is only six acquaintances from knowing every other person. Obviously overstated, Milgram's research does illustrate how amazingly connected even complex modern societies are.

[18] I am referring here to the importance of maintenance of interaction and the motivation to behave appropriately using social skills (Argyle 1988:52–56).

[19] Although within this network there will be considerable variation (Bott 1977).

[20] There has been considerable work done on why people form relationships, apart from structural or environmental factors. The research suggests that one important factor is 'solidarity' or having similarity in characteristics and interests (Brown 1965)

[21] Theoretical approaches to this question vary along a continuum. The ratio of the effect of environment vs intention (and therefore formation of connection) is very much in dispute (see Fischer 1977b:3).

[22] The difference between a network and a group is difficult to establish. Generally in the social sciences a group has members that have larger common aims, 'interdependent roles, and a distinguishable subculture'. In networks, only some of the actors have social relationships and they don't form a recognisable definable social whole (see Bott 1977).

[23] This approach is in line with the more sophisticated versions of rationality outlined in the Social Choice literature, or as Jackson et al. (1977:42) call it, 'structured choice'.

[24] Defining power, potential power and influence is surprisingly controversial. For discussion of this debate see Martin (1994), Clegg (1979:41–49), Molm (1987:101).

[25] Sometimes referred to in the economics literature as the 'moral cost' (see Groenendijk 1997).

[26] Information is clearly an important resource of power. In corrupt transactions it becomes crucial (Garson. 1977; Olsen 1970).

[27] Della Porta found, in her massive study of Italian corruption, that 'honesty' was a valuable trait among corrupt actors. If you were generally known to be 'honest' in your corrupt dealings then you were a person that could be dealt with (Della Porta 1996).

[28] In the author's experience as a corruption investigator with the NSW ICAC, this is a particularly common phenomenon. Della Porta (1996) also found that personalised relations were an important factor in ongoing corrupt transactions.

[29] It is axiomatic that low pay is one of the key causes of corruption in developing countries (see Palmer. 1983; Alatas 1990).

[30] Disagreement exists between the élitists and pluralists about how centralised decision making authority is. In Australian government, élites do exist and have significant power however it is mitigated (Higley, Deacon and Smart 1979). As Rose-Ackerman points out, in modern democracies the power of élites is mostly to block or deny others, rather than to act or approve (1996:377).

[31] The effect of such factors in potentially promoting corruption is brought out in Zipparo (1998).

[32] Martens (1999) provides practical detail as to how this occurs.

[33] Warren (1977) notes that formal positions in the organisation may not relate to actual power structures.

[34] By organisational power, I am not referring to the resources available to the organisation. I am referring to the ability of the actor to influence the workings of the organisation itself.

References

Abbott, A., 1983. 'Professional ethics', *American Journal of Sociology*, 88(5):855–85.

Alam, M.S., 1989. 'Anatomy of corruption: an approach to the political economy of underdevelopment', *American Journal of Economics and Sociology*, 48(4):441–56.

Alatas, S., 1968. *Sociology of Corruption*, Donald More Press, Singapore.

Alatas, S., 1986. *The Problem of Corruption*, Times Books, Singapore.

——, 1990 *Corruption: its nature, causes, and functions*, Avebury, Aldershot.

——, 1999. *Corruption and the Destiny of Asia*, Prentice Hall and Simon & Schuster, Kuala Lumpur.

Albritton, R.B., 2000. Senate Elections in Thailand'. Available online at <http://kpi.ac.th>.

Allars, M., 1997. *Administrative Law: cases and commentary*, Butterworths, Sydney.

Alston, P., 1995. The Rights Framework and Development Assistance. Paper presented at the Human Rights Council of Australia (HRCA) Symposium 'The Rights Way to Development: a human rights approach to development assistance', Canberra. Available online at <http://www.ozemail.com.au/~hrca/symposium.htm#The Rights Framework and Development Assistance>.

Argyle, M., 1988. *The Psychology of Interpersonal Behaviour*, Penguin, London.

Aristotle, 1988. *The Politics*, Cambridge University Press, Cambridge.

Aronson, M. and Dyer, B., 2000. *Judicial Review of Administrative Action*, LBC Information Services, Sydney.

Arthur, E.E., 1987. 'The ethics of corporate governance', *Journal of Business Ethics*, 6(1):59–70.

Asian Development Bank (ADB), 1995. *Governance: sound development management*, Working Paper, Asian Development Bank, Manila.

——, (forthcoming). *Report of Seminar on Corruption and Institutional Failure, Chiang Mai, May 2000*, Asian Development Bank, Manila.

Associated Press, 2001. Peru: now reviled ex-spy chief/presidential advisor maintains web of influence over country, 30 January, available online at http://www.ecountries.com/the_americas/peru/news/2798100.

Atkinson, R.L., Atkinson, R.C., Hilgard, E.R., 1983. *Introduction to Psychology*, Harcourt Brace Jovanovich, San Diego.

Ayres, I. and Braithwaite, J., 1992a. 'Communitarian Institutions: designing responsive regulatory institutions', *The Responsive Community: rights and responsibilities*, 2(3):41–47.

——, 1992b. *Responsive Regulation: transcending the deregulation debate*, Oxford University Press, New York.

Banerjee, A., 1997. *A Theory of Misgovernance*, Department of Economics Working Paper 97(04), Massachusetts Institute of Technology, Massachusetts.

Banfield, E.C., 1975. 'Corruption as a feature of governmental organisations', *Journal of Law and Economics*, 18(3):587–605.

Barber, B., 1983. *The Logic and Limits of Trust*, Rutgers University Press, New Brunswick.

Bardhan, P., 1997. 'Corruption and development: a review of issues', *Journal of Economic Literature*, 35(3):1,320–46.

Basel Action Network (BAN) website. Available online at <http://www.ban.org>.

Beare, M.E., 1997. 'Corruption and organized crime: lessons from history', *Crime, Law and Social Change*, 28:155–72.

Becker, G.S., 1968. 'Crime and punishment: an economic approach', *Journal of Political Economy*, 76(2):169–217.

—— and Stigler, G.J., 1974. 'Law enforcement, malfeasance, and the compensation of enforcers', *Journal of Legal Studies*, 3(1):1–19.

Beder, S., 1993. 'Engineers, ethics and etiquette', *New Scientist*, 139(1892):36–41.

Bierstadt, R., 1994. 'An analysis of social power', in J. Scott (ed.), *Power: critical concepts*, Routledge, London:5–15.

Birkinshaw, P., 1997. *Freedom of Information: the law, the practice, and the ideal*, Northwestern University Press, Evanston, Illinois.

Bliss, C. and Di Tella, R., 1997. 'Does competition kill corruption?', *Journal of Political Economy*, 105(5):1,001–23.

Bosch, H., 1997. The growing threat of international corruption, Paper presented to the Forum on Corruption in International Procurement, Canberra, 11 March.

Bossard, A., 1990. *Transnational Crime and Criminal Law*, The Office of International Criminal Justice, The University of Illinois, Chicago.

Bott, E., 1977. 'Urban families: conjugal roles and social networks', in S. Leinhardt (ed.), *Social Networks: a developing paradigm*, Academic Press, New York:253–92.

Bowie, N.E., 1990. 'Business codes of ethics: window dressing or legitimate alternative to government regulation', in M. Hoffman and J.M. Moore (eds), *Business Ethics: readings and cases in corporate morality*, McGraw-Hill, New York:505–9.

Braithwaite, J., 1989 *Crime, Shame and Reintegration*, Cambridge University Press, Sydney.

——, 1993. 'Power and the architecture of trust', Division of Philosophy and Law, The Australian National University, Canberra (mimeo).

—— and Makkai, T., 1993. 'Trust and compliance', *Policing and Society*, 4:1–12.

Brien, A., 1998. 'Professional ethics and the culture of trust', *Journal of Business Ethics*, 17(4):391–410.

Brooks, L.J., 1989. 'Corporate codes of ethics', *Journal of Business Ethics*, 8:(2,3):117–29.

Brown, L. (ed.), 1997. *State of the World 1997*, WW Norton & Co, New York.

Brown, R., 1965. *Social Psychology*, The Free Press, New York.

Burt R.S., 1977. 'Power in a social topology', in R.J. Liebert and A.W. Imershein (eds), *Power, Paradigms and Community Research*, Sage, London:251–334.

Buscaglia, E., 1997. 'Corruption and judicial reform in Latin America', *Policy Studies Journal*, 17(4):273–86.

Caiden, G. (ed), 1983. *International Handbook of the Ombudsman*, Volume 2, Greenwood Publishing Group, Westport, Connecticut.

Cartier-Bresson, J., 1997. 'Corruption networks, transaction security and illegal social exchange', *Political Studies*, 45(3):463–76.

Centre for Business Ethics, 1992. 'Instilling ethical values in large corporations', *Journal of Business Ethics*, 11(11):863–67.

Chaikin, D., 1983. *Mutual Assistance in Criminal Matters: a Commonwealth perspective*, Paper presented to the Commonwealth Law Ministers Meeting, Sri Lanka.

——, 1999. *Electronic Threat and Defence: the internet and Swiss banks*, Paper presented to the 4th International Financial Fraud Convention, London.

——, 1999. Affadavits submitted to the Philippine Senate Blue Ribbon Committee, The L2th Joint Public Hearing of P.S. Res. No 450 and 458, *Alleged existence of a PCGG-Swiss banker's conspiracy to hide the Marcos wealth*, Manila.

Chand, S. and Moene, K., 1997. *Controlling Fiscal Corruption*, IMF Working Paper 97–100, International Monetary Fund, Washington DC.

Chander, P. and Wilde, L., 1992. 'Corruption and tax administration', *Journal of Public Economics*, 49(3):333–49.

Chapman, A., 1996. 'A "violations approach" for monitoring the International Covenant on Economic, Social and Cultural Rights', *Human Rights Quarterly*, 18(1):23–66.

Chavez, F., 1999. *Criminal complaint about various Swiss banks, Swiss and Liechtenstein fiduciaries, and Swiss civil servants re Marcos case*.

Clark, T.N., 1968. 'The concept of power', in T.N. Clark (ed.), *Community Structure and Decision Making: comparative analyses*, Chandler, San Francisco:45–82.

Clegg, S., 1979. *The Theory of Power and Organisation*, Routledge and Kegan Paul, London.

Cockcroft, L., 1998. *Corruption and Human Rights: a crucial link*, Transparency International Working Paper, Transparency International, London and Berlin. Available online at <http://www.transparency.de/documents/work-papers/cockcroft.html>.

Cook, K.S., 1987. 'Emerson's contributions to the social exchange theory', in K. Cook (ed.), *Social Exchange Theory*, Sage, London:210-217.

Coulter, J., 1999. *Case Management in New South Wales Correctional Centres*, Independent Commission Against Corruption Research Report, Independent Commission Against Corruption, Sydney.

Credit Suisse v Republic of the Philipines, Swiss Supreme Court (15 January 1998).

Cressey, D.R., 1986. 'Why managers commit fraud', *Australian and New Zealand Journal of Criminology*, 19:195–209.

—— and Moore, C.A., 1983. 'Managerial values and corporate codes of ethics', *California Management Review*, 25(4):53–77.

Creusat, J-P., 1994. 'Year 2000 and LUCID© System', *The Narc Officer*, Jul./Aug.:69–76.

Criminal Justice Commission (CJC), 1993. *Corruption in the Workplace*, CJC, Brisbane.

Cullen, J.B., 1978. *The Structure of Professionalism: a quantitative examination*, Petrocelli Books, New York.

Dahl, R., 1994. 'The concept of power', in J. Scott (ed.), *Power: critical concepts*, Routledge, London:288–309.

Dankwa, V., Flinterman, C. and Leckie, S., 1998. 'Commentary to the Maastricht Guidelines on violations of economic, social and cultural rights', *Human Rights Quarterly*, 20(3):705–30.

Davis, M., 1991a. 'Do cops really need a code of ethics?', *Criminal Justice Ethics*, 10(2):14–28.

——, 1991b. 'Thinking like an engineer: the place of a code of ethics in the practice of a profession, *Philosophy and Public Affairs*, 20(2):150–67.

Dayag, C.D. and Laylo, P.R., 1994. 'Public opinion on graft and corruption in government', *Social Welfare Bulletin 94–3*, Social Weather Station, Quezon City.

Dean, P.J., 1992. 'Making codes of ethics real', *Journal of Business Ethics*, 11(4):285–90.

Della Porta, D., 1996. 'Actors in corruption: business politicians in Italy', *International Social Science Journal*, 48(3):349–64.

—— and Pissorno, A., 1996. 'The business politicians: reflections from a study of political corruption', in M. Levi and D. Nelken (eds), *The Corruption of Politics and the Politics of Corruption*, Blackwell, Oxford:76.

Department of Foreign Affairs and Trade (DFAT), 1998. *Human Rights Manual*, Department of Foreign Affairs and Trade, Canberra.

Diokno, M., 1995. 'Challenges and opportunities: a response'. Paper presented at the Human Rights Council of Australia (HRCA) Symposium 'The Rights way to development: a human rights approach to development assistance', Canberra. Available online at http://www.ozemail.com.au/~hrca/symposium.htm#Challenges and Opportunities.

Doig, A., 1995. 'Good government and sustainable anti-corruption strategies: a role for independent anti-corruption agencies?', *Public Administration and Development*, 15(2):151–65

Downer, A., 1997. *Promoting good governance and human rights through the aid program*, Address at the Department of Foreign Affairs/Non-Government Organisations Human Rights Consultations, Department of Foreign Affairs and Trade, Canberra, 27 August.

Dupont, A., 1998. Corruption in East Asia: how serious a problem is it?, Strategic and Defence Studies Centre, The Australian National University, Canberra (unpublished).

Dye, K.M. and Stapenhurst, R., 1998. *Pillars of Integrity: the importance of supreme audit institutions in curbing corruption*, World Bank (EDI), Washington, DC.

El Zein, S., 1998. 'What is international crime?', in Interpol, *Interpol: 75 years of international police cooperation*, Interpol, Lyon:27–30.

Elliott, K. (ed.), 1997a. *Corruption and the Global Economy*, Institute for International Economics, Washington, DC.

———, 1997b. 'Corruption as an international policy problem: overview and recommendations', in K. Elliott (ed.), *Corruption and the Global Economy*, Institute for International Economics, Washington DC:175–233.

Emerson, R., 1962. 'Power-dependence relations', *American Sociological Review*, 27:31–41.

———, 1970. 'Power-dependence relations', M.E. Olsen (ed.), *Power in Societies*, Macmillan, London:44–53.

Emirbayer, M., and Goodwin, J., 1994. 'Social network analysis, culture, and the problem of agency', *American Journal of Sociology*, 99:1411–54.

Etzioni, A., 1970. 'Power as a societal force', in M.E. Olsen in M.E. Olsen (ed.) *Power in Societies*, Macmillan, London:18–26.

Etzioni-Halevy, E., 1989. 'Exchanging material benefits for political support: a comparative analysis', in A. Heidenheimer, M. Johnston and V.T. LeVine (eds), *Political Corruption: a handbook*, Transaction Publishers, New Brunswick:287–304.

Euben, J.P., 1989. 'Corruption', in T. Ball, J. Farr and R.L. Hanson (eds), *Political Innovation and Conceptual Change*, Cambridge University Press, Cambridge.

Farrar, C., 1988. *The Origins of Democratic Thinking: the invention of politics in classical Athens*, Cambridge University Press, Cambridge.

Fasching, D.J., 1981. 'A case for corporate management ethics, *California Management Review*, Summer, 23(4):62–76.

Ferrell, O.C. and Gardiner, G., 1991. *In Pursuit of Ethics: tough choices in the world of work*, Creve Coeur, Smith Collins, Missouri.

Fischer, C.S., 1977a. 'Network analysis and urban studies', in C.S. Fischer, Jackson, R.M., Stueve, C.A., Gerson, K., Jones, L.M. and Baldassare, M.(eds), *Networks and Places: social relations in the urban setting*, The Free Press, New York:19–38.

———, 1977c. 'Perspectives on community and personal relations', in C.S. Fischer, Jackson, R.M., Stueve, C.A., Gerson, K., Jones, L.M. and Baldassare, M.(eds), *Networks and Places: social relations in the urban setting*, The Free Press, New York:1–16.

Fisse, B. and Braithwaite, J., 1993. *Corporations Crime and Accountability*, Cambridge University Press, Cambridge.

Fitzgerald, G.E., 1989. *Report of a Commission of Inquiry Pursuant to Orders in Council*, Queensland Government, Brisbane.

Fleming, J.E., 1984. 'Managing the corporate ethical climate', in W.M. Hoffman, J.M. Moore and D.A. Fedo (eds), *Corporate Governance and Institutionalising Ethics*, Heath, Lexington, DC:217–26.

French, J.R.P., 1956. 'A formal theory of social power', *Psychological Review*, 63:181–94.

Friedrich, C., 1989. 'Corruption concepts in historical perspective', in A. Heidenheimer, M. Johnston and V.T. LeVine (eds), *Political Corruption: a handbook*, Transaction Publishers, New Brunswick:15–24.

Fuller, L. 1969. *The Morality of Law*, Rev. ed., Yale University Press, New Haven.

Gans, J., King, S. and Mankiw, N.G., 1999. *Principles of Microeconomics*, Harcourt Brace and Company, Marrickville.

Garson, D., 1977. *Power and Politics in the United States*, DC Heath and Company, Toronto.

George, B.C., Lacey, K.A. and Birmele, J., 1999. 'On the threshold of the adoption of global antibribery legislation: a critical analysis of current domestic and international efforts toward the reduction of business corruption', *Vanderbilt Journal of Transnational Law*, 32(1):1–48.

Giddens, 1971. *Capitalism and Modern Social Theory. an analysis of the writings of Marx, Durkheim and Max Weber*, Cambridge University Press, Cambridge.

Glynn, P., Kobrin, S.J. and Naim, M., 1997. 'The globalization of corruption', in K. Elliott (ed.), *Corruption and the Global Economy*, Institute for International Economics, Washington, DC:7–27.

Gorta, A., 1988a. 'Minimising corruption: applying lessons from the crime prevention literature', *Crime, Law and Social Change*, 30:67–87.

———, 1998b. *Minimising Corruption: some lessons from the literature*, Independent Commission Against Corruption Research Report, Independent Commission Against Corruption, Sydney

———, 1999. *Taking an Informed Approach to Minimising Corruption*, Occasional Seminar at the Australian Institute of Criminology, Canberra, 3 March.

—— and Forell, S., 1994. *Unravelling corruption: A public sector perspective. Survey of NSW public sector employees' understanding of corruption and their willingness to take action*, Independent Commission Against Corruption Research Report, Independent Commission Against Corruption, Sydney.

—— and Forell, S., 1995. 'Layers of decision: linking social definitions of corruption and willingness to take action', *Crime, Law and Social Change*, 23(4):315–43.

Gould, D., 1991. 'Administrative corruption: incidence, causes, and remedial strategies', in A. Farazmand (ed.), *Handbook of Comparative Development and Public Administration*, Marcel Dekker, New York:467–84.

Gray, C.W. and Kaufmann, D., 1998. 'Corruption and development', *Finance and Development*, 35(1):7–10.

Greenberger, D.B., Miceli, M.P. and Cohen, D.J., 1987. 'Oppositionists and group norms: the reciprocal influence of whistle-blowers and co-workers', *Journal of Business Ethics*, 6:527–42.

Groenendijk, N., 1997. 'A principal agent model of corruption', *Crime Law and Social Change*, 27:322.

Harris-White, B., 1996. 'Editorial introduction: corruption, liberalization and democracy', *Institute of Development Studies Bulletin*, 27(2):1–5.

Heidenheimer, A., Johnston, M. and LeVine, V.T. (eds), 1989. *Political Corruption: a handbook*, Transaction Publishers, New Brunswick.

Henry, S., 1983. *Private Justice: towards integrated theorising in the sociology of law*, Routledge and Kegan Paul, London.

Higley, J., Deacon, D. and Smart, D., 1979. *Elites in Australia.* Routledge and Kegan Paul, London.

Hindess, B., 2000. 'Representation ingrafted upon democracy', *Democratization*, 7(2):1–18.

Hoffman, W.M., 1990. 'Developing the ethical corporation', in W.M. Hoffman and J.M. Moore (eds), *Business Ethics: readings and cases in corporate morality*, 2nd ed., McGraw-Hill, New York:628–34.

Hollinger, R.C. and Clark, J.P., 1983. *Theft by Employees*, Lexington Books, D.C. Heath and Company, Lexington, Massachusetts.

Hood, C., 1991. 'A public management for all seasons?', *Public Administration*, 69(1):3–19.

Horning, D.N.M., 1970. 'Blue-collar theft: conceptions of property, attitudes towards pilfering, and work group norms in a modern industrial plant', in E.O. Smigel and H.L. Ross, *Crimes Against Bureaucracy*, Van Nostrand Reinhold Company, New York.

Human Rights Council of Australia (HRCA), 1995. Human Rights Council of Australia (HRCA) Symposium 'The Rights Way to Development: a human rights approach to development assistance', Canberra. Available online at <http://www.ozemail.com.au/~hrca/symposium.htm>.

Hume, D., 1987 [1742]. *Essays: moral, political and literary*, Liberty Fund, Indianapolis.

Huntington, S.P., 1968. 'Modernisation and corruption', in S.P. Huntington, *Political Order in Changing Societies*, Yale University Press, New Haven:59–71.

——, 1993. 'The clash of civilizations?', *Foreign Affairs*, 72(3):22–49.

Imbaruddin, A., 1997. 'Corruption in Indonesia: causes, forms and remedies', *Development Bulletin*, No. 42, Australian Development Studies Network, Canberra:12–15.

Independent Commission Against Corruption (ICAC), 1992. *Report on Unauthorised Release of Government Information*, Independent Commission Against Corruption, Sydney.

——, 1994. *Community Attitudes to Corruption and the ICAC: ICAC public attitude survey 1993.* Independent Commission Against Corruption Research Report, Independent Commission Against Corruption, Sydney.

——, 1995. *Community Attitudes to Corruption and the ICAC 1994: Independent Commission Against Corruption community attitude survey*, Independent Commission Against Corruption Research Report, Independent Commission Against Corruption, Sydney.

——, 1996a. *Practical Guide to Corruption Prevention*, Independent Commission Against Corruption, Sydney.

——, 1996b. *Community Attitudes to Corruption and the ICAC 1995: Independent Commission Against Corruption community attitude survey*, Independent Commission Against Corruption Research Report, Sydney.

——, 1997a. *Corruption and Related Issues: an annotated bibliography*, Independent Commission Against Corruption Research Report, Independent Commission Against Corruption, Sydney.

——, 1997b. *Community Attitudes to Corruption and the ICAC 1996: Independent Commission Against Corruption community attitude survey*, Independent Commission Against Corruption Research Report, Independent Commission Against Corruption, Sydney.

——, 1998a. *Ethics: the key to good management—summary*, ICAC, Sydney.

——, 1998b. *A Major Investigation into Corruption in the Former State Rail Authority of New South Wales*, ICAC, Sydney.

——, 1998c. *Report on Investigations into Aboriginal Land Councils in New South Wales*, ICAC, Sydney.

——, 1999a. *Community and Journalists' Attitudes to Corruption and the ICAC 1999: Independent Commission Against Corruption community attitude survey*, Independent Commission Against Corruption Research Report, Independent Commission Against Corruption, Sydney.

——, 1999b. *ICAC 1998/99 Annual Report*, Independent Commission Against Corruption, Sydney.

——, 2000a. *What is an Ethical Culture? Key issues to consider in building an ethical organisation. A survey of NSW public sector agencies and local councils. Summary report*, Independent Commission Against Corruption Research Report, Independent Commission Against Corruption, Sydney.

——, 2000b. *ICAC 1999–2000 Annual Report*, Independent Commission Against Corruption, Sydney.

——, (forthcoming). *Unravelling corruption II: exploring changes in the public sector perspective 1993–1999*, Independent Commission Against Corruption Research Report, Independent Commission Against Corruption, Sydney.

Independent Commission Against Corruption website. Available online at <http://www.icac.nsw.gov.au>.

International Monetary Fund (IMF), 1998. *Good governance: the IMF's role*. Available online at <http://www.imf.org/external/pubs/ft/exrp/govern/govindex.htm>.

Jackson, R.M., Fischer, C.S. and Jones, L.M., 1977. 'The dimensions of social networks', in C.S. Fischer, Jackson, R.M., Stueve, C.A., Gerson, K., Jones, L.M. and Baldassare, M.(eds), *Networks and Places: social relations in the urban setting*, The Free Press, New York:39–58.

Jayawickrama, N., 1998. *Corruption—a violation of human rights?*, TI Working Paper, Transparency International, Berlin and London. Available online <http://www.transparency.de/documents/work-papers/jayawickrama.html>.

Johnston, M., 1986. 'Right and wrong in American politics: popular conceptions of corruption', *Polity*, 18(3):367–91.

Johnston, M., 1997. 'Public officials, private interests, and sustainable democracy: when politics and corruption meet', in K. Elliott (ed.), *Corruption and the Global Economy*, Institute for International Economics, Washington, DC.

Jones, C. and Menezes, F.M., 1995. *Auctions and Corruption: how to compensate the auctioneer*, Working Papers in Economics and Econometrics 291, The Australian National University, Canberra.

Joongi Kim and Jong Bum Kim, 1997. 'Cultural differences in the crusade against international bribery: rice-cake expenses in Korea and the Foreign Corrupt Practices Act', *Pacific Rim Law and Policy Journal*, 6(3):549–80.

Kaplan, R.D., 1994. 'The coming anarchy', *The Atlantic Monthly*, 273(2):44–76.

Karchmer, C. and Ruch, D., 1992. 'State and local money laundering control strategies', *National Institute of Research Brief*, United States Department of Justice, Washington, DC.

Kaufmann, D., Isham, J. and Pritchett, L.H., 1997. 'Civil liberties, democracy, and the performance of government projects', *World Bank Economic Review*, 11(2):219–42. Available online at <http://www.worldbank.org/wbi/governance/wp.htm#governance>.

Kaufmann, D., Kraay, A. and Zoido-Lobaton, P., 1999. *Governance Matters*, World Bank Policy Research Working Paper 2196, World Bank, Washington, DC. Available online at <http://www.worldbank.org/wbi/governance/wp.htm#governance>.

Klitgaard, R., 1988. *Controlling Corruption*, University of California Press, California.

Knightly, P., 1999. 'War on drugs lost to market forces', *The Weekend Australian*, 6–7 March:3, 6.

Kofele-Kale, N., 1995. *International Law of Responsibility for Economic Crimes: holding heads of state and other high ranking state officials individually liable for acts of fraudulent enrichment*, M. Nijhoff, Dordrecht.

Kofman, F. and Lawarrée, J., 1993. 'Collusion in hierarchical agency', *Econometrica*, 61(3):629–56.

Kotter, J.P. and Heskett, J.L., 1992. *Corporate Culture and Performance*, Free Press, New York.

Kraar, L., 1988. 'The drug trade', *Fortune*, 18(2):27–38.

L'Etang, J., 1992. 'A Kantian approach to codes of ethics', *Journal of Business Ethics*, 11(10):737–44.

Lamberth, J., 1980. *Social Psychology*, Macmillan, New York.

Langseth, P., Pope, J. and Stapenhurst, R., 1997. 'The role of a national integrity system in fighting corruption', *National Integrity System Country Studies*, World Bank (EDI), Washington, DC.

Larmour, P., 1997. 'Corruption and Governance in the South Pacific', *Pacific Studies*, 20(3):1–17.

——, 1998. *Making Sense of Good Governance*, State, Society and Governance in Melanesia Project Discussion Paper 98/5, Research School of Pacific and Asian Studies, The Australian National University, Canberra.

Lawrence, S.V., 1998. 'Excising the cancer', *Far Eastern Economic Review*, 161(34):10–14.

Leckie, S., 1998. 'Another step towards indivisibility: identifying the key features of violations of economic, social and cultural rights', *Human Rights Quarterly*, 20(1):81–124.

Legislating the Criminal Code: corruption, Law Com. No. 248 (1988).

Leinhardt, S. (ed.), 1977. *Social Networks: a developing paradigm*, Academic Press, New York.

LeVine, V., 1989. 'Transnational aspects of political corruption', in A. Heidenheimer, M. Johnston and V.T. LeVine (eds), *Political Corruption: a handbook*, Transaction Publishers, New Brunswick:685–99.

Lewis, J., 1999. 'Red channel funnel', *The Weekend Australian*, 6–7 March:20.

Luhmann, N., 1979. *Trust and Power: two works by Niklas Luhmann*, Wiley, Chichester.

Lupsha, P., 1996. 'Transnational organized crime versus the nation state', *Transnational Organized Crime*, 2(1):21–48.

Madison, J., 1857. 'Number 10: the utility of the Union as a safeguard against domestic faction and insurrection (continued)', in Hamilton, A., Madison, J. and Jay, J., *The Federalist: on the new Constitution, written in 1788*, Masters, Smith and Co., Hallowell:42–48.

Mailath, G. and Zemsky, P., 1991. 'Collusion in second price auctions with heterogeneous bidders', *Games and Economic Behaviour*, 3(4):467–86.

Maitland, I., 1990. 'The limits of business self-regulation', in W.M. Hoffman and J.M. Moore (eds), *Business Ethics: reading and cases in corporate morality*, McGraw-Hill, New York:509–18.

Mann, M., 1999. 'The dark side of democracy: the modern tradition of ethnic and political cleansing', *New Left Review*, 235:18–45.

Martens, F.T., 1999. 'Shaping the message in public corruption probes: a confidence game', *International Association for the Study of Organised Crime*, 13(1):5–8.

Martin, R., 1994. 'The concept of power: a critical defence', in J. Scott (ed), *Power: critical concepts*, Routledge, London:88–102.

Mathews, M.C., 1988. *Strategic Intervention in Organisations: resolving ethical dilemmas*, Vol. 169, Sage, Newbury Park.

Mauro, P., 1995. 'Corruption and growth', *Quarterly Journal of Economics*, 110(3):681–712.

——, 1997. 'The effects of corruption on growth, investment, and government expenditure: a cross-country analysis', in K. Elliott (ed.), *Corruption and the Global Economy*, Institute for International Economics, Washington, DC.

——, 1998. 'Corruption and the composition of government expenditure', *Journal of Public Economics*, 69(2):263–79.

McDonald, R., 1995. *The Work of the Financial Action Task Force in the Asian Area*. Paper presented at a Money Laundering Seminar for the Australian Financial Industry Regulators, Sydney, 15 May.

McDonald, W.F., 1995. 'The globalization of criminology: the new frontier is the frontier', *Transnational Organized Crime*, 1(1):1–22.

McFarlane, J., 1994. *The Current and Emerging Forms of Criminality Involving Organised Crime in the Asia Pacific Region: an Australian perspective*, Address delivered to the 3rd Multinational Asian Organised Crime Conference, Sydney, 1–3 November.

Mehmet, B., 1998. 'The scope, timing, and type of corruption', *International Review of Law and Economics*, 18(1):101–20.

Metropolitan Police, 1999. *Corruption and Dishonesty Strategy*. Available online at <http://www.met.police.uk/police/mps/mps/press/corrup.htm>.

Mihalic, F., 1957. *Grammar and Dictionary of Neo-Melanesian*, Mission Press, Sydney.

Mirrlees-Black, C. and Ross, A., 1995. 'Crime against retail and manufacturing premises: findings from the 1994 commercial victimisation survey', *Home Office Research Survey 146*, Research, Development and Statistics Directorate, Home Office, London.

Molm, L.D., 1987. 'Linking power structure and power use', in K. Cook (ed.), *Social Exchange Theory*, Sage, London:101.

Mookherjee, D. and Png, I.P.L., 1995. 'Corruptible law enforcers: how should they be compensated?', *Economic Journal*, 105(428):145–59.

Morgan, A., 1998. *Corruption: causes, consequences, and policy implications*, The Asia Foundation, San Francisco.

Mosely, R., 1995. 'High-tech crime looms as major global concern', *Criminal Justice Europe*, 5(4):1, 4.

Murphy, P.E., 1988. 'Implementing Business Ethics', *Journal of Business Ethics*, 7(12):907–15.

Myrdal, G., 1989. 'Corruption; its causes and effects', in A. Heidenheimer, M. Johnston and V.T. LeVine (eds), *Political Corruption: a handbook*, Transaction Publishers, New Brunswick:953–61.

Naples Political Declaration and Global Action Plan Against Organised Transnational Crime, 23 November 1994. Full text of this document is published in *Transnational Organized Crime*, 1(1):118–27.

Newton, L., 1986. 'The internal morality of the corporation', *Journal of Business Ethics*, 5(3):249–58.

——, 1982. 'The origin of professionalism: sociological conclusions and ethical implications', *Business and Professional Ethics Journal*, 1(4):33–43.

NSW Ombudsman, 1997. *Principles of Administrative Good Conduct*, New South Wales Office of the Ombudsman, Sydney.

Nye, J., 1967. 'Corruption and political development: a cost-benefit analysis', *The American Political Science Review*, 61(2):417–27.

——, 1979. 'Corruption and political development: a cost-benefit analysis', in M.U. Ekpo (ed.), *Bureaucratic Corruption in Sub-Saharan Africa: towards a search for causes and consequences*, University Press of America, Washington, DC: 411–33.

——, 1989. 'Corruption and political development: a cost-benefit analysis', in A. Heidenheimer, M. Johnston and V.T. LeVine (eds), *Political Corruption: a handbook*, Transaction Publishers, New Brunswick:963–83.

OECD Development Assistance Committee Expert Group on Aid Evaluation, 1997. *Evaluation of Programs Promoting Participatory Development and Good Governance: synthesis report*, OECD, Paris.

Olsen, M.E., 1970. 'Power as a social process' in M.E. Olsen (ed), *Power in Societies*, Macmillan, London.

Organisation for Economic Cooperation and Development (OECD), 1997. *Convention on Combating Bribery of Foreign Public Officials in International Business Transactions*, OECD, Paris.

——, (n.d) website. Available online at <http://www.oecd.org>.

Organisation of American States (OAS) website. Available online at <http://www.OAS.org>.

Pacific Islands Monthly, February 1999.

Palmer, L., 1983. 'Bureaucratic corruption and its remedies', in M. Clarke (ed.), *Corruption: causes consequences and control*, Frances Pinter, London:208.

Papua New Guinea, 1998. National Gazette No G4. Proposed Law to Alter the Constitution. Constitutional Amendment (Independent Commission Against Corruption). Port Moresby, 9 January 1998.

Pastin, M., 1986. *The Hard Problems of Management*, Jossey-Bass, San Francisco.

Pateman, C., 1988. *The Sexual Contract*, Polity, Cambridge.

Perry, P., 1997. *Political Corruption and Political Geography*, Ashgate, Aldershot.

Peters, T.J. and Waterman, R.H., 1982. *In Search of Excellence*, Harper and Row, New York.

Petri, H.L., 1981. *Motivation, Theory and Research*, Wadsworth, Belmont California.

Phongpaichit, P. and Baker, C., 1998. *Thailand's Boom and Bust*, Silkworm Books, Chiang Mai.

Phongpaichit, P. and Piriyarangsan, S., 1966. *Corruption and Democracy in Thailand*, Silkworm Books, Chiang Mai.

——, 1994. *Corruption and Thai Democracy*, Politics and Economics Study Institute, Chulalongkorn University, Bangkok (in Thai).

Pongpaijit, P., Pirijarongsan, S., Treerat, N. and Niyomsip, S., 1998. *Research Report on Corruption in the Thai Bureaucratic System*, reported to the Office of the Bureaucratic Counter Corruption Commission, Bangkok (in Thai).

Pieth, M., 1997. 'International cooperation to combat corruption', in K. Elliott (ed.), *Corruption and the Global Economy*, Institute for International Economics, Washington, DC.

Planning and Policy Department, 2000. *Legal Codes, Notifications and Regulations of the Office of the National Counter Corruption Commission*, Office of the National Counter Corruption Commission, Bangkok (in Thai).

Pleskovic, B. and Stiglitz, J.E. (eds), 1998. *Annual World Bank Conference on Development Economics, 1997*, World Bank, Washington, DC.

Pope, J. (ed.), 1996. *The TI Source Book*, Transparency International, Berlin. Available online at www.transparency.org.

Presidential Commission on Good Government, 1991. *Consolidated Report on Swiss Documents*, Presidential Commission on Good Governance, Manila.

Purcell, T.V., 1978. 'Institutionalising ethics on corporate boards', *Review of Social Economy*, December, 36(1):41–54.

——, 1984. 'Ethics committees on boards of directors?: The Norton experience', in W.M. Hoffman, J.M. Moore and D.A. Fedo (eds), *Corporate Governance and Institutionalising Ethics*, Heath, Lexington, DC:193–204.

Quah, J.S.T., 1982. 'Bureaucratic corruption in the ASEAN countries: a comparative analysis of their anti-corruption strategies', *Journal of Southeast Asian Studies*, 13(1):153–177.

——, 1988b. 'Corruption in Asia with special references to Singapore: patterns and consequences', *The Asian Journal of Public Administration*, 10(1):80–98.

Rashid, A. and Islam, S., 1997. 'Golden hoards', *Far Eastern Economic Review*, 160(42):18–20.

Reisman, W.M., 1989. 'Harnessing international law to restrain and recapture indigenous spoilation', *American Journal of International Law*, 83(1):56–59.

Riley, J.G. and Samuelson, W.F., 1981. 'Optimal auctions', *American Economic Review*, 71(3):381–92.

Roberts, J.T., 1994. *Athens on trial : the antidemocratic tradition in Western thought*, Princeton University Press, Princeton, New Jersey.

Robinson, J., 1996. *The Laundrymen: inside money laundering, the world's third-largest business*, Arcade Publishing, New York.

Robinson, M., 1998. 'Corruption and development: an introduction', *European Journal of Development Research*, 10(1):1–14.

Rogow, A.A. and Laswell, H.D., 1963. *Power, Corruption and Rectitude*, Prentice-Hall, Englewood Cliffs, N.J.

Rose, R., 1993. *Lesson Drawing in Public Policy: a guide to learning across time and space*, Chatham House, New Jersey.

Rose-Ackerman, S., 1975. 'The economics of corruption', *Journal of Public Economics*, 4:187–203.

——, 1978. *Corruption: a study of political economy*, Academic Press, New York.

——, S., 1996. 'Democracy and "grand" corruption', *International Social Science Journal*, 48(3):365–80.

——, 1997a. 'Corruption and development', in B. Pleskovic and J.E. Stiglitz (eds), *Annual World Bank Conference on Development Economics, 1997*, The World Bank, Washington, DC:35–57.

——, 1997b. 'The political economy of corruption', in K. Elliott (ed.), *Corruption and the Global Economy*, Institute for International Economics, Washington, DC.

——, 1999. *Corruption and Government: causes, consequences, and reform*, Cambridge University Press, Cambridge and New York.

Ruzindana, A., 1997. 'The importance of leadership in fighting corruption in Uganda', in K. Elliott (ed.), *Corruption and the Global Economy*, Institute for International Economics, Washington, DC:133–45.

Schedler, A. (ed), 1997. *The End of Politics? Explorations into modern antipolitics*, Macmillan, London.

Schutze, H, 1983. *Bank Secrecy and Mutual Assistance in Criminal Matters*, Swiss Bank Corporation,

Scott, C., 1999. 'Reaching beyond (without abandoning) the category of economic, social and cultural rights', *Human Rights Quarterly*, 21(3):633–60.

Senturia, J., 'Political corruption', in E.R.A. Seligman et al. (eds), *Encyclopædia of the Social Sciences*, Vol iv:448.

Shleifer, A. and Vishny, R.W., 1993. 'Corruption', *Quarterly Journal of Economics*, 108(3):599–617.

Skogly, S., 1993. 'Structural adjustment and development: human rights—an agenda for change', *Human Rights Quarterly*, 15(4):751–78.

Snape, T., 1997. 'Customs fraud unit to plug EU gaps', *The European*, 27 February–5 March:17.

Snoeyenbos, M. and Jewell, D., 1983. 'Morals, Management and Codes', in M. Snoeyenbos, R. Almeder and J. Humber (eds), *Business Ethics: Corporate Values and Society*, Prometheus, New York:97–108.

Special Committee on Public Accountability, 1991. *Report on the Inquiry on Operation Big Bird*, House of Representatives, Republic of the Philippines.

Speville, B.E.D., 1998. 'Hong Kong's quiet revolution', *Governance*, 1(1):29–36.

Stapenhurst, F. and Kpundeh, S.J. (eds), 1999. *Curbing Corruption: toward a model for building national integrity*, World Bank and International Bank for Reconstruction and Development, Washington, DC.

Starr, W., 1983. 'Codes of ethics—towards a rule utilitarian justification', *Journal of Business Ethics*, 2(2):99–106.

Stokes, D., 1997. *The Role of Development Assistance in Promoting Transparency and Good Governance*, Presentation to the Forum on Corruption in International Procurement, Canberra, 11 March.

Sullivan, G.R., 1998. 'Proscribing corruption—some comments on the Law Commission's Report', *Criminal Law Review*, August:547–55.

Swiss Federal Banking Commission, 2000. *Abacha Funds at Swiss Banks*, Swiss Federal Banking Commission,

Talcott, P., 1951. *The Social System*, The Free Press, Illinois.

Tampipi, R., 1997. 'Bureaucratic corruption: a Philippine public sector reform perspective', *Development Bulletin*, No. 42, Australian Development Studies Network, Canberra:16–18.

The Economist, 1997a. 'Money laundering: that infernal washing machine', 26 July:19–21.

Toffler, B.L., 1991. *Managers Talk Ethics*, John Wiley, New York.

Tomasic, R. and Bottomley, S., 1993. *Directing the Top 500: corporate governance and accountability in Australian companies*, Allen and Unwin, Sydney.

Transparency International, 1995a. *Submission to the Working Group on the OECD Recommendation on Cross Border Corruption*, August:7.

——, 1995b. *Ethics, Accountability and Transparency: putting theory into practice*, Paper presented at the 7th International Anti-Corruption Conference, Beijing, 6–10 October.

——, 1995c. *Introducing TI*, pamphlet, January.

——, 2000. *Annual Report*, Transparency International, Berlin. Available online at www.transparency.org.

——, (n.d.). Website. Available online at <http://www.transparency.de>.

—— and Worldaware, 1994. *Institutionalising the Fight Against Grand Corruption*, Seminar organised by Transparency International and Worldaware, London, 9 November.

Travers, J. and Milgram, S., 1969. 'An experimental study of the small world problem', *Sociometry*, 32:425–43.

UNICEF, 1999. *The State of the World's Children 1999: education*, UNICEF, Oxford University Press, Oxford.

United Nations Development Programme (UNDP), 1999. *Fighting Corruption to Improve Good Governance*, United Nations Development Programme, New York.

United Nations Drug Control Program, 1997. *World Drug Report*, Oxford University Press, Oxford.

United Nations General Assembly, 1996. *Declaration Against Corruption and Bribery in International Commercial Transactions*, United Nations, New York.

USAID Center for Democracy and Governance, 1999. 'The OECD Convention', *Democracy Dialogue*, June.

United States Information Agency Wireless File, 23 October 1995.

Uwanno, B., 1995. *Corruption Inspection System for High-Level Executives*, Thailand Research Fund, Bangkok (in Thai).

van Creveld, M., 1991. *On Future War*, Brassey's, London.

——, 1996. 'The fate of the state', *Parameters*, 6(1):4–18.

Van Duyne, P.C., 1996. 'The phantom and threat of organised crime', *Crime, Law and Social Change*, 24:341–77.

Wahlert, G., 1995. *Australia's Move Towards Electronic Commerce: some implications for law enforcement*, Office of Strategic Crime Assessments Assessment No. 2/95, Commonwealth Law Enforcement Board, Canberra.

Walsh, J., 1998. 'A world war on bribery', *Time*, 152(28):37–43.

Ward, P. (ed.), 1989. *Corruption, development and Inequality: soft touch or hard graft?*, Routledge, London.

Warren, R.L., 1977. *Social Change and Human Purpose: toward understanding and action*, Rand McNally College Publishing, Chicago.

Weber, J., 1983. 'Institutionalising ethics into the corporation', in T.L. Beauchamp and N.E. Bowie (eds), *Ethical Theory and Business*, 2nd ed., Prentice Hall, Englewood Cliffs:533–41.

Weeks, W.A. and Nantel, J., 1992. 'Corporate codes of ethics and sales force behavior: a case study', *Journal of Business Ethics*, 11(10):753–60.

Werner, S.B., 1983. 'New directions in the study of administrative corruption', *Public Administration Review*, 2:146–54.

Westney, D.E., 1987. *Imitation and Innovation: the Transfer of Western Organizational Patterns to Meiji Japan*, Harvard University Press, Cambridge.

White, D.R., Brudner, L.A., 1996. Network Theories of Social Structure. Course conducted at University of California, Irvine. Available online at http://eclectic.ss.uci.edu/~drwhite/netsyl96.htm.

Williams, P., 1995a. 'The new threat: transnational criminal organisations and internal security', *Criminal Organisations*, 9(3):3.

——, 1995b. 'Problems and dangers posed by organized transnational crime in various regions of the world', *Transnational Organized Crime*, 1(3):6. (special issue: *The United Nations and Transnational Organized Crime*)

Wood, J.R.T., 1997. *Report of the Royal Commission into the New South Wales Police Service*, New South Wales Government, Sydney.

World Bank, 1997a. *World Development Report 1997. The State in a changing world*, Oxford University Press, New York.

——, 1997b. *Helping Countries Combat Corruption: the role of the World Bank*, Poverty Reduction and Economic Management Network of the World Bank, World Bank, Washington, DC. Available online at <http://www.worldbank.org/html/extdr/corruptn/coridx.htm>.

——, 1997c. 'Helping countries combat corruption: the role of the World Bank—corruption and economic development', *Helping Countries Combat Corruption: The Role of the World Bank*, Poverty Reduction and Economic Management Network of the World Bank, World Bank, Washington, DC. Available online at <http://www.worldbank.org/html/extdr/corruptn/cor02.htm>.

——, 1997d. 'Helping countries combat corruption: the role of the World Bank—key messages', *Helping Countries Combat Corruption: The Role of the World Bank*, Poverty Reduction and Economic Management Network of the World Bank, World Bank, Washington, DC.. Available online at <http://www.worldbank.org/html/extdr/corruptn/cor01.htm>.

Yamin, A. and Maine, D.P., 1999. 'Maternal mortality as a human rights issue: measuring compliance with international treaty obligations', *Human Rights Quarterly*, 21(3):563–607.

Zipparo, L., 1997a. *Monitoring the Impact of the NSW Protected Disclosures Act 1994. Phases 3 & 4: NSW public sector employee attitudes to reporting corruption*, Independent Commission Against Corruption Research Report, Independent Commission Against Corruption, Sydney.

——, 1997b. *Monitoring the Impact of the NSW Protected Disclosures Act 1994: encouraging NSW public sector employees to report corruption*, Independent Commission Against Corruption Research Report, Independent Commission Against Corruption, Sydney.

——, 1998. *Ethics: the key to good management*, Independent Commission Against Corruption Research Report, Independent Commission Against Corruption, Sydney.

Zipparo, L. and Cooke, S., 1999. *Private Contractors' Perceptions of Working for the NSW Public Sector: a survey of consultants and contractors*, Independent Commission Against Corruption Research Report, Independent Commission Against Corruption, Sydney.

Zipparo, L., Cooke, S. and Bolton, S., 1999. *Tips from the top: senior NSW public sector managers discuss the challenges of preventing corruption*, Independent Commission Against Corruption Research Report, Independent Commission Against Corruption, Sydney.

Index

www.ingramcontent.com/pod-product-compliance
Lightning Source LLC
Chambersburg PA
CBHW061243270326
41928CB00041B/3391